Samuel Pepys' Penny Merriments

Samuel Pepys'

PENNY MERRIMENTS

Being a Collection of Chapbooks, full of Histories,
Jests, Magic, Amorous Tales of Courtship, Marriage and Infidelity, Accounts of Rogues and Fools,
together with Comments on the Times.

SELECTED *and* EDITED *by*

Roger Thompson

of the University of East Anglia at Norwich

To be sold at all *Good* booksellers.

Published by *CONSTABLE* and Company Limited,
at *10 Orange Street*, London 1976

First published in Great Britain 1976
by Constable and Company Limited
10 Orange Street London WC2H 7EG
Introduction, editorial matter and selection
Copyright © Roger Thompson 1976

ISBN 0 09 461130 0

Set in Monotype Garamond
Printed in Great Britain by
The Anchor Press Ltd and bound by
Wm Brendon & Son Ltd both of
Tiptree, Essex

The Contents of This Book

III. Courtship

IV. Social Comment

V. Jokes and Jests

List of Illustrations

Acknowledgements

This is the most pleasurable of any writer's tasks. First, I am grateful to the Master and Fellows of Magdalene College, Cambridge, for their permission to reproduce extracts from two volumes of the *Penny Merriments* and for their cooperation in this venture. One of their number, Robert Latham, Pepys Librarian and co-editor of the definitive edition of *The Diary of Samuel Pepys*, has been a constant source of help and kindness. His assistant, Mary Coleman, typed the selections, a forbidding task, with infinite care and despatch. I thank Alastair Maclean for his enthusiastic encouragement in the early stages of the project, Andrew Best for his able management of it and Elfreda Powell for her sensitivity to the material and understanding of the problems of selection. My colleagues John Broadbent and Bob Hodge read an early draft of the introduction, and made many valuable comments. My wife cheerfully, if a little enviously, held the fort during all those day-trips to Cambridge.

Introduction

Two months before he died in 1703, Samuel Pepys made his will. Being childless, he left his treasured library of three thousand volumes to his nephew John Jackson, with the stipulation that on Jackson's death the books should go either to his old college, Magdalene, or to Trinity College, Cambridge. In 1724, therefore, the *Bibliotheca Pepysiana* came to Magdalene, to be housed in their glass-fronted cases in the finely proportioned first-floor room of the recent building to which Pepys himself had generously contributed.

Among the meticulously arranged and catalogued books, mostly bound in calf and sheepskin leather, are three squat volumes, which Pepys entitled *Penny Merriments*. Beside them is a similar volume of *Penny Godlinesses*. The *Merriments* contain 115 small books, later known as chapbooks. The pages usually measure only 8·5 × 14 cm – a few are even smaller – and books in the first two volumes are sixteen or twenty-four pages long, that is, printed from a single sheet. The third volume contains longer 'histories' and 'romances'. The majority of the chapbooks are printed in black-letter type on very cheap paper, and many are illustrated with crude woodcuts. (A complete short-title list of the collection is to be found at the end of this book.)

These merriments are a vivid and invaluable source of popular culture for historians: a rare window on the minds of ordinary people. Such chapbooks formed a part of that ephemeral 'street literature' of the seventeenth century along with ballads, broadsides, almanacks, political propaganda and news-sheets. They cost a penny, or at most twopence, and were so cheaply and shoddily produced that very few have survived. The more popular titles were printed over and over again, possibly from the same typesetting; certainly the blocks for the crude woodcuts were re-used – sometimes with little or no reference to the text. The poor quality of the printing and the number of typographical errors suggest that this task was relegated to prentice work. How large editions were is not known, but it is probable that it was a good deal higher than the normal 1,500 copies for more respectable literature. In 1683 it was said that 20,000 copies of William Russell's speech from the scaffold were run off as a broadside. This example of street literature may be a better guide.[1]

Pepys was an inveterate collector. And he had the three personal attributes of a collector: insatiable curiosity, wealth, and a strongly developed acquisitive urge. He gathered books for his library with care and discrimination for over forty years. His collection of ballads is the finest in the world. He also accumulated manuscripts, prints, maps, plans, frontispieces and music. Why he bothered with popular ephemera he never tells us. It could be that as the son of a poor tailor he felt an urge to keep in touch with his humble roots. Or he may like other contemporaries, Thomason, Rawlinson, Luttrell, Wood, for instance, have had the conscious intention of preserving examples of his own culture for later generations. Like John Selden, whose collection of ballads he acquired, he may have felt that 'Though some make slight of Libells; yet you may see by them how the wind sits. . . . More solid Things do not show the complexion of the Times so well as Ballads and Libells.' Their 'simplicity and nakedness of style' probably appealed to him, as it did to other bibliophiles. Or, again, he may have felt an urge similar to Boswell's in 1763, to gain 'a great acquaintance with the humours and traditions of the English common people'. The market for ballads was declining in the last quarter of the seventeenth century, and the broadsheets were being replaced by chapbooks. The *Penny Merriments* may therefore be a reflection of this change in popular taste.

The chapbooks which are, or can be, dated suggest that Pepys was an active collector in the decade of the 1680s, when he rose to the height of his influence as a naval administrator, and then fell after the Glorious Revolution. At this time the lucrative ballad and chapbook market was dominated by two groups of publishers, who jealously guarded their copyrights registered with the Stationers' Company. The Coles-Vere-Wright-Clarke-Thackeray-Passinger-Millet partnership traced its origins back to the 1620s, and specialised in old popular favourites in black-letter type. The other group, including Brooksby, Deacon, Dennisson, Back, Blare, Conyers and Kell, seems to have been less tightly organised, and to have ventured on some more topical material. The two centres of the London chapbook trade were around Pye Corner – the ballad warehouse – and London Bridge. Londoners bought their pennyworths from booksellers' stalls or from hawkers; provincial readers relied on travelling chapmen, who set out like Autolycus in the spring, or booths at country fairs. The publishers of chapbooks were not fly-by-night pedlars, but usually substantial citizens, freemen of the Stationers' Company, and on occasion its masters or wardens.[2]

What was the readership that these experienced and successful stationers aimed at? Though research on seventeenth-century literacy in England is incomplete, there seems little doubt that the ability at least to read was spreading widely down the classes. The enormous expansion of publishing would support this view, and remarks in prefaces of popular books corroborate it.[3] It seems improbable that the poorest classes, cottagers, day-labourers – the frequent butt of chapbook humour – or unskilled workers in the towns would have the time, ability or motivation to read chapbooks. Women – another popular quarry – were similarly probably less literate than men. The most likely audience is the middle classes: the lower echelons, tradesmen, artisans, journeymen, yeomen and substantial husbandmen, for simpler jests, histories, romances and rogueries, the better educated for the subtler humour, the garlands, the satire and the complements. The themes of such tales as Jack of Newbery, Dick Whittington or Aurelius would certainly appeal to the aspiring lower-middle classes, who would likewise identify with many of the characters in other stories. The prevailing tone of merriness and uncorsetted ribaldry is again essentially that of the non-puritan bourgeoisie. A typical 'pill to purge melancholy' is 'Chaucer Junior's' *Canterbury Tales*. This 'Choice Banquet of delightful Tales' is dedicated to 'The Bakers, Smiths, Millers and other Readers'. Occasionally one finds a literary reference to chapbook readers; for instance, in Alexander Oldys's sophisticated *The Fair Extravagant* the hero wishes to write a note from a country inn, and calls for pen and paper. The hostess's paper is 'torn from *The Practice of Piety* or *The Famous History of Valentine and Orson*'.[4]

There is not space in this brief introduction to discuss the fascinating and complex question of the sources of these chapbook stories and jests. Many of the indigenous English myths and stories may well have been handed down orally, in their verse form, before they were first printed in the fifteenth, sixteenth and early seventeenth centuries. Other rich treasuries which were pilfered shamelessly by English hack writers were Italian *facetiae* and *novelle*, French *fabliaux* and Spanish and German rogue stories. Many of these, in turn, can be traced even farther back to Arabic origins.[5] Suffice it to say here that very few, if any, of the plots, situations, puns or jests are original to the editions selected here.

Most of the chapbooks were written anonymously. Writers were paid only about £2 for their work, and most of them were probably exploited denizens of Grub Street. Occasionally a popular author is cited, no doubt to boost sales. Thus we have Martin Parker and Lawrence Price, two of the most prolific and successful ballad writers of the early seventeenth century, and Thomas Deloney and Richard Johnson, equally famous as romanciers. Crompton, Crouch, Lanfier and Smithson were also well known to seventeenth-century readers of street literature. William Lilly and Richard Saunders were household words as astrologers and almanac writers. For the rest of the anonymous hacks, survival rather than fame was no doubt their prime consideration.[6]

Ideally, the whole of the *Penny Merriments* should be reprinted. A significant number of the chapbooks appear to be unique. Unlike ballads, very little chapbook material has ever been republished.[7] However, the cost of reproducing the more than 3,000 pages (all numbered in pencil by Pepys, who also produced his own index in red and black inks at the end of Volume I) would be prohibitive. A representative sample is a good deal better than nothing.

My basic principle in making the selections has been to give a taste of as many of the splendidly diverse collection as possible. I have included excerpts from 80 of the 108 chapbooks in the first two volumes. Some of the extracts are perforce brief, giving only one or two situations in a story which contains a dozen or a couple of pages of recipes from a twenty-four page book. I have aimed to give a balanced flavour of the original, while at the same time choosing examples which will most readily impart a feel of popular culture, thought-processes, sense of humour and preoccupations of ordinary people in the seventeenth century. The one group which I have had to cut most rigorously is the complements and 'Garlands', miscellanies of verse, amatory addresses and maxims. I have included sections from nine of the twenty-two books of this kind, whose contents tend to become repetitive and distinctly indigestible.

The books in the three volumes are not arranged in any apparent order, which in one sense is one of the delights of reading them, since one never knows what new gem will come next. In the interests of clarity and coherence, however, I have done violence to their haphazard medley, and arranged them into various rough groupings, giving the original volume and chapbook number at the end of each extract. The contemporary spelling, including compositors' errors, has been retained, except where the sense of a passage is obscured. I have limited notes to explaining difficulties of language and syntax and historical references. Most of the pieces speak clearly and wittily for themselves.

I have divided the 80 extracts into eight sections:

> Histories
> Magic
> Courtship
> Social Comment
> Jokes and Jests
> Practica
> Rogues and Fools
> Marital and Extramarital

Arbitrary patterns of this kind obviously lead to some overlapping, but I have been guided by what seems to be the main purpose of each piece.

The seventeenth-century use of the word 'history' was looser than our own. It covered not only verifiable events in the past, but what we should now call historical novels, and myths, legends and tall tales which had grown up round historical figures like Henry VIII, Robin Hood or Guy of Warwick, all of whom were immensely popular in the seventeenth century. The theme of most of these stories is of people in humble circumstances attaining fame and fortune through physical strength, or luck, or persistence or good fellowship. The Robin Hood philosophy prevails throughout. The examples of Whittington or Jack of Newbery would perform much the same function for ambitious apprentices or tradesmen in the seventeenth century, as did the uplifting rhetoric of Samuel Smiles in the nineteenth.

I use the term 'magic' in a similar sense to that of Keith Thomas in his brilliant study of popular beliefs in this period, *Religion and the Decline of Magic*, to include popular myths like Tom Thumb, Cupid and Friar Bacon, the arts of palmistry, fortune-telling and prognostication, the 'science' of astrology, which had, of course, an enormous following from Charles II downwards, and the macabre black magic symbolised by the Faustus story. In this section appears Mother Ursula Shipton, an archetypal 'wise woman' or conjuror, to whom country people resorted for help even up to the beginning of this century.

I have selected six pieces of broadly social comment attacking generally or specifically contemporary vices. The allegory of Diogenes is as universal and timeless as the seven deadly sins. The satire on the social effects of alcoholism, though at least sixty years older than our edition, does reflect a very strong contemporary concern, seen in protests against the increase in the numbers of inns and alehouses, against the use of arable land for growing malting barley, against drunkenness at court and as a cause of unemployment, beggary (also a topic) and vagrancy.[8] Miserliness and usuriousness are obviously perpetual targets both for the have-nots and those who believe in a glad-handed, neighbourly community. However, the spread in the seventeenth century of the philosophy of possessive individualism, and a practice of capitalism which more frequently exhibited its unacceptable and exploitative side, would give immediacy and sharpness to *The Death and Burial of Mistress Money*.

There is a miser too in *Make Room for Christmas,* a proto-Scrooge, as the cobbler's family are embryonic Cratchits. Yet the real enemy here is not avarice, but the apparent joylessness of puritanism, with its programme briefly enacted of an alternative, godly society. The cobbler and Christmas are symbolic of all the church-ales, sports, mayings, wakes and harvest homes so engrained in rural life, which the rule of the saints replaced with fasts and days of humiliation.

This contemporary application is even more marked in the satire of quakerism, *The Secret Sinners.* The amorous antics of James Naylor, Mrs. Attaway and other extreme antinomians during the Interregnum had given their opponents ample ammunition for bombarding the sects.[9] In the Restoration, the Society of Friends affronted ingrained popular prejudices by their liberation of women, their lack of respect for secular authority, their peculiar modes of address and their appearance of being 'holier than thou'. That the mode of attack on their presumed hypocrisy and self-serving antinomianism is sexual is due partly to the precedents of Cromwellian scandals and the stock situation of infidelity. Yet it may also mirror a new uncertainty about sexuality that was strongly marked, for instance, in that product of a puritan education and environment, Samuel Pepys. I have hesitated to include this piece because of its offensiveness, but its importance as an unique copy and as an excellent example of Restoration intolerance required its inclusion.[10]

The courtship pieces are of two types. On the one hand are the examples of complements, which are instructional examples on courtship etiquette, models, for an uncertain and gauche middle class, of poised addresses. The popularity of this type of book, as well as books on letter-writing and general social practice, suggests an increased social mobility, which men like Pepys exemplified. 'Manners' and 'form' so dear to the Restoration court and theatre had to be learnt by an aspiring bourgeoisie in an age still dominated by the aristocracy. On the other hand are stories of courtship, often featuring bumpkins. Some of these like the dialogues between Andrew and Joan or John and Kate give vivid details of Stuart wedding customs and the mechanics of setting up a humble household, vital episodes in everyday life about which all too little is known. I have included with this group a few examples of romances, so popular, according to dramatists, with chambermaids, and their mistresses, a taste apparently still unsated.

The section on jests and jokes gives an all too rare insight into seventeenth-century *popular* humour, as opposed to court wit, which is much more widely known from Restoration comedy, poetry and anecdote. Many of the jokes are extremely unsophisticated, even infantile, by modern standards. Many of these limping attempts at wit, and the comedies of situation owe their origins to famous humorists of the Renaissance, like Poggio Bracciolini, Boccaccio and Rabelais. Hardly any have a topical slant. Here too are extracts from a book of 'wonders', evidence of a certain popular credulousness. The scholarly investigations of such experts as Gershon Legman and John Wardroper on this topic excuse me from further comment.

The practical guides on cooking, medicine and the law must have been intended for the comfortable middle classes. The recipes are in one case addressed to a cookmaid and in the other are a gentlewoman's; the ingredients for recipes and prescriptions would have been way beyond the pockets of 'the poorer sort'. Similarly the model injunctions, bills of sale and powers of attorney in *The Country-Mans Counsellor* would only be of much use to the solid yeomanry and lesser squires, grudging fees to country attorneys.

The appeal of the rogue is eternal, but especially strong in hierarchical and authoritarian societies. The rogue cocks a snook at established conventions with engaging cheekiness, and gets away with it. Lesser mortals can safely fantasise his daring, resource, inventiveness and luck. The exploits of Guzman, the Spanish Rogue, were a palpable hit in Stuart England, and his fellow-countryman Lazarillo was widely read. Eulenspiel had been anglicised a century earlier as Howleglas, and other favourites were Scoggin, Armstrong and Latroon. The 'mad exploits' of the highwayman Hind, hanged in 1652, had occurred within the living memory of Pepys and his contemporaries, however much Deacon's hack had romanticised them in the telling.[11] Some fools had much of the rogue in them too, as their Shakespearean role clearly demonstrates. John Frank, an historical character, escaped unscathed from endless pranks by a combination of low cunning and imbecility. Other fools, like Boord's Gothamites or despised Welsh braggarts, have an almost surreal appeal, and their ludicrous stratagems and humiliating misadventures would boost the egos of the most exploited or unfortunate reader, provided he did not hale from Wales or Gotham.[12]

The last and in many ways most interesting section is devoted to pieces on marital and extra-marital relations. Erotic humour occurs in several of the other groups, among the jests and the rogues, predictably, but also in two of the pieces on social problems. There the relations between the sexes are incidental, here they are central. On the verbal level, here are several examples of 'flytings' or duels of words between less than devoted spouses, and demands for sexual liberation by frustrated females. On the plane of action, we have female infidelity with apprentices or gallants. In *The Female Ramblers* the style comes closest to the tone of Restoration comedy, with the important exception that the point of view is female rather than male.

In comparison with the verbal legerdemain of the jokes, the quality of wit in this section is strikingly more sophisticated, though few of the puns and innuendoes are original. Nonetheless the mental suppleness demanded by the symbols and metaphors suggests that bawdy was one of the most inventive and stimulating areas of everyday intercourse. It is as though readers would immediately attune to the indirections, nudges and winks of music-hall or working men's club comedian, but entirely miss the nuances and wit of a comedy of manners. Freud suggested that this kind of preoccupation stemmed from sublimation, which raises the possibility that a sense of shame about sex had permeated the middle classes of Stuart England.

Two of the most frequent obsessions of this section are male impotence and cuckoldry, with the obvious female counterpart of woman's insatiability. In large part these owe their origins to

Italian models. Poggio Bracciolini's *Facetiae,* for instance, are
studded with such types, as is *The Decameron.* January, *ipso facto,*
condones May's infidelity. Moreover, the triangle is eternal.
Yet, it remains to ask why such alien stock should retain its
hardiness when transplanted to Restoration England. Why
should 'cornumania' and the reversal of conventional sexual
roles, be so persistently popular with non-intellectual readers?
Answers to such questions of popular taste are bound to be
exceedingly complex. Here we can offer only hypothetical
answers.

   The period of the puritan ascendancy in the years 1640–1660
had had marked effects on social mores as they struggled to
impose an alternative society on a largely reluctant nation.
Their efforts to turn the world upside down were aimed at that
key unit of the community, the family. This was to become a
spiritual household, a little church. A concomitant of this expanded role was a new attitude to marriage: rather than a
quencher of sexual 'burning' and a means of responsible pro-
pagation of the species, puritan theologians increasingly stressed
the primary purpose of matrimony as companionship, loving
partnership and mutual, god-inspired caring. The negative side
of this reappraisal of the family, the death penalty for adultery,
swingeing punishment for fornication, has usually been high-
lighted, especially by anti-puritan commentators. Yet, more
positively, it produced far more important changes in the role
and status of women in the family, matched, incidentally by their
heightened esteem and independence in many of the puritan
sects. Indeed one of the persistent laments or lampoons of critics
of the puritan revolution was that the weaker half had been
allowed to get out of hand – strikingly illustrated by Sarah's
independence in *The Secret Sinners.*[13]

   The Restoration of 1660 returned not only king, lords, bishops
and commons, the old structure in local government and a more
worldly aristocratic culture. It also sought to restore the tradi-
tion of male-dominated family life, relegating women to their
former second-class citizenship and religious silence. Against
such a background, satire of women's insatiability and infidelity

takes on a deeper meaning. It is significant that the cuckolds in this section are drawn from tailors, clerks, men-midwives, shop-keepers, apothecaries and old fools, all traditionally effeminate. The exposure of the essential Eve and the execration of the unmanly would go some way to confirming a shaken but re-assertive masculinity.

Hyder Rollins once wrote that after the *Diary*, Pepys' collection of broadside ballads was 'perhaps the greatest treasure in his library'. For the social historian, there is much justice in this apparently perverse relegation of fine and rare editions, important manuscripts and prints to scruffy ephemera of the streets. The great paradox of historical research is that we know most about the few at the peak of the social pyramid, least about the many. Intensive work on parish, county and legal records in recent years has produced many invaluable additions and revisions to our conceptions of 'the inarticulate' in pre-industrial England, but the very nature of the evidence used tends to preclude answers to important questions like 'What made ordinary people laugh?' 'What were their everyday worries?' 'What were their fantasies?' 'What were their popular prejudices?' 'What were their ambitions?' 'How did they organise their day-to-day lives?' 'How did they spend their leisure time? 'What were their ideals?'

Obviously literary evidence of any sort must be handled with great circumspection by historical researchers. Anyone who assumed that Restoration comedy accurately and completely reflected the life and thought of the upper classes in later Stuart England would receive a nasty shock if transported back three hundred years. Nonetheless, the insights into the minds and lives of ordinary people which judicious reading of the *Penny Merriments* affords, places them alongside the five volumes of ballads as veritable treasures of the Pepysian Library.

Norwich 1976 Roger Thompson

Notes

1. On this genre, see Leslie Shepard, *History of Street Literature* (1973); on printing, D. F. Mckenzie, 'Printers of the Mind: Some Notes on Bibliographical Theories and Printing-House Practices', *Studies in Bibliography*, XXII (1969), 1–76.

2. This paragraph paraphrases the brilliant bibliographical research of Cyprian Blagden: 'Notes on the Ballad Market in the second half of the Seventeenth Century', *Studies in Bibliography*, VI (1954) 161–180. A chapman is portrayed in Sec. III, *A Country Garland*.

3. Roger Schofield, 'Measurement of Literacy in Pre-industrial England' in Jack Goody, ed., *Literacy in Traditional Societies* (Cambridge, 1968) pp. 311–325; H. S. Bennett, *English Books and Readers 1600–1640* (Cambridge, 1970) pp. 84–85, 180–181.

4. London, 1682; Bunyan's youthful reading of this class of literature is well known.

5. John Wardroper, *Jest Upon Jest* (London, 1970) pp. 1–25; Gershon Legman, *The Horn Book* (New Hyde Park, 1964) *passim*; invaluable reference works are Katharine M. Briggs, *A Dictionary of Folk-Tales,* 4 vols. (London, 1970–1971), and E. C. Brewer, *Dictionary of Phrase and Fable.* See also my source-tracing in the forthcoming Check list in *The Library* (1976).

6. Bennett, *English Books,* p. 229.

7. John Ashton, *Chap-Books of the Eighteenth Century* (London, 1882) is totally bowdlerised.

8. See Kenneth Wrightson, Puritan Reformation of Manners, Unpublished Ph.D. thesis, Cambridge University, 1973; C. MacAndrew & R. B. Edgerton, *Drunken Comportment* (London, 1970).

9. Christopher Hill, *The World Turned Upside Down* (London, 1972); K. V. Thomas, 'Women and the Civil War Sects' in Trevor Aston, ed., *Crisis in Europe,* 1560–1660 (London, 1965) pp. 317–340; Roger Thompson, *Women in Stuart England and America* (London, 1974) Ch. IV.

10. A book called *The Quaker and his Maid* was proceeded against as 'a grossly indecent production' by the Secretary of State in 1675; W. H. Hart, *Index Expurgatorius Anglicus* (London, 1872–1878) p. 195.

11. F. W. Chandler, *The Literature of Roguery* (New York, 1907, repr. 1958).

12. Wardroper, *Jest,* pp. 74–95.

13. See note 8, and Christopher Hill, *Society and Puritanism* (London, 1964); E. S. Morgan, *The Puritan Family* (New York, 1966).

I. HISTORIES

King Henry the VIII and a Cobler.[1]

CHAP. I.

How King Henry the 8th. used to visit the Watches in the City, and how he came acquainted with a merry and a Jovial Cobler.

It was the Custome of King Henry the 8th. to Walk late in the Night into the City Disguised, to take notice how the Constables and Watch performed their Duty; not onely in carefully Guarding the City Gates, but also in diligent Watching the inward parts of the said City, that so they might prevent those Disturbances and Casualties which often happens in great and Populous Cities in the Night. This he did oftentimes, without the least discovery who he was; returning home to White-hall early in the Morning. Now in his return home through the Strand, he took notice of a certain Cobler, who was constantly up and at work, Whistling and Singing every morning; he therefore resolved to see him, and be acquainted with him; in order to which he immediately knocks off the Heel of his Shooe, by hitting it against the Stones: having so done, he bounced[2] at the Coblers Stall; who's there? cries the Cobler. Here is one, said the King. With that the Cobler opened his Stall door, and the King asked him, if he could set on his Heel again? Yes that I can, says the Cobler. Come in Honest Fellow, and sit thee down by me, and I will do it for you strait; the Cobler scraping his Awls and Old Shooes to one side, to make room for the King to sit by him. The King being hardly able to forbear Laughing at the kindness of the Cobler, asked him if there was not a House hard by which sold a Cup of Ale, where the People were up? Yea, (said the Cobler) there is an Inn over the way, where I believe the folk of the house are up; for the Carriers

1. Cf. popular ballad of 1588. 2. Knocked loudly.

go from thence very early in a Morning. With that the King borrowed an old Shooe of the Cobler, and went over to the Inn, desiring the Cobler to bring his Shooe to him thither, so soon as he had put the Heel on again; the Cobler promised he would. So making what haste he could to put the Heel on, he carried it over to the King, saying; Honest Blade, here is thy Shooe again; I'le warrant it will not come off in haste. Very well, said the King, What must you have for your pains? A couple of Pence (answered the Cobler.) Well said the King, because thou art an honest merry Fellow, here is a Tester[3] for thee. Come sit thee down by me, I will drink to thee a whole Pot, here's a good Health to the King: with all my heart, said the Cobler, I will pledge thee were it Water. So the Cobler sat himself down by the King, and was very merry, and drank off his Liquor very freely. He also Sung some of his Merry Songs and Catches, whereat the King Laughed heartily, and was very Pleasant and Jocund with the Cobler; telling him withal, that his Name was Harry Tudor, and that he belonged to the Court, and if he would come and see him there, he would make him very welcome, because he was such pleasant merry Company, and charged him to be there, and not to forget his Name, but to ask any one for him about the Court, and they will bring you to him: For (said the King) I am very well known at the Court. Now the Cobler little dream'd that it was the King which spoke to him, much less that the Kings Name was Harry Tudor: Therefore with a great deal of confidence, he stands up and pulls off his Hat, and makes two or three fine scrapes with his Leg, gives the King many thanks, withal telling him, that he was one of the honestest Fellows he ever met withal in his Life-time. And (though he had never been at Court) yet it should not be long before he would make a Holiday to come and see him. Hereupon the King discharging the House for what he had drank, would have taken his leave of the Cobler: But the Cobler taking him by the hand, said; By my faith, you must not go yet, you shall first go and see my poor Habitation; I have there a Tub of good Nappy[4] Ale was never Tapt yet, you must needs go and taste of it; for you are the honestest Merriest

3. Sixpence. 4. Foaming, heady, strong.

Blade that I ever met withal, and I love an honest merry Companion with all my heart. . . .

CHAP. IV.

The Coblers Reception at Court, with the manner of his Behaviour before the KING.

The Cobler being thus set forth, strutted through the Streets like a Crow in a Gutter, thinking himself as fine as the best of them all. In this manner he came to Court, staring on this body, and that body, as he walkt up and down, and not knowing who to ask for Harry Tudor, at last he espyed one as he thought, in the Habit of a Serving-man, to him he makes his Address, saying, Dost thou hear honest Fellow, do you know one Harry Tudor, which belongs to the Court? Yes, said the Man, follow me and I will bring you to him: with that he had him presently up into the Guard-Chamber, telling one of the Yeoman of the Guard, there was one that enquired for Harry Tudor. Replyed the Yeoman, I know him very well, if you will please to go along with me, I will bring you to him immediately. So the Cobler followed the Yeoman, much admiring the Finery of the Rooms he went through, he thought within himself, that the Yeoman was mistaken in the person whom he enquired after: he therefore pulled him back by the Coat, and told him, that he did believe he was mistaken in the Person whom he enquired after. For (said he) him who I look for, is a plain merry honest Fellow, his Name is Harry Tudor: We drank two Pots together not long since, I suppose he may belong to some Lord or other about the Court. I tell you Friend, replyed the Yeoman, I know him very well, do but follow me, and I shall bring you to him strait. So going forward, he came at last to the Room where the King was, accompanied with several of his Nobles who attended him.

As soon as the Yeoman had put by the Arras, he spoke aloud, saying; May it please your Majesty, here is one that enquires for

Harry Tudor. The Cobler hearing this, thought he had committed no less than Treason, therefore he up with his Heels and run for it. But not being acquainted with the several turnings and Rooms through which he came, he was soon overtaken, and brought before the King, whom the Cobler little thought to be the Person he enquired after: Therefore in a trembling condition, he fell down upon his knees, saying; May it please your Grace, may it Please your Highness, I am a poor Cobler; and enquired for one Harry Tudor, who is a very honest Fellow, I mended the Heel of his Shooe not long since, for which he paid me nobly, and gave me two or three Pots to boot: And I had him over afterwards to my Celler, where we drank part of a Tub of nappy Ale, and was very Merry, until my Wife Joan began to Grumble, which put an end to our Merriment for that time. But I told him, I would come to the Court and see him as soon as conveniently I could. Well, said the King, be not troubled; do you know this honest Fellow again if you see him? Yea, that I do from a thousand (replyed the Cobler.) Then said the King, stand up and be not afraid, but look well about you, peradventure you may find this honest Fellow amongst this Company. Whereupon the Cobler arose and looked wishfully upon the King, and the rest of his Nobles, but to little or no purpose. For though he saw something in the Kings face which he thought he had seen before, yet he could not imagine him to be Harry Tudor . . .

CHAP. V.

The Coblers Entertainment in the King's Celler; and how he met with his new Friend Harry Tudor, and how he come to know him to be the King.

The Cobler had not been long in the King's Celler, before the King came to him in the same Habit which he had on when the Cobler mended his Shooe; whereupon the Cobler knew him, and run and embraced him, saying, Honest Harry, I have made a

Holiday on purpose to come and see you; but I had much ado to
get leave of my wife Joan, who was loath I should loose so much
time from my work; but I was resolved to see you, I therefore
made my self as fine as I could. But (i'le tell you Harry) when I
came to the Court I was in a peck of troubles how to find you out;
but at last I met with a man who told me he knew you very well,
and that he would bring me to you; but instead of doing so, he
brought me before the King, which had almost frightned me out
of my seven senses. But in good faith (added the Cobler) I am
resolved to be merry with you, since I have the good fortune to
meet with you at last. I that you shall, replyed the King, we will
be as merry as Princes. With that he call'd for a large Glass of
Wine, and drank to the Cobler the King's good Health. God-a-
mercy, said the Cobler, honest Harry, I will pledge thee with all
my heart. Now after the Cobler had drank about four or five
good Healths, he began to be merry, and fell a singing his old
Songs and Catches, which pleased the King very much, and made
him laugh heartily. When of a sudden several of the Nobles came
into the Celler, extraordinary rich in apparel, who all stood bare
to Harry Tudor, which put the Cobler into a great amazement at
first, but recovering himself, he lookt more wishfully upon Harry
Tudor: when presently he knew him to be the King, which he
saw in the Presence Chamber, tho' in other Habit, he immediately
fell down upon his knees, saying; May it please your Grace,
may it please your Highness, I am honest poor Cobler, and mean
no harm: No, no, said the King, nor shall receive none here. . . .

[Vol. I, no. 38]

The Pleasant HISTORY of
King *Henry* the Eighth,
AND THE
Abbot of Reading

Printed by *J. M.* for *C. Dennisson,* at the Stationers-Arms, within *Aldgate.*

CHAP. I.

How King Henry the Eighth Rode a hunting in Windsor Forrest, and how he lost his Company, and dined with the Abbot of Reading.

. . . The Table being spread with variety of dishes, the King sat down to his Meat, Eating very heartily of a Loin of Beef, commonly called a Sir-Loin of Beef; insomuch that the Abbot took great notice of him, to see how he laid about him, first cutting a good Sizeable piece, then calling for a Glass of his Clarret drank it off, and then fell to his Beef a fresh continuing eating until he had made a prety handsome hole in the Sirloyn of Beef; said the Abbot, much good may it do you Sir, I perceive you have a good Stomach to your meat, I would give a hundred pounds with all my heart, I had so good a stomach as you have; you see of all this variety of Meats here is, I can hardly eat any thing, a pestle of a Lark is as much as I have eaten. . . .

CHAP. II.

How the King sent a messenger for the lord abbot, and sent the abbot Prisoner to the Tower.

. . .

CHAP. III.

How the Lieutenant of the Tower went to the King in behalf of the Abbot.

. . .

CHAP. IV.

How the Abbot Dined in the Tower, and how the King Demanded his Hundred Pound, for bringing the Abbot to his Stomach.

Now when the Lieutenant of the Tower came to the King, he told him how hungry the Abbot was, and that he was ready to eat his own Flesh: Well, said the King, to morrow let him have a Loyn of Beef to Dinner, and let him have a Bottle or two of Clarret, but be you not known that you have Orders from me, but that you do it upon your own account, and let there be a Hole made out of the Abbots Room that I may come privately and see him eat; The Lieutenant told the King that all things should be done according to his Order.

He therefore went home again to the Tower and told the Abbot that the King was much enraged against him, insomuch that he could not prevail with him in the least to have any other Diet but Bread and Water; but that he so much pittyed him, and was troubled at his Condition, that he would venture his Place and Life to serve him: and that to morrow he should have a Dinner, and he would come and Dine with him himself; the Abbott was not a little pleased with this News, telling him he would not be Ungrateful to him for this great kindness, if ever he came for to have his Liberty; Now the Abbot was so overjoyed with the hopes of a Dinner the next Day, that he Slept Quieter that Night then he had done ever since he came into the Tower; the next day about twelve a Clock, the King came privately to the Tower, where he was conveyed secretly into a room adjoyning to the Lord Abbots, and a hole made so cunningly that he might see the Lord Abbot and he not see him again; it was not long before the Cloath was laid, and a proper tall Fellow brought in a lusty Loyn of Beef, and another two or three Bottles of Clarret, at which sight the Lord Abbot could[1] forbear laughing: Then came in the Lieutenant of the Tower, saying you see my Lord, I venture my Life to come and Dine with you, but no more

1. The printer has omitted 'not' or 'hardly' here.

words of that; but let us fall to as fast as we can, and be merry; so after the Abbot had said a short Grace he fell aboard on the Beef, cutting a swinging piece which he soon devoured then he calls for a Glass of Clarret, drinks it off, and then falls to his Beef again, insomuch that the King had much ado to forbear Laughing, to see how the Abbot had laid about him, seeing plainly the Abbot had gotten as good a stomach as he had; now when the Abbot had pretty well Dined, the King sent one of his Servants into the Room, saying aloud, the King: at which news the Lieutenant fell on his knees, and the Abbot was like to have fallen into a sound[2], but the King entring the Room, said, my Lord, be not dismayed, I come but to demand the Hundred Pound you owe me, pay me that, and you shall have your Liberty when you will. . . .

[Vol. I, no. 37]

2. Sc. swound, or swoon.

THE *Pleasant* HISTORY *of Thomas Hic-ka-thrift*.[1]

His Birth and Parentage, and the true manner of his performing many Many Acts, and how he Killed a Gyant.

Young man, here thou mayest behold what Honour Tom came unto.

And if that thou dost buy this Book,
Be sure that thou dost in it look;
And read it o're, then thou wilt say,
Thy money is not thrown away.

In the Reign before William the Conqueror, I have read in ancient Histories, that there dwelt a Man in the Marsh of the Isle of Ely, in the County of Cambridge whose Name was Thomas Hic-ka-thrift, a poor Man, and day labourer, yet he was a very stout Man, and able to perform two days works instead of one, he having one Son, and no more Children in the world, he called him by his own Name Thomas Hickathrift; this old Man put his Son to good Learning, but he would take none, for he was, as we call them now in this Age, none of the wisest sort, but something soft, and had no docity[2] at all in him: God calling this Old Man his Father out of the world, his Mother being tender of him, and maintained him by her hand labour as well as she could: he being sloathful and not willing to work to get a penny for his living, but all his delight was to be in the Chimney corner[3], and would eat as much at one time as might very well serve four or five ordinary men, for he was in length when he was but Ten years of age, about eight foot, and in Thickness five foot, and his Hand was like unto a shoulder of Mutton, and in all parts from top to toe, he was like a Monster and yet his great Strength was not known.

---

1. Also a nursery rhyme hero. 2. Gumption. 3. Warmest lounging place in a cottage.

How Tom Hic-ka-thrift's Strength came to be known; the which
if you please but to read, will give you full satisfaction.

THe first time that his Strength was known, was by his Mothers
going to a Rich Farmers House, (she being but a poor Woman)
to desire a Bottle[4] of Straw to shift[5] her self and her Son Thomas:
the Farmer being an honest Charitable Man, bid her take what
she would: she going home to her Son Tom, said, I pray thee to
to such a place and fetch me a Bottle of Straw, I have asked him
leave: he swore a great Oath he would not go; nay, prithee Tom
go, said his old Mother, he swore again he would not go, unless
she would borrow him a Cart-rope, she being willing to please
him, because she would have some Straw, went and borrowed
him a Cart-rope to his desire, he taking went his way; so coming
to the Farmers House, the Master was in the Barn, and two men
a Thrashing: said Tom, I am come for a Bottle of Straw: Tom,
said the Master, take as much as thou canst carry; he laid down
his Cart-rope, and began to make his Bottle; but, said they, Tom,
thy rope is too short, and jeer'd poor Tom, but he fitted the man
well for it, for he made his bottle, and when he had made it, there
was supposed to be a Load of Straw in it of two thousand weight;
but, said they, what a great fool art thou? thou canst not carry
the Tith[6] on't; but Tom took the Bottle and flung it on his
shoulder, and made no more of it then we do of an hundred
weight, to the great admiration of Master and Men. Tom Hic-ka-
thrift's strength being known in the Town, then they would not
let him any longer lye basking by the fire in the Chimney-corner,
every one would be hiring him to work, they seeing him to have
so much strength, told him that it was a shame for him to live
such a lazy course of life, and to lye idle day after day as he did.
So Tom seeing them bait at him in such a manner as they did, he
went first to one work, then to another, but at length came a Man
to Tom, and desired him to go with him unto the Wood, for he
had a Tree to bring home, and he would content him. So Tom
went with him, and he took with him four Men beside; but when
they came to the Wood, they set the Cart by the Tree and began

4. Bundle, bale. 5. Replace old straw. 6. Tenth.

to draw it up with Pullies, but Tom seeing them not able to lift it up, said Stand away you Fools, and takes the Tree and sets it on one end, and lays it in the Cart, now says he, see what a Man can do; Marry, it is true, said they: so when they had done, coming through the Wood they met the Woodman, Tom asked him for a stick to make his Mother a fire with; I, said the Woodman, take one what thou canst carry: so Tom espyed a Tree bigger then was in the Cart, and lays it on his Shoulder, and goes home with it as fast as the Cart went and six Horses could draw it: This was the second time that Toms Strength was known: so when Tom began to know that he had more strength then twenty Men had, he then began to be Merry with Men, and very tractable, and would Run, or Go, or Jump; and took great delight to be amongst Company, and to go to Fairs and Meetings, and to see Sports and Pastime: So going to a Feast, the Young Men were all met, some to Cudgels, some to Wrastling, some throwing the Hammer, and the like; So Tom stood a little to see their Sport, and at last goes to them that were a throwing the Hammer, and standing a little by to behold their Man-like Sport, at last he takes the Hammer in his hand, to feel the weight of it, and bid them stand out of the way, for he would throw it as far as he could: I, said the Smith, and jeer'd poor Tom, you'l throw it a great way i'le warrant you: but Tom took the Hammer and flung it, and there was a River about five or six furlungs off, and flung it into that: so when he had done he bid the Smith go fetch his Hammer again, and laught the Smith to scorn; but when Tom had done that, he would go to Wrastling, though he had no more skill than an Ass had, but what he did by Strength, yet he flung all that came, for if once he laid hold they were gone: some he would throw over his head, some he would lay down slyly and how he pleased: he would not lock nor strike at their Heels, but flung them two or three Yards from him, ready to break their Necks asunder: so that none at last durst go into the Ring to wrastle with him, for they took him to be some Devil that was come amongst them, so Tom's fame was spread more in the Country. . . .

[Vol. I, no. 3]

The Honour of the Gentle-Craft.[1] 1685.

CHAP. 3.

How Sir Simon Eyre[2],
A Shoomaker by trade,
A Feast for all the Prentices
Upon Shrove-Tuesday made.

Our English Chronicles declare
a story worthy to be known,
Of one by name Sir Simon Eyre,
who in short time full rich was grown,
His parentage mean, yet his name
Liveth still in lasting fame.

This man came young out of the North,
and here was a Prentice bound
Unto a Shoomaker of good worth,
his Master no dislike yet found
With his Prentice, but all was well,
And afterwards it thus befel.

Simon with other Prentices more
upon a Sunday morning went,
As they had often done before,
to eat some pudding-pyes was their intent
But when the shot came once to pay
Simon thus to them did say.

My Masters and my friends here all,
Of my empty Purse take pitty,
And I do vow if it so befall

---

1. Based on Deloney's *The Gentle Craft* (1598). The 'gentle craft' was shoe-making. 2. Died 1459; ebullient hero of Dekker's *Shoemakers Holiday* (1600); actually more likely to have been a draper!

That I'm Lord Major of this City,
If you my word will now but take,
A breakfast for you I will make.

The other Prentices took his word,
and for that time they paid the shot,
But afterwards it was restor'd,
for he such wealth and treasure got,
That in short time this Simon Eyre
Was made Sheriff, and after Major.

His promise then he kept in mind,
so that a Breakfast he did make
For all the Prentices he could find,
who kept it holiday for his sake,
And that his love might be exprest,
Upon Shrove-tuesday did them feast.

And afterwards Sir Simon Eyre
did build up Leaden-Hall,
That Shoomakers might so repair
unto the Tanners stall.
Thus for Shoomakers he did provide,
And afterwards in honour dy'd.

FINIS.

[Vol. I, no. 36]

The Famous History
OF
GUY Earl of WARWICK.

By *Samuel Smithson.*

Licensed and Entred accolding to Older.

Printed for J. Clark, W. Thackercy, and
T. Passinger. 1686.

Guy of Warwick.[1] By Samuel Smithson. 1686.

The Famous History of Guy Earl of Warwick.

CHAP. I.

In the blessed time of Memory, when King Athelstone wore the Imperial Diadem, and Reigned Regent of our English Nation, Sir Guy (Warwicks Mirror, and the Worlds wonder) was the chief Hero & Knight of Chivalry in the Golden Age, whose prowess and bold deportments, with his noble valour, became so peerless and excellent, surpassing all his predecessors that Fames loud Trumpet sounded Warwicks praise throughout the World, by which Jews, Turks & Infidels trembled at the name of Guy.

CHAP. III.

With speed Guy walks to the Garden, being entertained by a damosel that waited on fair Phillis, reposing her self in a Green Arbor of Pleasure, whom Guy salutes with bended knee, amazed with her love-enchanting eye, where Cupid appeared in every Corner, as Comets do in their etherial station, saying, All hail fair Phillis, fair flower of beauty, and jewel of vertue, 'tis love, fair Phillis, which was my conducter, and bound me in the burning Italian fire, where resting in torments, hoping in despair, I wait the hour of bliss or minute of misery.

Gentle Guy, said fair Phillis, love is not at my disposing, you know my Fathers name is great in the Nation, and I dare not Match without his consent. . . . make thy bold Atchievements & noble actions shine abroad as the glorious sun, that all opposers may tremble at thy high applauded name, and thy suit shall not be denied.

1. Based on fourteenth-century chivalric verse romance. Smithson's pretentious style contrasts starkly with the preceding histories.

Fair Phillis, said Guy, I ask no more, never did the Hound mind more his Game, than I do my Enterprize; Phillis farewel, take this joyal Kiss as a Signet from my heart. . . .

So Guy now travelling to the Duke of Lovain met by the way Earl Terry, set upon by sixteen Traytors in a wood, who had taken away his lady, Guy demands of the Earl which way the villains were gone, at last Guy overtook them, and fell upon these bloody Traytors, & kill'd eight of them presently; the Lady seeing so much Blood shed, desired Guy to spare their lives that were left, & according to her request he did, restoring the Lady to her own Lord and Husband. . . .

CHAP. X.

Gaining this freedome for the Captives, Guy went on his intended journey, and coming to a Grave, found a dead skull all worm-eaten, with which Guy conversed, speaking to the scalp, and making answer for the head; perhaps, said Guy, thou wert a Prince or Mighty Monarch, a King, Duke, or Lord? But the Beggar and the King must all to the earth, and therefore Man had need to remember his dying hour: Perhaps thou mightest be a Queen, Dutchess, or Lady, garnisht with beauty, but now thou art but worms-meat, lying in the Grave, a Sepulchre for all creatures. . . .

CHAP. XIII.

King Athelstone sent for his Champion to honor him, but Guy refused it, saying, my Liege, I am a mortal man, and therefore set the vain World at defiance, but by earnest request of the King upon promise of concealment, Guy told the King his name, which so much rejoiced his heart, that he embraced his worthy Champion; but Guy took leave of his Soveraign, and as an unknown stranger, went into the Fields, and made him a Cave, living very pensive & solitary: and his dying hour drawing on,

Guy sent a Messenger with a Ring to Phillis, which she seeing, came with all speed to her beloved Lord, where with weeping joy they embraced each other: Guy departed his life in her tender Arms, and was honourably interred; his Widow taking grief for the death of her Husband, dyed within fifteen days after him; but K. Athelstone, to grace the everlasting memory of Guy, caused many Monuments to be erected in Warwick Castle, that After-Ages might speak of the Noble Fame and Honour of GUY Earl of WARWICK.

Finis.

[Vol. I, no. 44]

The Life and Death of the Lady Rosamond.[1]

CHAP. II.

How King Henry the Second hearing of Rosamonds beauty, could not rest until he had seen her, and obtained her love

THe Kings unquiet thoughts would not suffer him to rest, till he had been made an eye-witness of Rosamands beauty: after some time passed, he beheld her whole countenance he had so long desired to see: and casting his eyes upon her incomparable favour, he perceived that those Encomiums which in his hearing had been bestowed on her, were but as the gloomy morning to the lightsom day, and came as far short of expressing her comlyness, as the sable night doth the glorious noontide, or the blackish smoak to the glittering flame: neither could he be satisfied onely with the view of this beautiful creature, but still his boyling breast was fiered with unlawful and lustful thoughts: desiring that there might be some nearer familliarity and accquaintance between them: his thoughts slept not long, but many snares were by him laid to intrap her, and many sorts erected so parted her her unstained purity:[2] many persons did he set at work soliciting her to yeild to his unchast desires: which solicitations were as darts cast against a brazen[3] wall, and could not enter: which when the King perceived, the next opportunity that presented her unto his view, he delivers his mind to her himself, manifesting his love to her, refusing all denials, and with gracious promises and inticing speeches, lefe her not till he had gotten her favour, and made her promise to fulfill his will.

1. Daughter of Walter, Lord Clifford, she died in 1177. Her bower is still at Blenheim. 2. Printer's error; the sense is 'to part her from her unstained purity'. 3. Bronze.

CHAP. 3.

The King hearing Queen Elenors[4] Jealousie, builded a Bower for Rosamond, in Woodstock.

AFter the King had for some time enjoyed the company of his late gained Lady, Elenor his Queen hearing that her Lord did too too much frequent the company of his loose Damosel, and perceiving his affection to be altered, & estranged from her, that was his lawful Queen, and to be fired on the beauty of another, used all the means that a womans wit sharpened with malice could invent, to untye the fast knit bands of their affections: which malice of the Queen towards this Lady, the King soon perceived, and fearing that which afterwards hapned, lest his dear Rose should come to any untimely death, erected for her Labyrinth, within his own Palace at Woodstock in Oxfordshire, a place under ground most curiously wrought, having many turnings, windings, and doors belonging to it, that it was impossible, being once entered, to find the way out of it, without the guidance of a clew[5] of thread. The charge of this place wherein this Paramour was inclosed, he committed to Sir Thomas Vaughan Knight, his sure & trusty friend. . . .

[Vol. I, no. 2]

4. Eleanor of Aquitaine. 5. Ball.

The Miller and the King.[1]

How the King was benighted in Sherwood, and lost his
Nobles, and of his meeting with the Miller.

Henry our Royal King,
would ride a hunting,
To the green Forrest
so pleasant and fair.
To have the Hart chased,
and dainty Does tripping,
Unto merry Sherwood
his Nobles repair,
Hawk and hound was unbound,
all things prepar'd,
For the same to the game,
with good regard.
All a long Summers day,
rode the King pleasantly,
With all his Princes,
and Nobles each one,
Chasing the Hart and Hind,
and the Buck gallantly,
Till the dark Evening
inforc'd him turn home,
Then at last riding fast,
he had lost quite,
All his Lords in the Wood,
late in dark night.
Wandring thus warily,
all alone up and down,
With a rude Miller,
he met at the last:

1. The miller was John Cockle of Mansfield, the King Henry II. This is a
chap book version of a ballad registered in 1675, but the story is much older.

Asking the ready way
unto fair Nottingham,
Sir, quoth the Miller,
your way you have lost;
Yet I think what I think,
truth for to say,
You do not likely
ride out of your way.
Why? what dost though think of me
quoth the King merrily,
Passing thy judgment
upon me so brief?
Good faith, quoth the Miller,
I mean not to flatter thee,
I guess thee to be,
but some Gentleman Thief:
Stand thee back in the Dark,
light thee not down,
Least that I presently,
crack thy Knaves crown.
Thou dost abuse me much,
quoth the King, saying thus,
I am a Gentleman,
and lodging do lack.
Thou hast not qd.[2] the Miller,
one Groat[3] in thy purse,
All thy inheritance
hangs on thy back.
I have Gold to discharge,
all that I call,
If it be forty pence,
I will pay all.
If thou be'st a true Man,
then, quoth the Miller,
I swear by my Cole-dish,[4]
i'le lodge thee all night.

2. Quod, or quoth, i.e. said. 3. Fourpence. 4. Cabbage.

Here's my hand quoth the King,
that I was ever,
Nay soft quoth the Miller,
thou may'st be a spright:[5]
Better i'le know thee,
e're hands I will shake,
With none but honest men
hands will I take.

How the Miller brought the King home to Ienny his
Wife and his Son Richard.

Thus they went all along,
unto the Millers house.
Where they were seething,[6]
of Pudding and Souse;[7]
The Miller first entred in,
then after him the King,
Never came he in,
so smoaky a house?
Now (quoth he) let me see,
here what you are,
Quoth our King look your fill,
and do not spare.
I like well they countenance,
thou hast an honest face,
With my Son Richard,
this night thou shalt lye:
Quoth his wife by my troth,
it is a handsome youth;
Yet it is best (Husband)
for to deal warily.
Art thou not a Run-away,
I prethee Youth tell?

5. Sprite. 6. Boiling. 7. Pig's trotters or ears.

Shew me thy Pasport,[8]
and all shall be well:
Then our King presently,
making low courtesie,
With his hat in his hand,
thus he did say,
I have no Pasport,
nor never was servitor,
But a poor Courtier
rode out of my way.
And for your kindness
here offered to me,
I will requite it,
in every degree.
Then to the Miller,
his Wife whispered secretly,
Saying it seemeth
this youth is of good kin,
But by his apparel,
and eke by his manners,
To turn him out certainly,
it were a great sin.
Yea, qd. he, you may see,
he hath some grace,
When he doth speak
to his betters in place.
Well, quoth the Millers wife,
young-man welcome here,
And though I say it,
well lodg'd thou shalt be,
Fresh straw I will have
laid on your bed so brave,
Good brown Hempton[9] sheets,
likewise quoth she:
I, quoth the good man,

8. A permit to travel, usually to a fixed destination. 9. Archaic form of hemp-
en, made of hemp like sacking.

and when that is done,
You shall lye with no worse,
then our own Son.
Nay, first, quoth Richard,
good fellow tell me true,
Hast thou no creepers
within thy gay hose?
Or art thou not troubled
with the Scabbado,[10]
I pray quoth our King,
what things are those?
Art thou not lowsie
nor scabby, quoth he,
If thou be'st, surely
thou ly'st not with me. . . .

How the Nobles and his Followers sought the King, and
found him at the Millers House.

At last at the Millers house,
soon they espy'd him plain,
As he was mounting
upon his fair Steed.
To whom they came presently,
falling upon their knee,
Which made the Millers heart,
wofully bleed:
Shaking and quaking,
before them he stood.
Thinking he should have been
hang'd by the Rood.[11]
The King perceiving him
fearful and trembling,
Drew forth his Sword,
but nothing he said.

10. Venereal disease. 11. Cross, thus gallows.

The Miller down did fall,
crying before them all,
Doubting the King would have
cut off his head:
But his kind courtesie
for to requite,
Gave him a living,
and made him a Knight.
When as our Noble King,
came home from Nottingham,
And with his Nobles
at Westminster lay,
Recounting the sports
and pastime they had tane,
In this late progress
along by the way:
Of them all great and small,
thus he did protest,
The Miller of Mansfield's sport,
liked him best:
And now my Lords, qd. the King,
I am determined,
Against St. Georges day,
a sumptuous Feast.
That this old Miller,
our last confirmed Knight,
With his Son Richard
shall both be my guest.
For in this merriment,
'tis my desire,
To talk with the jolly Knight,
and the young Squire. . . .

Long Meg.[1]

The Life and Pranks of Long MEG
of WESTMINSTER

CHAP. I.

Containing where she was born, how she came to London, and
how she beat the Carryer.

In the time of Henry the Eight, there was born in Lancashire a
Maid (for her excess in height) called Long Meg, at 18 years of age
she would needs come to London, to get a Service.[2] Father
Willis the Carrier being her Neighbour, was the Man she made
choice of to bring her up,[3] being accompanied with three or four
Lasses more. After a long travel, being come at last within the
sight of the much desired City, she observed her fellow Travellers
to wax sad, she demanded the cause of their heaviness? one of
them made answer, because the Carryer being a hard Man,
demanded more Money then they had in their Purses, for leting
them ride a little on his Pack-Saddle. Meg replyed, If that be all,
fear not, I will either speak him fair, or fall upon him so fouly,
that I will deal well enough with him for that. This put them in
some comfort, and as they were in this discourse, entring into
Saint-John-Street from Islington, Father Willis came to them,
and demanded Money for Riding. What will you have, quoth
Meg? Marry, said he, ten shillings a piece. What, quoth she, 'tis
more Money than we have in our purses, you are a merry Man
indeed; we will give you a Gallon of Wine, and make you
amends hereafter when we are more able; in the mean time, as
the earnest of it, you shall have of every one of us a Kiss. At
which the Carrier stormed, and Meg smiled, which so incensed

1. A ballad on this famous Robin Hood for women was registered in 1590.
2. This confirms the growing body of demographic data about widespread
migration to London from the provinces in the sixteenth and seventeenth
centuries. 3. Sc. to London.

him, that he swore if they would not pay him, he would cudgel ten Shillings out of their bones. Marry content, quoth Meg, and taking a staff into her hand, she did so belabour him and his Man that he desired her for Gods sake to hold her hands: Not I, quoth she, unless you first bestow an Angel on each of us for a handsel⁴ our good luck, and swear e're you depart London, to place us all three with Mistrisses. The Carrier having felt the weight of her Arm thought it better to give three Angels, then to receive so many blows as she should bestow on him, and therefore not only gave them the Money but swore not to remove from London till he had seen them all three plac'd.

CHAP. VI.

Containing a merry Jest, how she met with a Nobleman, and how she used both him and the Watch.

It chanced one Evening, that Meg in a frolick humour did put on a Suit of Mans Apparel, and with her Sword and Buckler⁵ walked the Streets; the same night it fell out, that a young Nobleman being disposed to be merry, would needs go abroad with his Man to see Fashions, and coming down the Strand, he espyed Meg, and seeing such a tall Fellow swinging up and down, thought to have a cast at him; and coming to him, How now Fellow (quoth he) whither walkest thou? Marry (quoth Meg) to Saint Nicholas Shambles to buy Calves Heads. How much Money (quoth the Nobleman) hast thou in thy purse? In Faith (quoth Meg) little enough, wilt lend me any? I marry (quoth the Nobleman) and putting his Thumb to Megs mouth, said, there's a Tester.⁶ Whereupon Meg up with her fist, and took him a good Box on the Ear and said, There (Sir Knave) there's a Groat⁷ again, and now I owe you but two pence: whereupon the Noble-

---

4. Token or present. The page has been shaved by the binder but the word after handsel must be 'For'. 5. Meg had already fought for Henry VIII in France. 6. Sixpence; probably a pun on taster. 7. Fourpence.

man drew,[8] and his Man too. And Meg was as active as they, and together they go, but Meg drave them before her, and Housed them in a Chandlers shop, insomuch that the Constable came in to part the fray, and having asked what they were the Nobleman told his name, whereat they all put off their Caps. And what is your name quoth the Constable to Meg? Mine, quoth she, is Cutbeart Curry Knave; Upon this the Constable commanded to lay hold on her and carry her to the Counter.[9] Meg out with her Sword, and did set upon the Watch, and behaved her self very resolutely: but the Constable called for Clubs, and then Meg was fain to cry out, Masters, hold your hands, I am Long Meg of Westminster. With that they all stayed, and the Nobleman would needs have her, the Constable, and all the rest, to the Tavern, and concluded the Fray in a Cup of Wine.

CHAP. XII

Containing a pleasant Jest, how she used the angry Miller of Epping, in Essex.

Meg going on foot one day with Sundry of her Neighbours, to make merry in Essex, it being a great frost, & none with them but a young stripling of fourteen years of age, it chanced that they went by Epping Mill, where the Miller looked out (for the wind blew fair, and the Sails went merrily) the little Boy, that was a Wag, thought to have been merry with the Miller, and therefore called to him, put out, put out Miller, put out: What shall I put out Boy, quoth the Miller? Marry, quoth the Boy, a Thieves head, and Thieves pair of ears, put out Miller, put out.[10]

At this the Miller in a great rage, came down and beat the Boy. Meg stepped to him, and would have staid his hand, and the Miller lent her three or four good bangs over the Shoulders, Meg

8. Sc. his sword. 9. Or compter: prison, mainly for debtors. 10. Millers were frequently depicted as swindling people through giving them inferior flour; they were also traditionally lecherous.

felt it smart, and getting in within the Miller, did wring the stick out of his hands, with which she cudgell'd him to some tune; and when she had done, she sent the Boy up the Millers stairs for an empty Sack, and put the Miller in it, all but the Head, and fastning him to the Rope, wherewith he pulled up the Sacks, she haled[11] him half way, and there let him hang. The poor Miller cryed out for help, and if by Fortune his Wife had not been coming, he had been almost killed; and the Mill (for want of Corn) set on Fire.[12] Thus Meg plagued the saucy Miller of Epping.

[Vol. II, no. 26]

11. Hoist. 12. Because of the friction between the two millstones.

The Excellent and Renowned
HISTORY
Of the Famous
Sir *Richard Whittington*,
Three times Lord-Mayor of the Honoura-
ble City of *LONDON*.

Giving an Account of all the Remarkable and noted
Passages of his Life.

This may be Printed, *R. P.*

Dick Whittington.[1]

CHAP. III.

How Whittington, by reason of his hard Usage, attempting
to run away, was brought back by the ringing of Bow
Bells; and of the great Riches he received for the
Adventure of his Cat, and how it came to pass.

Whittington being still in Mr. Fitzwarren's[2] house, under the
imperious Cook-maid; and she finding her power over him, used
it with such rigour, that it made him, in a manner weary of his
Life: which put him upon purpose of running away; and in order
thereto, early in the morning on St. Allhallows-day,[3] he packed
up his cloaths and went as far as Bun hill-fields where, it being
yet scarce day, he sate him down to consider whether or to what
place he should go; and to bewail his unhappy and uneasie
Condition: when, to his thinking, he heard the Bells at Bow-
Church in Cheap-side, in their tuning express these Words; viz.

> Turn again Whittington
> Thrice Lord Mayor of London.

> Turn again Whittington
> Thrice Lord Mayor of London.[4]

This made so deep an impression in his mind, that it quite
altered his former Determination and made him resolve upon
returning again to his Service; which he accordingly did, e'er
he was missed by any of the Family: where we must leave him
for a while to follow his drudgery, and bear patiently the Cook-
maids Doggedness and Cruelty. . . .
[Vol. II, no. 31]

1. A younger son of a Gloucestershire knight; 1358–1423. A popular ballad
about him was registered in 1605; he is also featured in Richard Johnson's
Crown Garland, III, 3 of *Penny Merriments*. 2. A relative, a merchant, and
Whittington's master. 3. All Saints Day, Nov. 1. 4. In 1397, 1406 and 1419.

A True Tale of *ROBIN HOOD.*

Or, A Brief Touch of the Life and Death of that renowned Outlaw *Robert* Earl of *Huntington*, vulgar-
ly called *Robin Hood*, who lived and dyed in A. D.
1198. being the 9th. year of the Reign of King
Richard the First, commonly called *Richard Cœur
de Lyon.*

Carefully collected out of the truest Writers of our
English Chronicles : And published for the satisfaction of those who desire truth from falshood.

By *Martin Parker.*

Printed for *J. Clark*, W. *Thackeray*, and
T. *Passinger*. 1686.

Robin Hood.[1] 1686.

Both Gentlemen & Yeomen bold
or whatsoever you are,
To have a stately story told
attention now prepare:
It is a Tale of Robin Hood,
that I to you will tell,
Which being rightly understood,
I know will please you well.
This Robin (so much talked on)
was once a man of Fame,
Instiled[2] Earl of Huntington,
Lord Robert Hood by Name.
In Courtship[3] and Magnificence
his Carriage won him praise,
And greater favour with his Prince
than any in our days.
In bounteous Liberality
he too much did excell,
And loved men of Quality
more than exceeding well:
His great Revenues all he sold
for Wine and costly chear,
He kept three hundred Bow-men bold,
he shooting lov'd so dear:
No Archer living in his time
with him might well compare:
He practis'd all his youthful prime
that Exercise most rare.
At last by his profuse expence
he had consum'd his wealth;

1. From the Lytel Geste of Robin Hood, published in 1490, the legendary outlaw was the most popular hero of ballad and chap book literature for the next two centuries. 2. Styled. 3. Courteous behaviour, or the state befitting a court.

And being outlaw'd by his Prince,
in Woods he liv'd by stealth.
The Abbot of St. Maries rich,
to whom he mony ought,
His hatred to the Earl was such,
that he his downfal wrought.
So being outlaw'd (as 'tis told)
he with a Crew went forth
Of lusty Cutters stout and bold,
and robbed in the North.
Among the rest one Little John
a Yeoman bold and free,
Who could (if it stood him upon)
with ease encounter three:
One hundred men in all he got,
with whom (the story says)
Three hundred common men durst not
hold combat any waies.
They Yorkshire Woods frequented much
and Lancashire also,
Wherein their practises were such
that they wrought muckle woe.
None Rich durst travel to and fro,
though ne'r so strongly arm'd,
But by these Thieves (so strong in show)
they still were rob'd and harm'd.
His chiefest spight to th' Clergy was
that liv'd in monstrous pride:
No one of them he would let pass
along the High-way side,
But first they must to dinner go,
and afterwards to shrift:[4]
Full many a one he served so,
thus while he liv'd by Theft.
No Monks nor Fryers he would let go,
without paying their Fees:

4. Penance; here, ironically, handing over their valuables.

If they thought much to be used so,
their Stones he made them lese:[5]
For such as they the Country fill'd
with Bastards in those days:
Which to prevent, these Sparks did geld
all that came in their ways
But Robin Hood so gentle was,
and bore so brave a mind,
If any in distress did pass,
to them he was so kind,
That he would give and lend to them
to help them in their need;
This made all poor men pray for him
and wish he well might speed.
The Widow and the Fatherless
he would send means unto:
And those whom famine did oppress
found him a friendly foe.
Nor would he do a woman wrong,
but see her safe convey'd
He would protect with power strong
all those who crav'd his aid. . . .

[Vol. II, no. 36]

5. Stones is slang for testicles; lese, archaic for lose, i.e. castrate. This strong
anticlericalism probably stems from the fifteenth and early sixteenth centuries,
and is reminiscent of Poggio and Rabelais.

Jack of Newbery.[1] By W.S.F.C. 1684.

The most delightful History of JACK of Newberry.

In the Reign of King Henry the Eighth, one John Winch-comb, being an Apprentice to a rich Clothier in the town of Newberry in Barkshire, a pretty handsome Youth, his Master dyed, and left his Mistress a widow; who perceiving Jack to be a faithful, careful, and trusty Servant, she put him in great trust in the House; who as carefully performed the trust reposed in him.

His Mistress having many Sutors coming to her, could not fancy any: for her man John had stoln away her Heart. The Parson of Spinhome-land[2] woo'd her, and often solicited with her to make her his wife, but could not obtain her love, because he was a Clergy-man; too much (she thought) devoted to his Study. A rich Tanner was a second wooer, but could not speed; for though he was rich, yet was he too old for her young and lusty desires. A Taylor was a third man, who was almost confident of her love; but all in vain, for her man John, oh! he was the man that had so wounded her heart that she could love no other man.

She seeing the backwardness of John, her man (after many occasions which she gave him to woo her) came at last, and told him plainly that she loved him, which secret she did earnestly desire him not to impart to any; but he very modestly blushing with a Rosie colour in his cheeks, not knowing how to express himself as he desired, being astonished hereat; answered: Sweet Mistress (quoth he) I am but a Child to undertake so great a thing! it is a charge, the discharge whereof me thinks I fear to undertake: At which answer, she was something discouraged in her sute for the present; and kissing of him, brake off discourse for that time; and night approaching, she went to Bed; . . . But when she had lain in bed an hour or two, she began to think

1. Died 1520. His classic success story was popularised by Deloney in 1597; eight editions in the next twenty years. The destructive side of the rise of the cloth industry is depicted in the opening of Sir Thomas More's *Utopia*.
2. Speenhamland, famed a century later than this edition for its poor law system.

it very long to lye alone; so she arose out of her bed, and went to her man John, shivering and shaking, and lifting up his bed-cloths, he started; Who is there, quoth he? It is I my sweet Iohn, quoth she, I am your Mistress; it is an extreme cold Night, and I, lying alone, am almost starved[3] in my Bed: Good Iohn afford me the favour of one Nights lodging by thy side, my Iohn, I pray thee. Alas, poor Mistress, quoth he, come come lie close: Yea, yea, quoth she, ah! poor sweet Iohn; oh! sweet, sweet, Iohn: oh! sweet and good Iohn; but here I leave them till the next morning.

She got up very early in the morning, and calling for John her man to go abroad with her, she took him to the Church of Saint Bartholomews; and calling for the Priest of the place, she, with him perswaded Iohn that they might then be married together; which with small intreaty he was perswaded to; and so they returned home; and when they went to dinner, she made him to sit in her old husbands Chair by her self at the end of the Table; at which his old fellow-servants began to smile: and before Dinner was ended, she took him about the neck and kissed him, and told her Servants that he was her Husband, and commanded them to give him the respects due to a Master. . . .

Shortly after the King was to raise an Army of Souldiers against the Scots, who was risen against the English;[4] and Iack of New-berry raised at his own charges an hundred and fifty men; and allowed white Coats, red Caps, and yellow Feathers; and led them himself: fifty of them were valiant Horsemen; fifty Pikes, and fifty Musquetiers; all brave Steeds, good Arms, and valiant men; who marching by before the Queen, Queen Katherine;[5] she called for him, and understanding what he was, after she had put forth her hand for him to kiss, she promised to acquaint the King's Majesty with his free and great service. . . .

Now to return again to Jack and his Wife, it fell out that she fell sick and dyed; and being buried, Jack fell in love with one of

3. Not a Freudian slip; to be starved with cold was a common usage in the seventeenth century. 4. Culminating in the Scots' defeat at Flodden, 1513. 5. Of Aragon.

his maids: and sending for her Father, to know what he would give with his Daughter: he came to Newberry, and seeing the wealth of his Daughters sweet-heart, and master, he was astonished: for Iack had, viz.

> In one Room two hundred Looms all going.
> Two hundred Boys making Quills.[6]
> A hundred Women Carding.
> Two hundred Maids in another Room spinning.
> An hundred and fifty Boys picking of Wool.
> Fifty Shiermen.[7]
> Eight Rowers.[8]
> Fourty Dyers in the Dy-house.
> Twenty men in a Fulling-Mill.
> Ten fat Oxen he spent every week in his house, besides
>   Butter, Cheese, Fish, etc.
> A Butcher ⎫
> A Baker   ⎬   for his own house.
> A Brewer ⎭
> Five Cooks.
> Six Scullion Boys.
> Divers Turn-spits, etc.

[Vol. II, no. 50]

---

6. For bobbins. 7. Sheep-shearers. 8. One who puts a nap on cloth.

'Jane Shore' (This is in fact a picture of Queen
Elizabeth, but it was common practice to use any
available woodcut as illustration.)

Cupids Garland.

The Contents.

> Cupids Garland here is set, with Guilded Roses round,
> And if the Reader like of it, the Garland then is crown'd.

[Vol. II, no. 38]

---

1. 1525-1578; supposedly bastard son of Henry VIII, gallant and adventurer, died at Battle of Alcazar. 2. Jane Shore, died a beggar. 3. Eleanor, mistress and second wife of Humphrey, Duke of Gloucester. Hanged in 1441 as sorceress. 4. Traditional romance, popularised by Johnson in *The Crown Garland*, of member of Mortimer family, who saw Isabel bathing in the Avon, carried her off to the Castle, where she killed herself to save her chastity.

II. MAGIC

Mother Bunch's Closet.[1] by T.R.[2] 1685.

Mother BUNCH's
CLOSET
newly broke open.
Wherein is discovered many Rare Secrets of
ART & NATURE;
Tryed and Experienced by Learned Phylo-
sophers, and recommended to all inge-
nious Young-Men and Maids.

Teaching Young-Men (in a natural way) how
to get *Good Wifes*, & Maids *Good Husbands*.
Experimented by ancient Authors, as, *viz. The
manner* of St. Agnes *Fast*,[3] the 21st. of *January*.
The washing of the Smock on Midsummer *Eve.*
The soweing of Hempseed. The Dutch Cake.
Teaching them how in sleep and Dreams to
see and know them perfectly.

> *No harm at all is in this set,*
> *But teaching Maids Husbands to get,*
> *And also young Men of each degree,*
> *Turn o're the Leaf and you may see*
> *What there is writ in merriment,*
> *Hoping to give you all content.*

By your Loving Friend poor *Tom* for the King a Lover of
Mirth, but a Hater of Traytors and Treason.[4] *T.R.*

Printed by *A.M.* for *P. Brooksby* in *Py-corner*, 1685.

1. Title-page. Mother Bunch was a famous alewife in Elizabethan London.
See Wardroper, *Jest*, pp. 154–5. 2. Probably Thomas Robins, a popular
seventeenth-century ballad writer. 3. When maids dream of future husbands.
4. This suggests that the first edition of this version was written during or
following the Civil War.

... Now for those poor young Creatures that have pined them-selves to the *Green Sickness*,[5] and neglect the Cure till it is almost past; those that are the worst Pretenders to Phisnomy[6] might easily guess their Distemper and prescribe their Remedy without the help of a Dispensatory:[7] And all those (of what constitution soever) that languish in single sheets till fifteen I will tell (if your courage will serve to try the Experiment) how you shall know & see the persons that shall ease you of the simple thing, so much talked of, called a *Maidenhead*, by him that must be your Husband; collected from the *Twelve Sybills*,[8] *Trismajistus*,[9] and *Cornelius Aggrippa*;[10] and this is

The first Way.

You that desire to know it this way must wait till *Midsummer Eve*, then at night three or four of you, or more, or less, must take your Smocks and dip them in fair water, then turn the wrong side outward and hang them on Chairs before the Fire, and have by you a Vessel with drink in it, and lay some Salt in another before the fire, and be sure not to speak a word whatever you hear or see; and in a little time the likeness of those persons you shall marry will come & turn your smocks and drink to you: now if there be any of you that will never marry, they will hear a Bell, but not the rest; but whoever hears this Bell, none of my Authors is positive that she shall dye a Maid.

---

5. Complaint, probably psychosomatic, suffered by virgins and cured by sexual intercourse; often mentioned. 6. Slang for physiognomy; here diagnosis from the face. 7. Medical book. 8. Classical prophetesses systematised by medieval theologians to twelve. 9. Hermes Trismegistus. 10. 1486-1535; German writer on the occult and hermetic philosophy.

Another : and quickly tryed.

Which is this: You are only to take a little Hempseed, and go
into what place you please by your self, & carry the Seed in
your Apron, and with your right hand throw it over your left
shoulder, saying thus,

> Hempseed I sow; Hempseed I sow;
> He that must be my true love come after me and mow[11]

and at the ninth time expect to see the Figure of him you are to
have, or else to hear a Bell, as before.

> Yet though you hear this sad & dismal Bell,
> 'Tis your own fault if you lead Apes in Hell.[12]

Another Way.

Which is this: You that dare venture your selves into a Church-
Yard, just as it strikes Twelve, take there a naked Sword in your
hand, and go nine times about the Church, saying only thus,
Here's the Sword, but where's the Scabbard? which continue all
the time you go round, and the ninth time the Person you are to
marry will meet you with a Scabbard & kiss you, if not a Bell,
as before.[13]

Another which is called the Dutch Cake.

Three or four, or more of you, are to make a Cake of half Flower
and half Salt (no matter what Flower it is) and some of every
one of your own water, make this Cake broad and thin, then
every one of you either make a mark that you know, or set the
two first Letters of your Name on it with a great Pin or Bodkin,

---

11. Sow and mow were often rhymed together, with obvious sexual
connotations. 12. Proverbial fate of old maids; apes symbolic of lechery.
13. This common phallic symbolism would seem more suitable for intending
husbands.

but leave such a distance that it may be cut, then set it before the Fire to bake, but all this while speak not one word, turn it every one of you once, then let it bake a little more, and then throw on every one a little Salt, and she that turn'd it first let her turn it again, then the person to be her Husband will cut out her name and break it in two & give her one half; and so the next, and the next, till the last; If there be any so unfortunate to hear a Bell, I wish I had them to my Bedfellows this night, to prevent leading Apes in Hell.

Lady Fortune *gave such a Purse in* Spain,
When it was empty, strait 'twas full again.

Fortunatus receiving the purse from Lady Fortune.[2]

Of Wives, Husbands and Children.

Lines reaching from the mount of the thumb, over the mount (towards the line of life) shew the number of wives or husbands;[3] therefore observe how many there be; and if it be a man, he shall certainly have so many wives, or (as the fashion is) Town

1. Saunders and Nathaniel Colson were both well-known astrologers and competitors with William Lilly. 2. Famous legend, see short-title list, Vol. I, no. 18 of eastern origin. Fortune gives a young wanderer a self-replenishing purse of gold. 3. In an age when the mortality rate was far higher, remarriage was far more frequent, and step-parents, wicked or otherwise, a commonplace.

Misses;[4] if it be a woman-kind, she shall have so many husbands, or at least a Bolus[5] to keep her from the Green-sickness.

As many lines as cut the first joynt of the Ring-finger, so many Husbands or Wives shall the party have.

Certain little lines cutting the line of Life, being well colour'd, so many as there be, so many children they promise either in man or woman.

Now having laid open the significations of those lines and signal observations which tend to prosperity, I will proceed to those which portend or foreshew want or poverty, infirmities, imprisonment, untimely Death, and universal misfortune; of this I shall treat more largely than of good hap,[6] it being far more requisite to prevent or lessen an evil, than to be fond of pleasure or profit. . . .

Of Whoredom and Lust.

The sister of the line of life, on the mount of the Thumb, long and reddish, in the hand of a Woman, intimates she will kiss in a corner, or (in a plainer sence) is a little whorish.

The Mount or rising of the Thumb big, and elevated with many cross disordered lines, is a sign the person is a light[7] Huzzy.

The Table-line small and forked, and the Mount of the fore-finger rising high, in the root of which are little marks like pricks, usually signifieth a man to tread more hens than his own, and a woman to beat her puff-past with her neighbours rowling-pin.[8]

Lines chequerwise near the wrist of the hand denotes a woman excessively wanton; one that cannot fix her humours[9] to a constant Diet, but wholly delights in variety.

---

4. A mistress. Cf. *The Character of a Towne Miss* (London, 1675). This term was very popular in the Restoration period. 5. A medicinal capsule, but here, probably, a dildo, or penis-substitute. 6. Fortune. 7. Lecherous, wanton. 8. Both metaphors for sexual promiscuity. 9. Wishes or constitution.

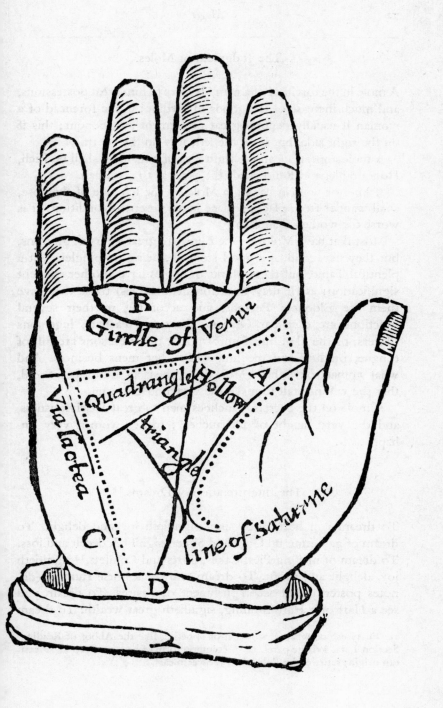

The Judgment of Moles.

A mole in the forehead of a man, denotes to him great possessions, and much increase of the goods of fortune; in the forehead of a woman it usually denotes great preferment and honour; this if on the right side, but if on the left, it is on the contrary.

A mole appearing on the right Ear of a man, he shall be Rich, Honourable, and Renowned; the same as to a woman.

A Man or woman having a Mole on the left side of the nose, shall wander from place to place in an unsettled condition: It is worse for women than men.

Most that have Moles on their lips, are great eaters or gluttons, but they never fail of a good stomach, being no pinglers[10] at a plentiful Table, but these Marks or Moles have another eminent signification; as (if they were fortunate Moles) those that have them are Eloquent Persons, and according to their several functions are excellent Orators, Famous Preachers, ingenious Players, or the like: but if unfortunate, those Persons are full of tongue, pratling and medling with other mens business. And what woman soever has a Mole there, she is so notorious a Scold, that she will not fail to make the very house to ring.

A mole on the Secrets,[11] inclines men to great Lasciviousness, and the very height of Debauchery: makes women very unhappy. . . .

The Interpretation of Dreams.[12]

To dream you hear Birds sing, signifieth joy and delight. To dream of gathering up Gold and Silver, signifieth deceit and loss. To dream of making Pies, Cakes, Tarts and Comfets,[13] signifieth joy, delight and profit. To dream you see a horse running, denotes posterity and accomplishment of desires. To dream you see a Hart or a Hare running, signifieth great wealth. To dream

10. Fussy eaters, without stomach or appetite, like the Abbot of Reading, Section I. 11. Private parts. 12. A common form of prognostication, of eastern origin; satirised by Rabelais. 13. Sweetmeats.

of hearing Bells ringing, signifieth an Alarm or Disturbance amongst Citizens. To dream you hear singing or playing upon Instruments, denotes recovering of health to those that are sick. To dream of seeing a Comedy Acted, denotes good success in Business. To dream one plays at Cards or Dice, signifies deceit and craft, and being cheated. To dream you won at Dice, denotes that some Inheritance will fall to you by the death of some of your Relations. To dream one is married, signifies sickness. To dream one hath Gloves on his hands, denotes Honour. To dream a man is in bed with a handsome woman, denotes deceit.

[Vol. I, no. 50]

The Mirror of Natural Astrology:
OR,
A NEW BOOK
OF
FORTUNE.
SHEWING,

The Nature of *planets*, how any one may know
what their fortune is, born under such a *planet*.

Written by Mr. *LILLY*.

Printed for *W. T.* and Sold by *J. Deacon*, at
the Angel in *Guilt-spur-Street*,

Mr. Lilly, 1602–1681; Mr. Lilly's first almanac appeared in 1644. He was
widely read in England and even in Europe.

Lilly's New Erra Pater.[1]

Notable Observations on the most remarkable
days in every month throughout the year.

January.

If on New-years day in the morning, the Clouds be red, there
will be much anger, war, and great tempests that year.

If the Sun do shine on the twenty second day of January, there
will be plenty of Wine that year.

If the Sun do shine on St. Paul's day, being the 25. day, it
shall be a fruitful year, and if it rain or snow, there will be neither
much plenty nor much scarcity. If it be very misty on that day, it
betokens great death, if thou hear it thunder that day, it foreshews great wind, and great death, especially among rich men, as
saith Erra Pater, junior.

February.

On Shrove-tuesday, whosoever doth plant or sow, it shall remain
alwaies green: also how much the Sun doth shine that day, so
much he shall shine every day in Lent; & when on that day the
Sun shineth early, then doth all manner of fruit prosper, and
Thunder on that day betokeneth great winds and much Fruit.

March.

The more mists there be in March, the more good it doth; and
as many days as be in March, so many heavy Frosts shall be after
Easter, and so many mists in August.

1. Erra Pater was supposedly 'a Jewe born in Jewery' who published a
perpetual almanac c. 1535.

All manner of trees that shall be cut down[2] on either of the two last holidays in March, shall never fail.

If on Palm Sunday be no fair weather, it foreshews good; if it do thunder that day, it signifieth a merry year and death of great men. . . .

Infallible Signs of Rainy Weather, deduced from the Observation of divers Animals.

If Ducks or Drakes their wings do flutter high,
Or tender Colts upon their backs do lye,
If Sheep do bleat or play or skip about,
Or Swine hide Straw by bearing on their snout;
If Oxen lick themselves against the Hair,
Or grazing Kine to feed apace appear,
If Cattel bellow gazing from below,
Or if Dogs Intrials rumble to and fro;
If Doves or Pigeons in the Evening come
Later than usual to their Dove-house home;
If Crows and Daws do oft themselves bewet,
Or Ants and Pismires[3] home apace do get;
If in the Dust Hens do their Pinions[4] shake,
Or by their flocking a great number make;
If Swallows fly upon the Water low,
Or Wood-Lice seem in Armies for to go;
If Flies, or Gnats, or Fleas infest and bite
Or sting more than they'r wont by day or night,
If Toads hie home, or Frogs do croke amain,
Or Peacocks cry, soon after look for Rain.

[Vol. II, no. 19]

2. Trimmed or pruned? 3. Another word for ants. 4. Outer part of wing.

The most Pleasant and Delightful[1] Art of Palmistry,

Wherein every Man or Woman may give Judgment on themselves or others, by the exact tracing the Lines of the hand, which is shewed by many familiar Examples, whether good or bad Fortune attends them: in Riches or Poverty. In health or sickness.
Sickness, whether it shall end in life or death.
Whether a man or woman shall marry to their future happiness.
If any thing stolen or lost shall be had again.
If a person shall win at play.

With exact Tables demonstrating the same.

As likewise, the Names and Characters of the Planets; with a perfect description of their power and rule in the Bodies of Men and Women.
Also the Art of using the Mosaycal Rod,[2] to find out hidden Treasure, the manner and time of gathering the same Rod.
Out of the Learned *Sacrobosco*,[3] Cardinal *Morbeth*,[4] *Tricassus*,[5]
Mr. *Saunders, and* Mr. *Lilly*, etc.

To which is added,

Mr. Saunders's Art of *Dyalling*, to know the hour of the day by the hand; *necessary for all Travellers.*
Faithfully Collected by J.M. to prevent superstitious ones.

With Allowance.[6]

Printed by *A.M.* for *J. Deacon* and *C. Dennisson*, and are to be sold at either of their Shops, at the Angel in Guiltspur Street,[7]

[Vol. II, no. 8]

---

1. This is the title-page. 2. Divining rod; *Exodus*, ii, 2–5. 3. John Holywood, mathematician and astronomical author, ob. 1244 or 1256. 4. I cannot trace him. 5. Patricio Tricasso of Mantua wrote on Chiromancy in 1525. 6. Sc. of the Licenser of the Press. 7. Shaved by the binder.

Mother Shipton[1].

CHAP. I.

Of Mother Shiptons strange Parentage, and the place of her Birth.

Mother Shipton (as all Histories agree) was a Yorkshire woman; but the particular place is very much disputed, because several Towns have pretended to the honour of her Birth; But the most credible and received opinion ascribes it to Nascborough, near the dropping Well, in the County aforesaid: concerning her Pedigree or Parentage there is likewise very various Report. Some say, that her Father was a Necromancer and that skill in the Black Art thereby became intail'd upon her by inheritance; but the common Story (which therefore I shall follow, yet without forcing the Reader to believe it whether he will or no) is, That she never had any Father of humane Race, or mortal wight, but was begot (as the great Welsh Prophet Merlin was of old) by the Phantasm of Apollo, or some wanton Airial Daemon, in the manner following.

Her Mother (whom some Records call Agatha, and others Emmatha) being left an Orphan about the age of sixteen, very poor, and much troubled with that grievous, but common disease, called by some Idleness, and by others Sloth; as she was once upon a time sitting, bemoning her self on a shady bank by the Highway side, this spirit appear'd to her in the shape of a very handsom young man, & smiling on her, Pretty maid, quoth he, why dost thou sit so sad? Thou art not old enough to have thy Head pestered with the cares of the World; prithee tell me the business, and doubt not but I will help thee out of all thy troubles. The Maid (for Maids there were in those days at her age) casting up her eyes, and not suspecting a devil in so comely a countenance, related to him her wants, and that she knew not

1. Popular cunning woman; first published in 1641.

how to live; pish! said he, that's nothing, but be ruled by me and thou shalt never lack; she hearing him promise so fairly, told him she would; and thereupon to draw her in by degrees to destruction he first tempted her to Fornication, and prevailed so far as to gain her, but his Touch as she afterwards confessed to the Midwife were as cold as Ice or Snow. From this time forward she was commonly once a day visited by her Hellish Gallant, and never wanted money, for still as she swept the House, she should find some odd pieces, as Ninepence[2] Quarters of thirteen-pence-half-pennys,[3] and the like, sufficient to supply all her occasions.

CHAP. 2.

How Mother Shiptons Mother proved with child; How she fitted the severe Justice, and what hapned at her delivery.

The Neighbors observing Agatha without any Employ to live so handsomly, wondred exceedingly how she came by it, but were more surprized shortly afterward, when they perceiv'd her to be with child, which she could not long hide, for before her delivery, she was as big as if she had gone with half a dozen children at once; whereupon she was carried before a Justice,[4] who chid & threatened her for her incontinency, but he was soon silenced, for his Wife and all his Family being present, Agatha said to him aloud, Mr. Justice, gravely you talk now, and yet the truth is, your Worship is not altogether free, for here stands Two of your Servant wenches, that are both at this time with Child by you;[5] pointing to them severally with her finger: at which both himself and the two Girls were so blank, that his wife plainly saw what she said was true, and therefore fell upon two poor Harlots like a fury, so all Mr. Justice and the Constable

2. Silver coin, often given as love-tokens. 3. Popular slang for a hangman, from his pay. 4. Probably because her bastard would become a charge on the parish. 5. A not uncommon comic situation; cf. speech of Polly Baker, attributed to Benjamin Franklin.

could do was not enough to keep the peace, and the whole family
was in such confusion, that Agatha for that time was dismist, and
soon after was brought to bed in the Month of July, in the 4.
year of the Reign of K. Henry the 7th. which was in the year of
our Lord, 1488. Her Travel[6] was very grievous, and a most
terrible Clap of thunder hapned just as she was delivered of this
strange birth, which afterward was so famous by the name of
Mother Shipton. Nor could the Tempest affright the women
more than the prodigious Physiognomy of the Child; the body
was long, but very big-boned, great gogling eyes, very sharp and
fiery, a Nose of unproportionable length, having in it many
crooks and turnings, adorned with great pimples, which like
vapours of brimstone gave such a lustre in the night, that her
Nurse needed no other Candle to dress her by; and besides this
uncouth shape, it was observ'd, that as soon as she was born,
she fell a laughing and grinning after a jeering manner, and
immediately the Tempest ceased.

CHAP. 3.

By what name mother Shipton was christened and how her Mother went into a Monastery.

The Child being thus brought into the World, under such strange
circumstances was (though not without some opposition) ordered
at last by the Abbot of Beverly to be christened, which was
performed by the name Ursula Soothtell:[7] for the later was her
mothers, and consequently her Maiden Sirname, and as for
Shipton, it was the name of her husband, whom she afterwards
married. . . .

---

6. Labour. 7. I.e. truthtell.

CHAP. 4.

Several other merry pranks plaid by Mother Shipton, in Revenge
to such as abused her.

As our Ursula grew up to riper years, she was often affronted, by
reason of her deformity, but she never fail'd to be revenged on
those that did it: As one day all the chief of the Parish being
together at a merry meeting, she coming thither occasionally[8]
on an Errand, some of them abused her by calling her, The Devils
Bastard, and Hag-face, and the like; whereupon she went away
grumbling, but so ordered affairs, that when they was set down
to Dinner, one of the principal Yeomen, that thought himself
spruce and fine, had in an instant his Ruff (which in those days
they wore) pull'd off, and the Seat of an House of Office[9] clapt
in its place; he that sate next him bursting out into a laughter
at the sight hereof, was served little better, for his Hat was
invisibly convey'd away, and the Pan of a Close-stool[10] which
stood in the next Room, put on instead thereof. Besides this, a
modest young Gentlewoman that sate at the Table at the same
time, looking at these two worthy Spectacles of mirth endeavour'd
all she could to Refrain laughing, but cou'd not, and withal
continued breaking of wind backward for above a quarter of an
hour together, like so many broad-sides in a Sea-fight, which
made all the company laugh so extremely, that the Master of the
house (being the chief Inn in the town) was alarm'd below therewith, and desirous to share with his Guests in their mirth, came
running up Stairs as fast as his legs would carry him, but being
about to enter the door, he could not, and no wonder, since the
oldest Man living never saw a larger pair of Horns than he had
on his Head.[11] But whilst they were gazing on one another, as
more than half distracted, they were all reduc'd to the same
condition they were in at first, after which followed a noise, as if

8. By chance. 9. Privy, lavatory. 10. Commode. 11. The sign of a cuckold,
from the Actaeon story.

more than a hundred persons were laughing together, but nothing was seen.

CHAP. 6.

Her Prophecy against Cardinal Woolsey.

By these and several the like exploits, Mother Shipton had got a name far and near for a cunning woman, or a woman of the foresight, so that her words began to be counted Oracles, nor did she meddle only with private persons, but was advised with concerned people of the greatest Quality; among which number at that time was Cardinal Woolsey, when it was reported, that he intended to live at York,[12] she publickly said, He should never come thither; which coming to his ear, and being much offended, he caused three Lords to go to her, who came disguised to Ring-house hear York, where leaving their men, they took a Guide and came to Mother Shipton's, where knocking at her door, she cryed out within, Come in Mr. Beasly (their Guide) and those Noble Lords with you. Which much surprized them that she should know them, for when they came in, she called each of them by name and treated them with Ale and Cakes, whereupon said one of the Lords, If you knew our Errand, you would not make so much of us, you said the Cardinal should never see York. No, said she, I said he might see York, but never come at it; Well saies the Lord, when he does come thou shalt be burnt.[13] Then taking off her Linnen Kerchief from her head, saies she, If this burn, then I may burn; and immediately flung it into the fire before them, but it would not burn, so that after it had lain in the flames a quarter of an hour, she took it out again not so much as singed. Hereupon one of the Lords askt her what she thought of him, My Lord, said she, the time is coming when your Grace will be as low as I am, and that is a

12. In early 1530, after his dismissal by Henry VIII. He had been archbishop of York since 1514, but had never visited his province. 13. Common Roman Catholic punishment for witches.

low one indeed. Which proved true, for shortly after he was beheaded.[14]

Nor was her speech of the Cardinal less verified, for he coming to Cawood, went to the top of the Tower, & askt where York was, which being shewn him, he enquired how far it was thither, For (qd. he) there was a Witch said, I should never see York. Nay, says one present, your Eminence is misinformed, she said you should see it, but not come at it. Then he vow'd to burn her when he came there, which was but eight miles distant, but behold, immediately he was sent for back by the King, and dyed of a violent Loosness at Leicester.

[Vol. I, no. 56]

14. Correctly contradicted in next paragraph.

The Fryer and the Boy.

. . . You oft have read that merry toy
Of the Fryer and the Boy,
    how sweetly he did play
Upon a sweet and merry Pipe,
That made mens senses quick and ripe,
    and dance both night and day.
And of his Step-dames cruelty,
And the report that she let fly,

1. This excerpt is from the second part, the only one in the collection. The first stanza is 'the story so far'. This is based on French *fabliau*, and may reflect medieval St. Vitus and tarantella cults. Cf. Pied Piper of Hamelin.

and of the Fryers intent,
And of his dancing in the bush,
When that he went to catch the Thrush,
how all his Clothes were rent,
How every man start up and danc't,
Proctors, Priests and Sumners[2] pranc't,
so long as they could stand.

His manly tricks I will recite,
Filled with mirth and much delight;
how he revenge did take,
Upon Tobias that stout Fryer,
And for his tricks gave him his hire,[3]
himself amends to make.

Jack departed from his Step-dame,
And went to serve a Gentleman,
and pleas'd him wondrous well,
And with his maid he fell in love,
Which unto him did faithless prove,
for truth as I here tell.

This Fryer us'd to her bed-side,
And did no more but up and ride;[4]
all this poor Jack beheld;
This caus'd Jack her to despise,
To see her fall and the Fryer rise;
revenge in's heart then swell'd. . . .

Above you may behold and see,[5]
How he is prostrate on his knee,
and in his hands a Cat;

Desiring that his love may turn
Into that shape, and ever mourn,
and catch both Mouse and Rat.

2. Proctors and summoners are both officials of ecclesiastical courts. 3. Paid him in his own coin. 4. A cliché sexual metaphor; friars were notoriously lecherous, at least among such detractors as Poggio. 5. In a woodcut.

Go on and prosper Venus said,
Fall to thy sports, be not afraid
to use thy utmost skill.

I granted have thy full intent,
But see thou use't in merriment,
no blood of life to spill,

The Fryer he was kneeling there,
And when he these words did hear,
they pierc'd him to the heart:

Now out alass the Fryer said,
I am in danger and afraid,
'tis I shall feel the smart,

Next night after he did spy
The Fryer in the maids bed to lye,
stark naked both they lay;

Then he pul'd out his Pipe and play'd,
And he like one that was afraid,
ran into the high way:

Both Fryer and maid leapt out o'th bed,
The Fryer fell down and broke his head,
thus danc't into the street;

Both old and young, both rich and poor,
Some out at window some, at door,
laughing each other greet.

The Cattel hearing of the same,
Straightway from their pastures came,
and merrily did dance;

The horses that most fast were ti'd,
Came galloping on every side,
and stately they did prance;

Also the swine aloud did cry,
And presently pull'd down their sty,
and these full high did capor,

Also the Bears began to roar,
And presently the stable tore,
they altogether vapor.

Like wild the Cats came dancing in,
Each one of them did youl and grin,
and made such harmony;

The Dogs came skipping and did houl,
Also much store of feather'd foul,
they danc't prodigously;

Also the Goats hearing the same,
From the mountains skipping came,
and knock't their horns together.

Their clattering horns made such a noise,
No man could hear each others voice,
like wind and stormy weather;

Mean while a mighty storm did rise,
And darksome clouds made dark the skys,
snow, rain and hail together;

Which did so supple[6] their joynts,
Made many of them untruss their points,[7]
in spight of wind and weather.

At this sight all men did amuse,
That stood on hills, how could they chuse?
but none durst come them near;

Thinking both men and cattel mad,
This made the Country-men full sad,
and run away for fear,

But one more wiser than the rest,
Remembring the former jest,
with wool stopt both his ears,

6. Archaic verb: to make supple, soft. 7. Garters made of leather thongs or ribbons.

And whilst Jack did pipe aloud,
The old man prest into the croud,
as one quite void of fears,

And from him snacth't his pipe away;
Fryer take the pipe, thus did he say,
I give it unto thee,

Jack said, Fryer give to me my pipe,
Or it shall cost thee many a stripe,
assured shalt thou be:

Thy pipe he said thou shalt not have,
For thou art an unlucky knave,
I know unto my sorrow;

Seest thou not how we are tir'd,
We never yet the pipe desir'd,
call thou again to morrow.

At this the rabble did still stand,
And those that danced hand in hand,
the Fryer and the maid.

Every one at them did scoff,
To see them naked and clothes off,
how they were both betray'd. . . .

[Vol. II, no. 23]

TOM THUMB,

His Life and Death.

Wherein is declared many marvellous acts
of Manhood, full of wonder and
strange merriment; which little
Knight lived in King *Ar-*
thurs time, in the Court
of *Great-Brittain.*

Printed by I. M. for I. Clarke, W. Thackeray, and T. Passinger.

THE
Life and Death
OF
TOM THUMB

Of the Birth, Name, and bringing up of Tom Thumb, with the
    merry Pranks he play'd in his Child-hood.

In Arthurs Court Tom Thumb did live,
    a man of mickle might,
The best of all the Table round,
    and eke a doughty Knight:
In stature but an inch in height,
    or quarter of a span,
Then think you not this worthy Knight,
    was prov'd a valiant man.

His Father was a Plow-man plain,
    his mother milkt the Cow,
And yet a way to get a Son,
    these couple knew not how:
Until such time the good old man
    to learned Merlin goes,
And there to him in deep distress,
    in secret manner show.

How in his heart he wisht to have
    a Child in time to come,
To be his heir, though it might be,
    no bigger then his Thumb:

1. Traditional story; cf. Richard Johnson's History, 1621.

Of which Old Merlin was foretold,
that he his wish should have,
And so his Son of Stature small,
the Charmer to him gave.

No blood nor bones in him should be,
in shape, and being such,
That he should hear him speak, but not
his wandring shaddow touch,
But so unseen to go or come,
whereas it pleas'd him well,
Begot and born in half an hour,
to fit his Fathers will.

And in four minutes grew so fast,
that he became so tall,
As was the Plow-mans Thumb in length,
and so she did him call:
Tom Thumb, the which the Fairy Queen,
there gave him to his name,
Whom with her train of Goblins grim,
unto the Christening came.

Whereas she cloath'd him richly brave,
in Garments richly fair,
The which did serve him many years
in seemly sort to wear:
His hat made of an Oaken leaf,
his Shirt a Spiders web,
Both light and soft for these his limbs,
which was so smally bred.

His hose and Doublet thistle down,
together weav'd full fine,
His Stockins of an apple green,
made of the outward Rhine:[2]

2. Finest quality hemp.

His Garters were two little hairs,
pluckt from his Mothers eye,
His Shooes made of a Mouses skin,
and tann'd most curiously.

Thus like a valiant gallant he,
adventures forth to go,
With other Children in the streets,
his pretty tricks to show;
Where he for Counters, Pins and Points,[3]
and cherry-stones did play,
Till he amongst those Gamesters young,
had lost his stock away.

Yet he could soon renew the same,
when as most nimbly he,
Would dive into the cherry bags,
and there partaker be:
Unseen or felt of any one,
until a Schollar shut,
This nimble youth into a box,
wherein his Pins were put.

Of whom to be reveng'd, he took,
in mirth and pleasant game,
Black pots and Glasses, which he hung
upon a bright Sun beam,
The other Boys to do the same;
in pieces broke them quite,
For which they were most soundly whipt,
whereat he laught out-right. . . .

[Vol. II, no. 22]

3. Ribbons.

The three Famous Conjurers.[1]

CHAP. III.

How Lacy Earl of Lincoln[2] was sent by Prince Edward[3] to fair
Margaret[4] of Harlestone; and how Lacy woo'd for himself, and
how Bacon[5] struck Fryer Bongy[6] dumb.

In Suffolk dwelt a beauteous maid,
  Fair Margaret call'd by name,
Whose modesty was spread abroad
  through England by sweet fame.
Prince Edward hearing of her worth
  the Earl of Lincoln sent,
To gain fair Margaret for his Wife,
  if that she gave consent:
When Lacy came unto the Maid,
  that was so lovely and so bright,
He was enamoured on her face,
  Cupid had wrought that spight,
As he forgot Prince Edward clean,
  and for himself did sue
For love unto this beauteous Maid,
  proving to th' Prince untrue.
Quoth he, Fair Margaret lovely one,
  O grant to me thy love,
And Lincolns Countess thou shalt be,
  besides I'le faithful prove.
She then could not say the Earl nay,
  but thereto gave consent:

1. Based on medieval prose romance, popularised by Greene in 1591. 2. Henry
de Lacy, third earl, ob. 1311. 3. Later Edward II. 4. Daughter of Earl of
Salisbury, ob. 1309. 5. Roger Bacon, philosopher and scientist, 1213–1293,
about whom myths gathered, the most famous being his brazen head which
could foretell the future. 6. 15th-century necromancer. The third conjurer
was the evil Vandermast.

Then Fryer Bongy was the man
would wed them incontinent.[7]
But mark how things contrarily
were brought by Fate to pass,
Prince Edward he at Oxford was,
where Bacon in a glass[8]
By Magick skill did shew the Prince
how they were hand in hand;
And Bongy reading in his Book[9]
to tye a fastning band
Of Marriage-rite betwixt the two,
which Bacon did prevent,
And by his charms struck Bongy dumb
and then a spirit sent,
To fetch him straight from Harlestone,
to Oxford with all speed,
The Spirit flew as swift as air,
for to perform this deed.
This being done, Prince Edward then
did haste to Harlestone,
To be reveng'd of Lacy straight,
by his destruction.
But they both kneel'd before the Prince,
and did desire his Grace
Not for to seek to cross their Loves,
which time could not deface.
He was amaz'd for to behold
their faithful constancie,
And gave consent with willing heart,
that they should wedded be,
Which was perform'd in Royal state,
with mirth and jollity,
Margaret a Countess was made,
for her true modesty. . . .

[Vol. I, no. 1]

7. Immediately. 8. Method commonly used by cunning men and white witches. 9. The marriage service.

Cupids Sports and Pastimes. 1684.

***

CHAP. I.

How Cupid took leave of Venus, and how he deceived the Shepherds Boy.

The Histories of Guy and Bevis[1] are grown very old, therefore new conceits may be more pleasing; for where as Robin Conscience[2] travelled about the World unregarded, and found cold entertainment, Cupid desir'd leave of his Mother Venus to descend unto the earth in a disguise, that he might unknown play some wanton tricks, which might at his return make his mother Venus laugh. Venus moved with a Mothers affection, granted his desire. Whereupon Cupid merrily departs, and goes to Mercury his old witty companion desiring him to set his fancy on work to invent a fitting disguise for him, which he did in this manner, Cupid, or Love (by Fancies direction) did put on a Canvas doublet, Leather breeches, white Stockings, red Cadiz-garters, and black high shooes, with a blew Velvet Cap, and a Staff in his hand so that he was like a Country boy, or Foot-Page, Being thus attired, he came unto his Mother, who smiled at his conceit,[3] and having given him some admonitions, concluded all with a parting kiss. Now Cupid spreading his wings abroad, soared in the Air, in his Leather breeches, and at last espying a Shepherds boy lying in the fields fast asleep with his mouth wide open, and his gray Coat hard by him (which he had put off because it was very hot weather) Cupid bended his course thither, and alighted softly upon the ground, and put on the Lads Coat: But as he busled to get it on, the Dog Patch barked, and waked his Master, who perceiving that another Boy had got on his Coat, began to challenge it; and a bloody fray had like to have been between Cupid and the Shepherds boy; but as they were contending, it

1. Guy of Warwick, and Bevis of Southampton. 2. Cf. I, 29 in Short-title list.
3. Whim.

chanced that Thump, his Fathers Ram, was hung in a bush, and was ready to break his neck with striving to get out, so that the boy seeing the Ram in this miserable case, thought to run and help him out, but yet he durst not do so, for fear Cupid (whom he took to be another boy) should run away with his Coat; but as he was looking upon the Ram in the bryars, and did very much pitty his distress, Cupid drew out his invisible bow, whose string was made so small that it could not be seen, and fitting an arrow thereunto, let it fly, and wounded the shepherds boy a little beneath the breast; the effect whereof was presently discerned: for the boy that before pittied the Ram, grew now in Love with him, supposing that he was more fair than any Lass upon the Plains: and so went to pluck the Ram out of the bryers and having got him out, he fell down upon his knees, and offered to kiss the silly creature: but the Ram could not endure to be affronted or mock'd as he supposed; and therefore run full butt against the boy, and beat him backward, so that he lay in a Trance.

CHAP. II.

How Cupid served an Old VVoman his Hostess, and her Landlord.

Now Cupid having got on the boys Gray Coat which hid his wings, went to the next Village Town, where he asked for lodging, and was entertained by an Old Woman[4] that Sold strong Ale, at the sign of the bottle[5] of Hay. While Cupid sat here full of merry conceits, to think how he had couzened the Shepherds boy of his Coat, it chanced that his Hostess Landlord[6] being a handsome young Gentleman, who had bin hunting abroad with his hounds, came into the Room, and called for a Pot of Ale; but as the Old Woman went to draw it, Cupid drew an arrow, which pierced her side, having no less power than the

4. To be an alewife was often one of the few alternatives to the workhouse for aged widows. 5. Bale or bundle. 6. The owner of her house.

other; for as soon as she had delivered the Pot of Ale to the Gentleman, she began to love him in an extream and passionate manner, and to kiss him with her cold lips; at which suddain Kindness and fulsome Kisses, the Gentleman admired,[7] conceiving that the Old Woman doated,[8] and so went home, never dreaming that she was in Love with him. As soon as he was gone, Cupid desired that he might go to Supper: his old Hostess set Meat[9] before him, and presently ran over to her young Landlord, and began to ask him, if he could love an old woman of threescore and ten years old? and so she took him about the neck, and gave him a sower kiss. Her Landlord supposing that age made her doat, went away and left her; who being much discontented, mourned to Cupid her young guest; who pittying her distress, Mother, says he, I see you are in love. Sayst thou so my boy, says she, if I am in love, 'tis since your coming gentle boy. But Cupid made her no answer, but desired to have a Candle to go to bed. . . .

[Vol. I, no. 43]

---

7. Was surprised. 8. Was senile, weak-minded from old age or dotage.
9. Food.

CHAP. I.

The place of his Birth and Education.

Strange news I from the German Empire bring
A true account of a most horrid thing;
Done by one Doctor Faustus call'd by name,
Who by delusion Satan overcame.
At Wittenberg[2] this Faustus he did dwell,
A place in Germany is known full well;
His Uncle brought him up most carefully,
Putting him to the University,[3]
It was his good old Uncles plain design,
That he should study what is call'd divine;
But he inclined was to Sin by Nature,
And minded not the will of his Creator:
Giving himself to wicked exercise,
Forsaking that which only makes men wise;
And Negromancy he did study so,
That thereby he wrought his souls overthrow:
In sinful manner then by day and night,
He spent his precious time, and took delight
In nothing else but what we count most Evil,
Offending God, to gratifie the Devil.

---

1. The legend of Faust was well-known in Germany before the Historia von D. Johann Fausten was published at Frankfurt in 1587. An English ballad on 'the great congerer' was published in 1588. Marlowe's masterpiece was written some time between 1588 and his death in 1593, and first performed in the following year. 2. Wurtemberg. 3. According to legend, at Cracow.

CHAP. VI.

Faustus warms his Blood in a Sawcer and writes as followeth.

I Doctor Faustus do confess your due
Is for to have both Soul and Body too;
I with my Pen the same do now declare;
Writ with my hand, seal'd with my blood they are
Provided you your promise do make good,
Which by the Lines above are understood:
That after twenty-four years do expire,
If I before satisfie my desire.
And what I do command you do obey,
You then shall carry Faustus hence away:
In the mean time I do expect to have
The power to raise dead bodies from the grave;
And have at will whatever I desire,
By your assistance, e're these years expire:
And if what I desire you grant to me,
Then Lucifer, Faustus shall come to thee.[4]

CHAP. VIII.

Faustus's Damnable Proceeding, and the Devils diligence.

When Faustus finisht had his curst design,
He then grew bold, & did no whit repine,
His Hellish Servant still was diligent,
To fill his Masters mind with all content:
For what soe're he did desire to eat,
Though hollow Fowls,[5] or any other meat;

4. The academic hubris of the historical Faustus, and of Marlowe's portrait, is here, significantly, hardly mentioned. 5. Poultry not sold by butchers.

Or did he wish to tast all sorts of Wine,
That were on this side or beyond the Line,[6]
Or were it all the World, be't what it will.
This Devil would his lustful mind fulfil,
And from great Dukes would steal them all away
What he desire'd was quickly made his prey,
So by this means his God he soon forgot,
And that he mortal was supposed not.

Dr Faustus.

6. Possibly south of the equator.

CHAP. XV.

Faustus desires to know more of Hell, and whether
the Devils might ever come into Favour
with God.

Faustus dispairing of all mercy then,
Doth call his spirit to discourse agen;
Tell me, quoth he, how do the Damned dwell?
What pains do they endure that are in Hell?
Will the Almighty e're be reconcil'd,
To him who fain would have his God beguil'd?
Forbear, quoth he, do not such questions raise,
They breed but trouble to thee all thy days.
Quoth Faustus, I must know or i'le not live,
Then did the Spirit him this answer give:
Forth from the Lake of Hell, 'twas never known
That ever any came, except 'twere one;
With him thou nothing hast to do, 'tis plain.
Those that are Damn'd must still in Hell remain.
There is such pains that tongue cannot express,
The wrath of God, and endless bitterness:
Sometimes they burn in flames, none can endure,
And sometimes frosts their torments do procure,
To go about to tell you, all's in vain,
For tongue cannot express their endless pain
That damned Souls do feel, in Hell that lye,
Both burn and freeze, and yet they cannot dye:
And now O Faustus! let me tell to thee,
All this and more will sure thy portion be. . . .

[Vol. I, no. 54]

III. COURTSHIP

A Merry DIALOGUE Between Andrew and his Sweet heart Joan.[1] by L.W.

. . . *And.* So now for my poor sweetheart Joan, the flower of all sh————heels,[2] whom I more long to see, than a hungry Plowman does for his Dinner; nay, I am so Love-sick, that I had rather lye with her than eat a quart of Pottage as cold as I am, nay I swear if you will beleive me, I had rather lodge with her in her smock than Mr. Mare in his Furred-Gown:[3] but hold I think this is the door, ile knock and see if Joan be within.

Ioan. Who is there that keeps such a dinn below at this unseasonable time of night?

And. Tis I Joan.[4] Who are you? Your old sweetheart Andrew. Is it you, poor dear Andrew, I am coming running sweet Andrew. What come in thy smock down two pair of Stairs? Yes Andrew, rather than you should stay long at the door I would have come down naked. Thanks Ioan. Prithee Andrew whats a Clock? Truly Joan I think it may be about three hours after seaven.

Ioan. But prithee Andrew tell me what makes you come at this time of night?

And. Truly Joan the cause of my coming is to finish our old Love that is between us, and to joyn in the way of matrimony, that is to mock a marriage together, this has been long talked of.[5]

Joan. Andrew but when will you be as big as your word?

And. Even when you will Joan; but first let's try if all things will agree together when they meet.[6]

Joan. Fy Andrew fy, you talk idle for want of sleep.

And. Truly Joan I have not slept since I first opened my eyes

1. Countrymen's wooings were a frequent source of townee humour. I have been unable to identify the author. 2. Shitten-heels, from working in the farmyard. 3. Mayor, or joke about horses? 4. The compositor has here lost his way in the dialogue. 5. Mock-marriages, a commonplace of Restoration comedy. 6. The sexual innuendo is obvious here.

in the morning at ten a clock: but prithee Joan let's pass away the night in Love-toys, for I came for the same intent to be merry, and not to sit like a sot and a drone by such a handsome, black, brown, neat, sweet, comely Lass as thou be'st; Oh Joan thou hast an eye like a Prune, but they may look in thy A - - - for beauty.

Joan. Pish Andrew, now you talk as if you did not love me.

And. Nay Joan, now you do me wrong; for shall I tell thee in downright Dunstable words, I love thee more far than a Bear loves Honey, and I hope you'l affect me as much as a Sow does a bunch of Carrots, there is a loving Complement Joan.

Joan. Truly Andrew you are deeply learned.

And. Yes Joan, I was brought up in a well: But Joan, I must kiss thee, ay, and again, yes, and again too: pish, fy,[7] you'l break my neck: Oh Joan, 'tis nothing but pure Love.

Joan. Come pray Andrew be civil, and leave off such childish doings.

And. Nay Joan, 'tis but a folly to persuade, for flesh and blood can't indure it, therefore I must kiss thee.

Joan. Pish, fy, nay pray be civil, why are you so rude? hy-day, I think you'l put me into the fire by and by.

And. Oh Joan, that will be hot love then.

Joan. I think so too, but in troth I do not care for such hot Love, because the old Proverb says, hot love is soonest cold; therefore pray leave off such idle talk and simple doings or else I will stay no longer.

Andrew. And is it so Joan, that you will stay no longer. Your Love faints weak, whilst mine does grow the stronger. . . .

[Vol. I, no. 5]

---

7. Joan, in common with many innocent country maids when faced with such ardour, says pish, fy.

Cupids Love-Lessons by H. C. 1683.

. . . A complemental speech, fit for a young Maid to
use to one she loveth; and is more bold
with her then he should be, or is
fitting.

Dear Friend, whom my heart affecteth and who is near and dear
unto me in affection, I say not that the vehement shews of your
faithful Love towards me, hath brought my mind to answer it in
so due a proportion,[1] that contrary to all general rules of reason,
I have laid in[2] you my estate, my life, my honour, it is your part
to double your former care, and make me see your vertue no
less in perceiving then obtaining, and your faith to be a faith, as
much in freedom as bondage. Tender now your own workman-
ship,[3] and so govern your Love towards me, as I may still remain
worthy to be loved. Remember your Promise, which I conjure
you to observe: let me be your own, as I am, but by no unjust
conquest. Let not your joys (which ought ever to last) be stained
in our own Consciences: Let no shaddow of Repentance steal
into the sweet consideration of our mutual happiness, I have
yielded to bee your Wife, stay then till the time that I may
rightly be so, let no other defiled name burthen my heart; what
shall I more say? if I have chosen well, all doubt is past since
your actions must determine whether I have done vertuously or
shamefully, following you.

His Answer.

Sweet Virgin, what I am, Heaven I hope will shortly make your
own Eyes Judges and of my mind towards you. (the mean time
sholl be my pledge unto you,) your contentment is dearer to me
than mine own, and therfore doubt not of his mind, whose

1. But, with since after that makes her meaning clearer here. 2. Furnished
you with. 3. An obscure phrase; in this context, it seems to mean reduce
your passionate advances.

Cupid.

houghts are so thralled unto you as you are to bend and slack hem, as it shall seem best unto you; you do wrong unto your elf, to make any doubt that a base estate should ever undertake so high an enterprize, or a spotted mind be able to behold your vertues. Thus much only I confess, I can never do th[4] to make he world see you have chosen worthily, since all the world is not worthy of you.

Vol. I, no. 47]

4. The page is torn here; 'that' seems to be the word needed, meaning that which is necessary.

Cupids Master-piece. 1685.

. . . Instructions for Lovers.

Teaching them how to demean themselves towards their Sweet-hearts.

You must not accost them with a shrug, as if you were lowsie: but with your Lady, Sweet Lady, or most Super-excellent Lady; neither must you let your words come rambling forth, ushered in with a good full-mouthed Oath, as I love you: but you must speak the overcoming Language of Love. I do not mean those strange Pedantick Phrases, used by some gallants who (aim at wit, but make themselves stark Asses by it) praise their Mistriss by the Sun, Moon or Stars, whilst the poor girls imagine, they mean the signs their Mercers or Perfumers live at.[1] But you must in fine gentle words, deliver your true Affection; praise your Mistrisses Eyes, her Lip, her Chin, her Nose, her Neck, her Face, her Hand, her Feet, her Leg, her every thing   ,[2] and leave your Lillies and your Roses, for the Countrey Froes[3] to make Nose-gays with.

$$\left.\begin{array}{l}\text{Thoughts}\\\text{Searching}\end{array}\right\} \text{C} \left\{\begin{array}{l}\text{Valued}\\\text{Love}\end{array}\right\} \text{may B.}[4]$$

. . . A pleasant discourse between a Bridegroom and a Bride on their Bridal night.

Bridegr. Will you not come to bed my dear why do you so delay? come let me help you.

    Bride. To bed! sweetheart, why are you so sleepy?

---

1. I.e. the signs hanging outside their shops. 2. There is a half-line gap here in the text. 3. May be anglicisation of frau, housewife. 4. A typical posy, or motto.

Bridegr. No, but I shall de[5] worse if you look sad and melan-cholly; come prithee my dear lets to bed: Why dost thou blush? let me undress thee, be not coy, but smile.

Bride. Alas I feel my self not well my love.

Bridegr. It's only bashfulness my dear, i'le make you well, there's no such Physick as your Husbands warm harms.[6]

Bride. Be not so hasty my Dearest, we steal not out content, 'tis time enough.

Bridegr. Do you then already cease to love me?

Bride. No think not so, for I love thee dearly.

Bridegr. To bed, then I shall give better credit to thee, be not so cold a Lover.

Bride. My passion[7] is now over, and now my dearest, I haste to thy embraces.

Bridegr. Welcome my comfort and delight, and thus I fold my Arms about thee.

Bride. And thus about thee my dear bliss I twine like the Female Ivy.

Bridegr. Come then let me kiss thee, let me kiss again and again, and multiply them to an infinite increase.

Bride. Spare not, for they are you own dear heart. . . .

[Vol. I, no. 33]

5. Misprint for doe, i.e. do. 6. Arms. 7. Here, anger at his urgency.

The Art of Courtſhip.

This may be Printed R. L. S.

Printed for _I. Back_, on _London-Bridge_.

The Art of Courtship.

Complemental Expressions, and Love Posies.

Sir, the joy to see you is more then words can utter.

Sir, 'tis you alone, next Heaven, on whom I must rely; your favours are so many, that my heart has scarcely room to contain them.

Sir, your Wisdom and Eloquence is so Charming, that I must needs admire you.

Madam, your Beauties are so rare, and your actions so tempting, that I must wear your Chains, and count it a blessing to be your slave.

Madam, wounded by your fair Eyes, I languish.

Madam, you are the fair Physitian that can only cure the Distemper of my mind.

THE
Art of LOVE,
OR,
The new School of Complements
Adorned with Love Letters.

Verses in Praise of his Mistriss.

Such brightness in her Angellick Face,
As make a Sun shine in a shady place.

On her Forehead.

Her stately Front, was figured from above
Majestick fair, well polisht, high and pale;
Pure white, which dims the Lillies of the Vale.

On her Eye-brows and Cheeks.
Each Eye-brow hangs like Iris[1] in the Skies,
On either Cheek a Rose and Lilly lyes.

Her Smiles.
Her tempting Smiles, so sweet and nice;
On earth doth make a Paradise.

On her Lips.
Her Lips like Roses, over-washt with Dew;
Do by their Breath their Beauties still renew.

On her Mouth.
Sweet Mouth that sends a Musick Rosie breath,
Whose very Words dart me a living death.

On her Arms.
Her Twin-like Arms, that stately pair;
Fit for a King's Embraces are.

[Vol. II, no. 16]

1. Goddess of the rainbow.

J B

John Back, at the *Black-Boy*, on *London-Bridge*, Furnisheth any Gentlemen or Chap-Men with all sorts of *BOOKS*, *BALLADS* and all other Stationary-Wares, at Reasonable Rates.

... A Song of Amorous Jockey.[1]
To a pleasant New Scotch Tune.

1.

Jenny my blithest Maid,
Prithee listen to my true Love now,
I am a bonny Lad,
Gang along with me to yonder brow,
Au the boughs shall shade us round,
while the Nightingale and Linnet,
Teach us how the Lads and Lasses can Wooe,
Come and i'le shew my Jenny what to do.

2.

I ken full many a thing,
I can Dance and Whistle too,
I many a Song can sing,
Pitch the Bar,[2] and I can Wrestle too,
The bonniest Lasses of au our Town,
Gave me head Lace and Kerchiefs many,
Only Jenny 'twas could win,
Jockey from all the Lasses of the Green.

3.

Then lig thee down my bearn,
I'se not spoil thy gaudy shining Gown,
I'se make a Bed of Fearn,
And I'se gently press my Jenny down,
Let me lift thy Petticoat,
And thy Kerchief which hides they bosom,
Shew thy only Beauties there,
Jenny's the only Lass that I Adore.

1. Jock. Scots ballads and love songs were popular. 2. Similar to tossing the caber, i.e. throwing a heavy wooden or iron pole in competition as a feat of strength.

4.

Jenney shall ne'r repent
For I bravely will behave me,
But to her Hearts content,
Send mere[3] pleasure back then she gave me,
Then lig thee by me Jenny my dear,
And I will lay my self upon,
Never was less cause of fear,
Nor Jenny should say I am undone.

[Vol. I, no. 32]

3. More; the dialect may well have been written by an Englishman.

Cupid's Posies.

... Another in Letters.

My Love is true which IOU,
As true to me, then CUB.

The Posie of a Ring sent to a Maid from her Lover.

My constant love shall ne'r remove.
This and I, until I dye.
Memento mei.
When this you see, remember me.
Like to a circle round, no end in love is found.
Take me with it, for both are fit.

A young mans conceit to his dear Love, being wrought upon a Scarf.

This Scarf is but an embleme of my love,
Which I have sent, with full intent,
　　my service to approve.

Another, wherein the Lover seeketh her love.

One was the Bow, one was the Dart,
That wounded us both to the heart:
Then since we both do feel one pain,
Let one Love cure us both again.

A young-mans Posie to his Sweet-heart,
shewing, that love is most violent
in absence.

Love is a flame, that with a violent desire,
Doth burn us most when we are farthest from the fire.
As those that dye are said for to depart,
So when you went away,
all life forsook my heart:
For though with inward pain
I draw my very breath,
Yet this I will maintain,
departure is a Death. . . .

[Vol. I, no. 21]

A Pleasant DIALOGUE Betwixt Honest John and loving Kate. The Contrivance of their Marriage and way how to Live. 1685.

. . . Jo. Be not angry my dear, if thou hast not a Smock to thy back I would have thee, but in knowing what each other hath, we shall know the better how to improve it, do thou the same by me.

Ka. Truly I have but ten pounds my father left me, and that is in my Uncle Hodge's hands.

Jo. Tis sure I hope.

Ka. You need not doubt that, for he cannot keep it from me, and five pound I have gathered since I came to service, besides my Mistress owes me above half a years wages.

Jo. O what a happy man shall I be, what a good housewife thou hast been, thou hast good cloathes too.

Ka. They will serve.

Jo. Now Kate I will tell thee what I have, my father gave me ten pounds when I came from him, and told me as I did improve that, he would give me more, and with my Masters leave, I have imployed it in his Mault-house,[1] and have encreased it; besides my master doth owe me my wages ever since I came to him, he would not let me have it for fear I should play the ill husband,[2] and if I please him, I know he will give me something when I marry, and so will thy Mistriss, will she not?

Ka. I hope so too.

Jo. Now for the best advantage, thy stock and mine together, will amount to something; and when we have concluded our marriage day, ile try if my Master will let me have a little house and ground thou knowest hard by William Jacksons, that will make a great house for us,

Ka. And a great Rent too, what should we do with such a house, one Room will serve our turn.

1. As an investment. 2. Husbander, saver. At the end of the seventeenth century the average wage of a spinster was fourpence a day, or about £6 p.a.; this was without food or lodging. See J. E. Thorold Rogers, *History of Agriculture and Prices in England* (Oxford, 1887).

Jo. Ay to sleep in my dear.

Ka. But what trade do you intend to drive?

Jo. Give me leave and ile tell thee, and if thou wilt help me a little, it will be the better, for two heads are better than one, we must not take care only for sleeping places, but a place to get mony in.

Ka. How, that pleases me well to be getting of Money, for I love it dearly.

Jo. I have almost broke my Brains with studying & contriving, but now I think I have hit ont.

Ka. Tis long coming out.

Jo. If my master will let me have the house we will brue good Ale, and we will have mault of our own, for we'l keep a stock going in my Master's Mault-house, with his leave, and there is pasture enough to keep two beasts, and conveniences for hogs and poultery, so thou mayest have all things about thee, and keep a maid and live like a Lady.

Ka. This will be brave indeed John, but what shall we do with our Ale.

Jo. Sell it my sweet one; Let me see, there are eight rooms in the house besides the Cellar, and with a little painting and a few benches it will be very fine, & a handsome sign to draw in company.

Ka. What shall that be.

Jo. The three fair maids, I think.

Ka. Not for a hundred pound I would not have such a sign.

Jo. Why prithee.

Ka. Why man they'd think surely we kept a bawdy house[3]. . .

Ka. What shall be do for Clothes.

Jo. In troth Kate we will save that money, those that we have will serve very well.

Ka. I think so too.

Jo. Only I will have a hat & a Gold ring for thee.

Ka. Who shall we bid to our Wedding.

3. Country inns had an unsavoury reputation as places of assignation in the seventeenth century.

Jo. All who we can think of, the more the merrier.

Ka. What Musick shall we have.

Jo. We will have old Rowly and his company.[4]

Ka. They will make a roaring noise.

Jo. And they will sing well too, to please the young people; why dost laugh, does the thoughts of it please thee.

Ka. I laugh to think how the young men will turn the Lasses about in dancing, and how they will buss them, methinks I see them already, but good Jack how shall I do to behave my self at that time amongst so many; I shall be so ashamed I shant know what to do.

Jo. Why priethee all people will adore thee that day, and I shall be woundy[5] proud of thee my Dear to see thee sit as a Virgin-Bride, and I shall wait upon thee too that same day, as it is my duty.

Ka. Is that the fashion.

Jo. Yes my dear, hast thou never observed it at weddings.

Ka. I shall observe my own the more, but you must not look towards me, for then I shall laugh and that will shame me quite.

Jo. No my dear a smile sometimes will do well they'l think there's the more love.

Ka. Must I dance too.

Jo. Ay pretty one, every body will strive to dance with the Bride.

Ka. Ide rather dance with thee John, than with them all.

Jo. So thou shalt my dear.

Ka. What Favours[6] shall we give.

Jo. Red and blew I think.

Ka. They will look gloriously, but all this while who shall lead us to Church.

Jo. Tom Sims, and Roger Blackwel shall lead thee, and Mary Tomkins and Bess Ruglas shall lead me.[7]

Ka. I shant be able to go along the street, the folk will so look at me.

---

4. Popular nickname of Charles II, after his stallion; it may just be an abbreviation for Roland. 5. Very, extremely. 6. Ribbons or rosettes. 7. The roles of bridesmaids and groomsmen have changed.

Jo. No matter for their looking, 'ile warrant thee who ever sees thee will wish her self in the same condition, who are not married already.

Ka. Will they think you.

Jo. I faith i'l warrant you.

Ka. Who shall marry us.

Jo. M. Timson.

Ka. Oh dear he will keep such a do to have me speak out that I shant know what to do with my self.

Jo. Thou must not be ashamed my dear, for it is an honour to be a bride.

Ka. Who shall be my Father to give me.[8]

Jo. Thou mayest ask Jack Wheeler, but I know he had rather had thee himself.

Ka. Oh fie no, I will not ask him, he will take it for an affront, I will rather ask old father Bandol for he us'd to call me Daughter, and he will take it kindly.

Jo. Do then.

Ka. Does it not make you ashamed to talk of these things.

Jo. No I promise thee, I am proud of it, and so art thou I believe, but that thou wilt not confess it.

Ka. I would it were once over.

Jo. So would I, i'd as live as a groat.[9]

Ka. Who shall make the Sack Posset.[10]

Jo. The Bride-maids will take care of that.

Ka. Good lack they will keep such a do when they come in to eat it, and taking their leaves of us, and throwing the stocking,[11] and one thing or other, that I shall wish them all far enough.

Jo. So shall I but we must lye the longer next morning.

Ka. But I forgot one thing, who shall dress me.

Jo. It is a thousand pities but thou shouldst marry, thou thinkest of every thing so, the Bride-maids my dear will dress thee.

8. The implication is that either the parents are dead, or that John and Kate have both moved a considerable distance from their parents. 9. As gladly as have fourpence. 10. Traditional wedding night drink, thought to have aphrodisiac qualities. 11. The bride's stocking was thrown from the bed after the couple had been bedded. Whoever caught it would marry next.

Ka. Where shall we lye the next night.

Jo. In our own house that will be the best, and therefore we must furnish it before, and lay in some Ale, that we may be able to invite all the wedding people to drink with us, and then we shall have good handsel[12] indeed, and we will also have a good Gammon of Bacon, and that will make the drink go down merrily.

Ka. What maid shall we have?

Jo. We will have a lusty wench, who may be able to do our work, for fourty shillings the year we may have one. . . .

[Vol. I, no. 10]

12. Wedding presents.

Loves School. 1682.

Loves New School,
OR,
A New Book of Complements.

A Complemental Dialogue between a Young-Man and a maid,
Licensed by her Father to make her own choice of a Husband.

Man.
Now Lady, your Fathers goodness hath left you to your self:
I, the admirer of your vertue, present my best affections: then
save that treasure,[1] whose life dependeth upon you, to whom my
heart presents its first devotion, and in a holy flame remains a
sacrifice till you accept of it.

Maid. I should prove my self unjust, in neglect of one that
nobly loves me, therefore that affection I may bestow, I were
ungrateful should I not present it.

Man. May I become a scorn of time, and all mens hate persue
me, when I prove so foul, as to give you occasion to call back
your love.

Maid. Cease to use hasty Protestations, I assure my self the
pureness of your Soul is without spot, and whilst you so continue,
I shall think my self happy in such a choice.

Man. Then let me flee into your bosome, and on your lips
confirm my happiness.

Maid. Fie, fie, leave for shame I esteem not golden Language,
because it's seldome bestowed on man but to guild over a Copper
Soul within.

Man. Can you be so cruel as to deem my language feigned? Far
be it from me to speak a word should displease you.

Maid. Well, more Oratory would but bring the rest into
suspicion, let it suffice I love you. Farewell.

Man. Farewell my excellent Mistris.

1. I take this to refer to her 'vertue'.

A constant heart within a Womans Breast,
Is Ophir Gold within an Ivory Chest;
Then happy sure am I, and blest,
That thou hast such a heart in such a breast.

. . . A Parson to his Mistris.

My Person is Divine,
my Parsonage fat and fair:
Then let us joyn in Love,
and make a loving pair.

Her Answer.
Your Person is Divine,
your Parsonage during Life;
But if the Parson dye,
pray where's the Parson's Wife?

[Vol. II, no. 15]

Simon and Cisley. by J.P.

THE
Merry Conceits and Passages
OF
Simon and Cisley.
Two Lancashire Lovers.

How simple Simon came to fall in love with simpering Cisley at a Wedding.

Simon & Cisley had formerly seen one another, but never had the fortune to be acquainted, until accidentally there happened to be a Wedding at the same Town where Simon lived, to which Cisley was invited (she living but a mile off with her Father, who was a Widower, and had no more Children.)

Being thus met at the Wedding, the Bride came to distribute her Favours[1] amongst her friends, so Simon and Cisley had each of them one. Cisley pinn'd hers upon her sleeve, and Simon seeing her do so, was about to pinn his upon his sleeve too: But Cisley smiling at his mistake, told him it was the fashion for men to wear them in their Hatbands, and if he pleased she would tye it for him.

Says the Clerk of the Church, (who saw her tying it) in truth Neighbour Simon, that Courtesie deserves a kiss; say you so, quoth Simon, marry then i'le be sure to give her one, and a good one too; so he clapt his Arms about her neck, and gave her a great smacking kiss, after his own Country fashion. But after Simon had once tasted the pleasure of Cisleys sweet lips, he was so over head and ears in love, that he could scarce eat any Dinner at all: which the Clerk observed and askt him (after Dinner) if he were in love, because he forsook his Victuals? A shame take you, quoth Simon, you made me kiss Cisley for nothing, but that you might get money for another Wedding.

1. Ribbons or rosettes.

How Simon conducted Cisley home, and he wooed her
Father, that he might have her for his
Wife.

After much mirth and dancing past at the Wedding, when it was
time to part, Simon told Cisley, that he had a great desire to see
her home, and she thought it no wisdom to refuse his courtesie,
in regard it was almost night, and she wanted company: so they
took their leaves and went together.

The first Style they came to, Simon made a stand; why do you
stay, quoth Cisley? (thinking he staid to kiss her) pray go over;
nay truly, quoth Simon, you go oftener this way, and know it
better than I do, pray go you over first: she argued the case with
him a good while, but for all she could say, she was glad to go
first over every Style they came to, a fair opportunity for him to
see her lusty leg, which made him more in love with her than
ever he was before. After they had gone a prety way farther
Simon began to discover his affection to her in such a manner, as
would have done a wise Woman good to have heard him. Cisley
thankt him for his Love, and told him she could not dispose of
her self whilst her Father was living, without his consent.[2] Simon
told her he did not fear that at all; so they trudg'd on till they
came to her Father, whom they found sitting at the door, waiting
for her coming home.

As soon as Cisley was gone in, Simon being a little elevated
with the wedding Ale, began to wooe her Father more earnestly
than ever he did her: & for a good while would take no denial,
until at last the old man perswaded him to get his Daughters
consent, and then he would tell him more. When Simon had told
Cisley what her father had said, she promised to meet him the
next Market-day and there to conclude the bargain at the Tavern:
and so after a parting kiss, Simon went whistling hom jovially,
to tell his mother the good news, (for his father was dead.)

2. This was, of course, normal practice; in richer families parents took a
much more positive approach, selecting partners, rather than merely con-
senting.

... How Simon put a trick upon the Miller that thought to
deceive him of his Sweetheart.

In the same Town where Simon lived, there dwelt a miller which
had a months mind[3] to Cisley and resolved if he could possibly
to deceive Simon of his Beloved: so it happened that the same
night that Simon promised to be at her Fathers, the miller chanced
to ride thither, upon this black mare, which he used to carry
Sacks on: he had been there several times before, but never
found Cisley so Coy as she was now grown, since she made a
Promise to Simon. Whilst they were together, Simon chanced to
take Old Roan, and away came he ambling in the dark to Visit
his dear Duck: but when he came to put his Horse into the
Stable, he found the Millers mare there before him: he knew the
Millers business well enough and therefore he resolved to fit him
for coming there a Wooing again: so he would not put his horse
into the stable but tyed him under a Hedge, (intending to go to
Cisley as soon as the miller was gone) and takes out the millers
mare into the Yard, where he found an old Wheel-barrow, which
he tyed fast to the mares tail, and when she was in her way home,[4]
he gave her three or four good jearks,[5] and set her a running
ding dong: but when the Mare felt the wheel-barrow ratling at
her arse, she ran as if the Devil had been upon her back, so that
she frighted all the people that ever came in her way, and set all
the Town where the Miller lived, in a great uproar, every one
concluding it was the Devil, because she made such a noise in the
night, and was black.[6]

Well, when the Miller took his leave of Cisley, and went to
bring out his Mare, he could not tell what to think, when he
found her not in the Stable: but hoping she was broke loose, and
run home, he made all the laste[7] that ever he could after her.

When the Miller was gone, Simon went to his sweet-heart, &

3. Burning desire or fancy; Brewer suggests that it might come from the
obsessions of women in the first months of pregnancy, which were frequently
alluded to in Restoration literature. 4. Facing homeward. 5. Clouts, thwacks.
6. An interesting sidelight on popular superstition; there was a widely-pub-
licised witchcraft trial in Lancashire in 1612. 7. Misprint for haste.

told her what he had done, which made her laugh heartily, but the poor Miller quite out of breath when he came to the Town, he found all his Neighbours up in arms: he askt the reason, they told him, the devil was in their town, and had almost frighted them out of their wits. Then he told them he had lost his Mare, and desired them to go with him, and see if she were at home: when they came there, they found the black she-Devil in a dropping sweat, with an old Wheelbarrow at her Arse, and had almost run her self to death. The Miller suspecting that Simon had done it, went to see if he were at home: but finding he was not, he resolv'd to be quit[8] with him before it was long, and so it fell out accordingly.

. . . There lived a Conjurer[9] within two miles of them, that was very notable in that Art; but the miller suspecting such a thing, had been with him before, and told him the whole jest, and had given him a share of the money; so that when Simon came to him and desired to know who got his money, the man seemed to be very diligent to pleasure him, and fell to his study for a matter of half an hour, and then told him, that if they were men that rob'd him, the chief Actor among them, was one that got his living by the wind: and if he knew any man of such a profession, it might be easie to find out them that robbed him, otherwise he could do no more by his Art. Simon satisfied him for his pains, and went home to consult with his friends, who this person should be, that got his Living by the wind; but when they came to consider if it, they never thought of the Miller, who was their Neighbour, but gave the money for lost, concluding it must be either a Seaman or a Trumpeter, & therefore never likely to be recovered again.

---

8. Quits, or equal. 9. Cunning or wise man, much resorted to by countrymen to help them find something lost or stolen, or to identify someone who had done harm.

. . . How the Parson with much ado got Simon and Cisley
married after a mad fashion.

The former invited guests came upon the Holiday appointed,
according to promise, against which time Simon had once more
got all things in readiness; and to make sure that he should not
be serv'd as he was before, he had both laid a broader Bridge, and
bought Cisley a pair of lower-heel'd Shooes: So now they were
fixt, and away they went to the Church; but when they came
there, the Parson fell to work to marry them; but when he came
to ask Simon, wilt thou have Cisley to thy wedded Wife? Yes
sir (qd. Simon) if she be as willing as I, or else I would not
have her for all the World. The Parson then askt Cisley, wilt
thou have Simon to thy wedded Husband? yes sir quoth Cisley,
(making a low courtesie) if you please; which made the company
smile: but the Parson seeing their ignorance, was glad to direct
them, and so with much ado he got them married after a mad
fashion, and home they went with great joy, where they had a
dinner of Simons mothers own dressing[10] who was very glad
that her only Son was so well married, and so was Cisleys old
Father too for his Daughter.

After dinner they had a Cup of good Ale of their own brewing,
and the lame Fidler to make them merry, with which they past
on the time till Supper, and from that time, until they had gotten
the Bride to Bed; but they had much ado to get Simon to go to
bed to her whilst they were there; but at length he was perswaded
to venture upon it, and then the Company left them, and wisht
them a good night.

FINIS.

[Vol. I, no. 57]

10. Preparation, cooking; common term, still used of salads.

The COUNTRY
Garland,

Hey for our TOWN.

This may be Printed, R. P.

Printed for *P. Brooksby*, in *Pye-Corner*, 1687.

THE
Country Garland
Of Delightful Mirth and Pastime; Set forth
and adorned with sundry pleasant and
delightful New SONGS.

1. The Plain-dealing Pedlar.
2. The two united Lovers Robin and Dolly.
3. The Dutiful Daughter, and the most indulgent Mother; set forth in a Dialogue betwixt them about her earnest Desire for a Husband.
4. The Broken Grasier, or the dutiful Daughters trouble after her hasty Wedding.
5. The Good-Fellows Resolve.
6. A tryal of Constancy: A Pastoral Song, between Damon and Celia.
7. The Libertine.[1]
8. He wou'd, and he wou'd not.
9. The Pollititian, or Loyal Subject.[1]
10. The Passionate Lover.
11. True Love in its Purity; Or, the Loyal-hearted Seamans farewel to his Beloved Nancy.

All very Pleasant and Delightful for Young MEN and MAIDS.

Printed for P. Brooksby, at the Golden-Ball, in Pye-Corner, 1687.

---

1. Court songs, rather out of keeping with the rusticity.

The Plain-Dealing Pedlar well furnished with sundry sorts of
choice wares.
To the Tune of, *The Journey-man Shooe-maker*.

I am a Pedlar here's my pack,
now you that are at leasure,
Come take a view see what you lack,
I have great choice of treasure
To furnish you, then now draw near
each little pritty Maiden,
For now my Pack is open here,
I hope to have good trading.

I have the greatest choice for you,
both Ribbons Gloves and laces,
With powder, paint, black patches too,
and Masques to hide your faces;
There's ne'r a man in all the fair,
as I the truth may tell you,
That has such choice of dainty ware,
as I have here to sell you.

A Powder for your Teeth I have,
my pritty Maids now buy it,
The which will make you white and brave,
if you will please to try it;
And though they are decay'd, they'l vamp,
and make them more compleater,
I have a Ring to Cure the Cramp,[2]
in e'ry Female Creature.

Those Gallants that hath been at France,
and by their fond Embraces,
Have lit of some unhappy chance,
to spoil their handsome faces;
Here is a Remedy for those,

---

2. Worn on the finger to ward off cramp and other diseases. Hallowed by
royalty on Good Friday and distributed to sufferers before the Reformation.

undone by Lawless doings;
It is a dainty Silver Nose,
that will repair such ruins.[3]

If you have any loving Friend,
whose Head his Wife has horned,
I have a Cap I will commend,[4]
most richly is adorned;
I pray present now one of these
unto you honest Neighbour,
For it will give him present ease,
he'l thank you for your labour.

Few Pedlars can with me compare,
i'le venture Forty Shilling,
For why, I deal in Grocers Ware,
to please you I am willing;
I'le put choice Nutmegs in your hand,
with dainty curious Pepper.
Ther's ne'r a Grocer in the Land,
can furnish you with better.

Come taste and try, before you buy.
so may I be believed,
And what I sell, may please you well,
and you no ways deceived:
Where I have been, I go agen,
so just I am in Dealing;
My Credit I did never stain,
by Cheating nor by Stealing.

[Vol. II, no. 41]

3. The effects of veneral disease on noses was a commonplace joke; nose
is also slang for penis. 4. A cuckold's cap had two peaked crowns, resembling
stumps of horns.

THE
DEATH and BURIAL
OF
MISTRESS MONEY.

with her WILL she made at her departure, and what hap
-pened afterwards to the USURER that buried Her.

LONDON, Printed by *A. Clark*, and are to be sold by
T. Vere and *J. Clark*. 1678.

IV. SOCIAL COMMENT.

Mistress Money.[1] 1678.

THE
DEATH
AND
BURIAL
OF
MISTRESS MONEY.

When the earth for her wantonness in Summer did pennance in a white sheet of Snow; and when the short days, and long Evenings gave assured tokens that it was the depth of Winter: The covetous wretch, old Avarez, to save fire and candle, went to Bed, where having meditated a while on his Trunk of Golden earth which stood in his Chamber, and now finding himself disposed to sleep, he made this short Prayer.

Whether I do sleep or rest,
Pluto still defend my Chest.

And no sooner had he spoke these words but he fell fast asleep before he could say Amen. But yet though his senses were bound up with the silken chains of sleep, yet his mind (ever watchful over his gold) and jealous of the losing it, drew him into a fearful dream, Which was that thieves had assaulted his house (he living alone with an old Maid called Kerdona) and that they were ready to break open that Chest wherein all his treasure lay. The fear of this dream had so surprised his fansie, that thinking he heard the lock crack, and that his angels[2] were taking their flight, he leapt out of his bed; and his cloaths hapning to ly upon his

1. Stock type and situation exploited most brilliantly by Chaucer, and by Jonson in *Volpone*. Previous edition 1664. 2. Possible pun on the coin, worth about ten shillings, last minted in Charles I's reign.

Trunk, thinking it to be one of the Thieves, catching fast hold thereon; and so holding the Trunk and cloaths fast in his arms, calls out aloud for help. Kerdona his Maid hearing this noise, and having laid by her Smock when she went to bed, because it should not wear out, came running unto him stark naked: Where you may think what a strange sight it was to see the maid perswade her Master that there was no cause of fear? No, says old Avarez, why I have one of the thieves under me, come help me to hold him fast. Alas says the Maid, it is your own cloaths. I will not believe that, says he, till I see more. With that the Maid lights a candle, and coming towards her Master, I hope sir says she, you will now see the truth of all: with that her Master looking upon her, and seeing her stark naked, hee falls backward into a swound, crying, O Cupid, I never knew the power of thy bugle[3] bow till now, 'tis pitty (says he) thou shouldst live a Maid longer, and therewithal embracing his Maid Kerdona, he fitted his own Arrow to her Bow-string, and that night got a bastard on her, called Ten in the hundred.[4]

How Kerdona did rise from
her Master Old Avarez: and how
he went the next day to Bury
his Gold,

KERDONA having all this night lain with an old Man, and being weary with his tedious fumbling,[5] at last lightly slipt out of the Bed, as good a Maid as she came in. And so stealing down she intended to send for her sweet-heart, who should finish that task of pleasure which the other had so slightly begun, and accordingly she sent a messenger for him. Now in the mean time Old Avarez calling to mind the terrour and fear of his former Dream, presently resolves upon a new course, which was, to avoyd the like perplexity he meant to bury his Money, being the safest way, (as he thought) that possibly could be invented, For says he, then I may

3. Possibly, a bow made of bugle, or buffalo horn. 4. The rate of interest he charged. 5. Commonly used for inept efforts of impotents.

sleep securely on my pillow, nor can any Dreams affright me with the fear of losing my beloved Gold. Being thus resolved, up he gets, and having put on his old furred Gown, away he goes into the fields, with a spade in one hand, and a great bag of Gold in the other hand, meaning to bury his money privately without any Ceremonies, himself being both Priest and Sexton. . . .

Mistress Money, being sick in body as you may perceive by her pale look, but healthfull in mind, bequeaths her body to be buried under this Tree, and her soul to the infernal Vault below.

Also he[6] gives and bequeaths unto her Friends in manner and form as follows—

To Young Mistress Tireby, who for my sake first lost her maidenhead, and afterwards turned a common whore, I give five pound to fetch her best gown out of pawn.

To young Master Rastley a Gamester, who hath often quarrelled in my behalf, I give forty shillings to swear and drink sack[7] withall.

To master All-sup the Broker I give sixe pence for a halter.[8]

To master Fatling an Inn-keeper, I give twenty shillings to paint his sign withal.

To the incurable Hospital of Knaves and Fools I give three pence per annum for ships and Coxcombs.[9]

To the Scholars I give nothing.

Item to those Drunkards that have spend all their money overnight, I give six pence for a mornings draught.

Item, to master Nonsense a young heir, I give four pence to buy Greens Groatsworth of wit.[10]

Item, to Maids that have no portions, I give five shillings to buy a chain to lead Apes in hell[11] withal.

Item, to him that hath a scolding wife, I give twelve pence to go to the alehouse; and if she follow him thither, I give him six pence to buy holly wands to swaddle[12] her withall.

6. Should read she. 7. Dry, *sec,* white wine. 8. Noosed rope; either for hanging, or for public humiliation.
9. Coxcombs were worn by fools; ships I cannot explain. 10. Robert Greene published this autobiographical piece in 1592. 11. Fate of old maids. 12. Sticks of holly to beat her.

Item, to Maids that are in Love, I give pence a piece, to buy the next new ballet[13] of Love, that so they may sing it over their milking pails.

Item, to a grave chamber-maid that very gracelesly has lost her maiden-head, I give six pence to carry her water to the Doctor.[14]

Item, to Tobacconists, I give Six pence for a brush to scour their smoaky throats.

Item, to the poor of the Town of Nonesuch, I give three pounds lacking threescore shillings[15].

Item, to them that keep the Road way of preferment, other ways called highwaymen or thieves, I give five shillings for a false Beard and Pistol.

Item, to Country Book-sellers, I give three pence to buy this new book withal.

And to him that writ it, I give what he can get, and so he will thank you for nothing. . . .

> How Kerdona and her Sweet-
> heart having stood by all
> this while unseen, found
> Avarez gold.

No sooner was the old Avarez gone home, reioycing that his money was now past thieves handling, when Kerdona and her sweetheart came forth from behind a bush, where they had lain in amorous dalliance, and had beheld what had past between Avarez and the spirit; and had seen how injuriously he stifled and then buried mistris money. But Kerdona a long time through duty to her Master, perswaded him to let the body rest: How? says her lover, I will not be guilty of her death for a Hundred pounds, and therefore let us make haste to dig her up again, for perhaps the warmth of my pocket may recover her. . . .

And thus have you seen that marriage and hanging goes by destiny, for the finding of this Gold made Kerdona and her

13. Ballad. 14. Pregnancy test. 15. I.e. nothing.

sweet-heart marry, & the losing of this gold made the Usurer hang himself, which was a fit end for an Usurer and so I end with Finis Funis.[16]

The Moral Meaning of this BOOK.

Avarez fearful dream shews that the poor man sleeps more quietly than the Rich. Kerdona is as much to say Gain, from *lucrum*; so that Avarez geting his Maid Kerdona with child, does shew that Usury does beget upon Gain, ten in the hundred. Avarez burying his gold and yet losing it, does shew that we should rather lay up our Treasure in heaven then in Earth. Kerdona's marrying with a young gallant and making him find Avarez gold, does shew that which is gotten miserably does at last come to some prodigal hand, and so is spent wickedly. And this is the moral meaning that this short story both afford.

[Vol. II, no. 24]

16. Literally, the end is the rope.

The Arraigning and Indicting of Sir John Barley-Corn.[1]

O Yes, O Yes, O Yes; if any Man or woman, in Country, Town or City have any Suits or Bills of indictments again Sir John Barley-Corn, let them appear this day, and they shall either hear or be heard.

Vulcan the Black-Smith appears, and give in his Bill. Be it known to you all, Gentlemen: that this Sir Iohn Barley-Corn hath been a sore Enemy to me, and to many of my Fellows: for many a time when I have been busie at my work, not thinking any harm to any man, but having a Fire-spark in my Throat, I one time going over to the Sign of the Cup and Can, for one penny-worth of Ale, there I found Sir Iohn I thinking no hurt to any Man, civilly sat me down to spend my honest Two-pence, but in the end, Sir John began to pick a quarrel with me, and then I started up, thinking to go my way, but then Sir John had got me by the top of the head, that I had no power to help my self: and so by his strength and power he threw me down, broke my head, broke my face, and almost all my bones, that I was not able to work three days, I was so sorely tormented in my head and other parts of my body. Nay, more than this, he pickt my Purse, and left me never a Penny, and therefore he doth deserve to dye.

Will the Weaver. Now Gentlemen, I do beseech you to hear me speak; I am but a poor Man, and have a Wife and a charge of Children, and a poor Weaver by my Trade, yet this in-knowing Companion will never let me alone, but he is always inticing me from my work, and will not be quiet till he hath got me to the Ale-house, and then he quarrels with me, and abuseth me most basely; and sometimes he binds me hand and foot, and throws me in the Ditch, and there stays with me all night, and the next Morning leaves me, but not with one Penny in my Pocket: and therefore if you hang him, I will never grieve. . . .

---

1. This well-known allegory of the evils of alcoholism is of west country origin; also ballad subject.

The Plow-Man Enters

Gentlemen, I pray may a Man speak without offence, that do intend to speak nothing but the truth, and no more?

The Judges. Yes, thou mayest be bold to speak the very Truth, and no more, for that is the cause we sit here for: therefore speak boldly, that we may understand thee.

The Plow-man. Gentlemen, in the first place, let me hear what bold impudent Rogue dare speak one word against Sir Iohn Barley-Corn? whoever he is he is no better than a Rogue, a Thief, a Vagabond, a Traytor to the Brown Loaf, a Thief to the Brass Pot, the Oven, and the Spit. Nay, he is a Traytor to the whole world, that would take away the Life of so noble a Man as Sir Iohn Barley-Corn, for he is a Man of an antient House, and is come of a Noble Race; there is neither Lord, Knight, nor Squire, but they love his Company, and he theirs, as long as they do not abuse him, he will abuse no Man, but doth a great deal of good, as can make it appear in many kind of ways. And in the first place, few Plow-Men can live without him; for if it were not for him, we could not pay our Landlords their Rents, and then I pray, what would such men as you do for mony and fine cloaths? Nay, your gay Ladies would care but little for you, if you had not your rent coming in to maintain them: and we could never pay you, but that Sir John Barley-Corn feeds us with Mony, and yet would you seek to take his Life? for shame let your malice cease, and pardon his life, or else we are all undone.

Enter in Bunch the Brewer

Gentlemen, I beseech you hear me speak, my name is Bunch, a Brewer, & I do believe few of you can live without a Cup of good Liquor, no more can I tell how to live without the help of Sir John Barley-Corn. As for my own part, I maintain a great charge, and keep a great many Men at work: I pay taxes forty pound a year to the King, God bless him and all this is maintain'd by the help of Sir John, then how can any Man for shame seek to take away his Life?

Enter in Mistris Hostis.

Take his Life, I pray who is that which they would take his Life? It is Sir John Barley-Corn, Mistris Hostis. . . .

[Vol. I, no. 4]

CHAP. II.

How Monford arrived in England, and of the cold Entertainment
he found amongst his Relations; how he came to Bednal-Green,
and settling himself there, he continued to Begg for his Living,
etc.

Monford escaping a Storm at Sea, in his Return Landed with his
Vertuous Wife on the Coast of Essex, where he had some considerable Relations, to whom in this necessity they applyed
themselves for succour, but they either not desirous of his
Company, who after the death of his Parents had wasted much of
his Patrimony, or fearing in that condition he might be chargeable
to them, would not know him, and those that were convinced he
was the same Monford that went over into France, gave him but
cold Entertainment, insomuch that scorning to rely upon their
Charity, he told the kind Partner of his joy and sorrow, that he
intended early in the morning to hast towards London, and that
he would rather trust to Providence then to the ingratitude of
those who in his prosperous days had Carressed him in a high
manner; and so without taking Leave of any, Early in the
morning they departed; and in two days travelling (having spent
the little Money they had reserved) necessity that has no Law, so
far humbled his high Spirit, that he did not think it amiss (especially in places where he was not known) to crave the Charity of the
People as he passed through several good Towns, who understanding that he came by his misfortune in fighting for the
Honour of his Country, gave very Liberally, insomuch that he
resolved to be of good chear, and thereupon considering with
himself that he was never brought up to Labour, or if he had,

1. A popular play of the same title by Chettle and Day was performed in
1600; a ballad registered in 1624. The life and cant of beggars, a major social
problem exacerbated by returning war veterans, was a subject of wide
interest around 1600.

the Loss of his Sight had rendred him incapable of business; he resolved to embrace what Providence had cast in his way: Which was, to live upon Charity, which he found to flow in upon him faster then he expected: Whereupon arriving at Bednal-Green, a place near London, he with the little Money he had got, hired a small Cottage for his Wife and himself, and daily appearing publick to crave Alms, was from thence called the Beggar of Bednal-Green, and in a short time found it a thriveing Trade, insomuch that his Bed of Straw was changed into Down, and his Earthen Platters and other Utensils into a better Sort. His Wife whilst he begged abroad not being idle at home, but Laboured at the Wheel and such other matters as in her younger years she had learned.

CHAP. III

How Monford happened to meet with Snap[2] an Old Experienced Beggar, who gave him an insight into the mistery of the canting Tribe, and how he invited him to their general Randesvouze, etc.

Monford resolving in this kind of way to spend the remainder of his Days, that he might humble himself for his former offences, having plyed it with good success in the place where he lived, by the Road side he was incountred one day by an Old Proficient at that Trade, who seeing him Diligent, became greatly desirous of his acquaintance, and to know what Gang he belonged to, and began to Cant (as is usual amongst such seasoned Sticks of that Profession) of which kind of Speech being known to none but themselves, Monford being ignorant, could make him no direct answer; which the other, whose Name was Snap, perceiving, and thereby knowing him to be a young beginner, invited him to their Feasts or rendesvouze in White-Chappel, whither he having promised to come, and they between them tip'd off four Black Pots of Hum[3] they at that time parted.

2. Cant term for a swindler or sharper who goes halves with the actual thief·- foist or nip. Possibly a fence, or receiver of stolen goods. 3. Strong ale.

CHAP. IV.

How Monford went to the Beggars Feast, and of his Entertainment as also of the Present they made him, etc.

Monford upon his coming home, declared to his Wife what a merry Companion he had met with, and what discourse they had, as likewise what he had promised, entreating her to get things in a readiness, that she might be at leasure to conduct him thither, where appeared, instead of a ragged Regiment of Lame, Blind, and Dumb, there was a rout of jovial Dancers, as gay as the Spring, and as merry as the Maids; which made them imagine they were either mistaken in the place, or had been imposed upon, and therefore were about to retire, had not Snap who knew Monford at the first Blush, started from his Chair where he sat Supervizor in all his Gallantry, and taking him by the hand, let him know who he was, and afterward presented him to the whole Assembly, who received him as a Brother or Member of their Society, each (by the order of Snap) paying him a Complement: and that for the future he might not want a Guide on all occasion, Snap in the name of the rest presented him with a Dog and a Bell trained to the Business, and had before been the Companion of an Eyeless Beggar deceased; and so having Feasted him and his Spouse in a Splendid manner, they dismissed him, upon his promise that he would not be wanting at that yearly meeting; and being dismissed, he trudged home with his tractable Guide, which ever after proved serviceable to him. . . .[4]

[Vol. 1, no. 15]

4. Monford eventually grows so rich through begging, that when his beautiful daughter is married to a knight, he receives a £3,000 dowry with her. At the wedding feast, Monford announces that he is really Henry de Montford, son and heir of Simon.

At the Sign of the *Stationers-Arms* within *Aldgate*, any Country Chapmen may be Furnished with all Sorts of BOOKS and BALLADS.

Dennisson's Sign.

Make Room for Christmas. Written by Lawrence Price.[1]

... The Citizens Entertainment to Christmas.
Make Room for Christmas.

Honest Christmas, thou art the very last man that I thought upon, and now I see the old Proverb is true, *Long look'd for is come at last*: Why surely Christmas thou look'st, God be thanked, more fresh and fairer then thou didst for almost twenty years ago:[2] I think now thou hast Conquered and overcome most of thy Enemies, and since thou art come in a manner as one unlook't for, I have provided that which I think thou never lookest for, which is a gallant wreath of Rosemary and Bays to wear upon thy Head in token of Victory. And I'le warrant thee that here is more than Ten Thousand in London, that will make thee as welcome as my self can do, and if thou wilt be pleased to stay with us for twelve days, thou shalt be feasted with Turkies, Capons, Pigs, Rabbits, and all other sorts of dainty fare: thou shalt also have thy choice of curious Down-beds and feather-beds to lay thy weary bones upon after thy long and tedious Journey, with variety of Musick to play thee asleep.

> If thou wilt there be plea'sd to stay,
> We'l dress thee in most rich array,
> Even such as thou desir'st to have,
> Holly and Ivy, fresh and brave:
> And thou shalt every day be seen,
> More famous than was George-a-Green.[3]

1. One of the most popular chapbook and ballad writers of the middle years of the century, noticed in *D.N.B.* 2. Suggests date of composition was 1660, after puritan hegemony. Christmas was decreed a fast day in 1644. There was much opposition to this, and in 1656 a bill was introduced in parliament on Christmas Day to prevent superstition in the future. 3. The Pinner of Wakefield, who resisted Robin Hood, celebrated in Greene's comedy (1599).

A Greedy Misers Complaint against Christmas.

Fie upon't, is Christmas come to Town again: I thought he had been hang'd seven years agon.[4] And I think my Servants be mad to let him come so near my Door, for he never come yet, but he brought one base rabble or other after his heels. I'le warrant you that Christmas when he comes, brings more Beggars to town, then all the other quarters of the year, let them come when they will; and therefore I hate him with all the veins of my Heart, and if he do not depart the sooner, I will so soundly remember his Box,[5] that I will make him repent the time that ever he came this way to trouble me or my friend: for he gets nothing of me, except it be a Whip and a Bell,[6] or a kick in the breech.

The Misers New Carrol, or Song, The Tune is, A Faithful Friend.

I'de have proud Christmas for to know,
That I no love to him did owe;
Before that I will part from money,
Or give the poor one single penny,
I'le lock it up until it rust,
Or quite dissolve to slime or dust:
I'le give my broken Meat to'th Hogs,
And throw the scraps to Cats and Dogs,
Rather then Beggers I'le relieve,
Or any comfort to them give,
Go Christmas, go and Ring thy Knell,
I long to hear thy Passing-Bell.[7]

[Vol. I, no. 22]

The Secret Sinners:
OR,
A most Pleasant DIALOGUE Between a Quaker and
his Maid, and his Wife Sarah.[1]

Enters the Quaker.

Quaker. I What a War is there even now, betwixt the Inward and
the Outward Man! Satan, Satan, I say unto thee, avoid, by Yea
and by Nay, I charge thee tempt me not: Oh! how the Outward
Man prevails! and I can hold no longer; nay, the Light within
does say unto me, That Mary is a Sister, and that Gods Lambs
may play, so that they can but keep it secret from the Wicked;
therefore Satan, though I defie thee and all thy Works, yet will
I go in unto Mary as I have said: Mary, why Mary, I say unto
thee Mary.

Mary. Here, here, thy Hand-man is even here.

Quak. Are all the Prophane[2] departed as yet from our Habitation? is there none of the Wicked to observe us?

Ma. Yea, verily, they are departed, not one of the Children
of Perdition remain with us.

Quak. But as I have said unto thee, I again say unto thee,
where is thy Dame?

Ma. Even now departed to hold forth amongst the Congregation[3] of the Righteous, in the full Assembly of the Righteous.

Qua. What to the Hill of Sion, that the wicked do prophanely
call the Bull-and-Mouth?[4]

Ma. Yea, verily; for having on the sudden a strong Impulse by
the operation of the Spirit, she said unto me, Mary, and I answered
I am here; whereupon she answered and said, she was going to
instruct our Friends.

1. A unique copy and a rare example of popular prejudice against the recently
founded Society of Friends, c. 1675. The parody of 'sanctified language' is
obvious. 2. Quaker self-righteousness and exclusiveness were resented.
3. Most felt much the same about women speaking in church as did Dr.
Johnson. 4. A public house where Quakers held meetings in London. Their
irreverence for steeple-houses was matched by popular ribaldry about their
meeting house.

Qua. Then Mary, I plainly say unto thee, sit thee down, by yea and nay I must Touze[5] thee, ingeniously[6] I must.

Ma. I fie, Master, fie; what is't ye do? the Saints ought not to defile each other, we shall lose our Credit among the Prophaned; nay, Master, why Master, O fie! wherefore is it you Kiss me so? O if my Dame should know on't!

Qua. I say unto thee, fear not, fear not I say, thou art a Sanctified Sister, and one of the Infallible Congregation; and as for thy Dame, I say she is departed; therefore Mary, again I say unto thee, that the Spirit within does move me to refresh thee; I burn, I fry, and can forbear no longer.

Mary. Oh! Master, Master, I adjure thee, that thou forbear, nay, Master, Master, O Master!

Qua. By yea and by nay, I charge thee to take patiently the refreshing of a Brother, when the inward Light[7] says yea.

Ma. O fie! Hast not thee declared among the Brethren, that it shall not be lawful for a Sister to defile her self?

Qua. Yea, with the prophaned I hold it is not Lawful, but dost thou conceive that Saints can play with each other? nay, for I say unto thee, if thou dost not thou art not a Sanctified Sister: O the motion of the Spirit, how strongly it rises, nay, I must, I must, and thou must not at this time say me nay.

Ma. O fie! take away thy hand, what is't thee dost? I say unto thee, nay, nay, I say unto thee nay; O let me alone, why dost thee tempt me to go astray like one of the Wicked?

Quak. Thou canst not Err, therefore prepare thy Vessel to receive the motions that approach unto thy Tabernacle.

Ma. Yea, now thy Wickedness is entred and has put out all the Light within, nay, now I am left in darkness, and thou mayest proceed, now I swim in delight, O the happiness of us Saints above the rest of the Wicked.

Q. Yea, Mary, thou hast even said, and now this first refreshment is over, let us wait another motion from the Light within and till then, if thou shalt think fit, we will sing a Song of Son.[8]

---

5. Romp with. 6. A Quaker cliché. 7. The dangers of antinomianism had been emphasised by opponents in Massachusetts in the 1630s and throughout the Interregnum in England. 8. Sexual pun on *The Song of Songs*.

Ma. Yea, verily, I would gladly bear a part with thee, but that I fear my Dame being out of breath with holding forth among the Brethren, should return, and then if she find us on the Bed, she will verily conceive that we have gone astray, and Erred from the Light.

Quak. I say unto thee, fear not, Mary, she knows we cannot fall, nor will she conceive that a Sanctified Sister and a zealous Brother, can be wrought upon to act Carnally like the Wicked.

M. Then if it please thee to begin, thy Hand-maid shall bear a part, but be sure let it be such pure Language as is used among our Friends when assembled at Bull-and-Mouth.

Quak. Yea, Mary, it shall. . . .

Mary. I say unto thee forbear a while, by yea and nay I hear a noise, and I fear the Wicked are approaching.

Qua. As thou has said, I hear the same, and do forbear.

Sarah returning from holding forth,
speaks as she Enters.

Sarah. Why Mary, mary.

Mary. O Master Master, by and by, nay, 'tis my Dames voice, whether shall I depart? where shall I run to hide myself from Sarah? O how I tremble, I quake, I shake, now a fit of the inward man has seized me, nay, the Light does Whisper in my   and saith unto me, that I have Wronged my Dame.

Quak. Yea, thou hast said, it is my Yoak-mates voice; but fear not, Mary thou has not erred, step, step in there, step in and I shall declare unto her that thou, according to the Light, art praying for a Holy Sister, whom one of the Prophaned caused to go astray.

Ma. Yea, I shall step, but see, she's even now Administring unto thee; alas, good Woman, quite out of breath with her loud instructing our Friends, but I am safe, she cannot see me now.

Dame. Husband, Husband, I say unto thee, why hast thou neglected to appear among the Brethren?

Qua. Sarah, I say unto thee, I have been staid by a dispondancy, even in the Outward man; O the War that it raises between the Flesh and the Spirit! hadst thou even beheld what a Grumbling the Outward man kept when the Light within prevailed against him, by yea and by nay, thou wouldst have thought me all in a Feavor, nay, he assaults me yet, O he rises, he rises, O how strong he prevails! the Light is half departed, and dost thou behold again how he strugleth to take away the other part, and leave a Brother in the Dark.

Dame. Yea verily, I do, and pitty thee; Satan, Satan, I say unto thee, avoid; O Holy Man, he strives against the temptations of the Flesh, but where is Mary? O Mary, Mary.

Qua. Thine Hand-maid is even praying for a Sister that is lately gone astray.

Dame. What, with a Brother?

Qua. Nay.

Dame. With the Wicked.

Qua. Yea verily, thou hast said.

Dame. O Pious Mary, I say unto thee, come forth and Administer unto thy Master; O how the number of the Ungodly increase? come forth I say.

Ma. Lo, thy Hand-maid is even here.

Dame. Look, look, I say, nay, again I say unto thee, look, nay, Administer as a Holy Sister ought unto thy Master, least the Outward Man prevail against the Light, whilst I even go the Congregation of the Brethren, and exhort them, nay, all our friends, to pray for a falling Brother, that Satan may not buffet him.

M. Yea, yea, I shall administer according as thou hast said.

Qua. O good Wife make haste, the Flesh grows stronger, I say unto thee again, make haste, nay, run, run unto the Brethren.

Dame. Yea, yea, I shall.   [She goes out.]

Qua. Now Mary I plainly say, thy Dame is again departed.

M. Yes, verily, thy Hand-maid doth see, and how easily good Woman, she is deceiv'd by the working of the Inward man; nay, Master, Master, 'tis enough, I dare not wrong my Dame too much, reserve some refreshment for our Sister Sarah.

Qua. By yea and nay, I say unto thee Mary, by reason she hath kept all her Light within, and held none forth till now of late, it has dryed her up, nay, burnt her to a Charcole; and again I say unto thee, she is stricken in years, and regardeth not the Flesh, therefore Mary, I say I must, nay, I will, and if thou deniest the refreshing of a Brother, thou are not worthy to be called a Sister.

M. Nay, I even see thou are resolved and I shall not at this time resist thy good motion, nay, thou mayest do if it shall so please thee.

Qua. Yea, I shall.

Ma. But by yea and nay, if thine Hand-maid prove with Child, what must be done with the sanctified Babe?

Qua. I answer thee, I shall send it to some of our Friends at Clapham, there to be instructed by a Holy Sister, so that the prophaned shall not be able to reproach our Congregation with the same.

Ma. Then I plainly answer thee again, and say, that thine Hand-maid shall as often as the Spirit moves, so that Sarah nor none of the Wicked observe, prepare her Vessel to receive thy refreshments: but now Sarah is returned from the Brethren, I hear her voice and must be gone, or she will observe my rumpled Handkerchief.

Qua. Yea, thou sayest well, but lay it by and here is another, depart not, I say depart not.

Dame. O Husband, Husband, pray how is it; is the Outward man yet quiet? O had you heard the Brethren groan, and Holy Sisters weep, when I speak, and said that you were fallen from the Light.

Qua. Yea, verily they have prevailed, Satan is departed for this time, and thou mayest thank thy Hand-maid too, for she, like a pious Sister, has been very diligent since thy departure.

Dame. Yea, I say unto thee, I shall thank her, O Mary, I shall ever commend thee for a sanctified Sister among our friends, and now let all our mourning be turned into joy, yea, we will sing a Hymn for joy the inward Man has wrastled and prevailed.

Qua. Yea, yea, Sarah; if thou wilt begin, I and thy Maid will bear our parts, in spight of all the Wicked. . . .

Dame. Now let us part, and rejoyce with our Friends for the Mastery, that the inward Light has obtained over the Carnal, and that thou art not fallen like one of the Wicked.

Qua. Yea verily, as thou hast said, so it shall even come to pass; Come Mary, we will depart unto the Congregation of those Saints that be of our Notions.

Ma. Yea, yea, let it even be so. . . .

CONCLUSION.

Now Reader, see what here is plainly shown
The Character of such who weep and groan
Who hate all sins but such as are their own.

Divide us from the Wicked, still they cry,
And whilst they seem the Flesh to mortifie,
They hatch vile frauds, and close Adultery.

For when they say, *in pleace lets take our flight,*
And leave this Babel in the shades of night,
A Sisters Placket[9] puts out all their Light.

FINIS.

[Vol. I, no. 51]

---

9. Slit in petticoat.

DIOGENES

His Search through

ATHENS

With Candle and Lanthorn, when the Sun shin'd
I sought Honest Men, but none could I find.

Printed for **J. Wright, J. Clarke,**
W. Thackeray, and T. Passinger.

Diogenes[1] His Search through Athens.

Diogenes being in a pleasant humour, would needs make a Search through Athens at noon day with Candle and Lanthorn to find out an honest Man; and so having snuffed his Candle, and left his Tub to defend it self; he walks through every Street, Lane, or Alley, in all the City of Athens: But yet, *Non est Inventus*, This honest man is not to be found; for instead of honesty, he found Knavery in several shapes. And the first he met withal was Bribery, who was taken for an honest grave substantial Citizen; but Diogenes knew him to be a Knave, and so past by him, grumbling out these two verses.

> Farewel Bribery, what ere befal,
> Thou has got the Devil and all.

He had no sooner spoke these words, but he saw cruelty and Extortion comming towards him, and a great Company putting off their Hats to him, because indeed he was one of the principal and best men in the Parish, but Diogenes passed by him with his Cap on, and pointing at him, said:

> Yonder goes one that would be glad
> To sell his Soul, if he a chapman had.

As soon as he had spoken thus, he looked up, and straight espyed Prodigallity and his Whore, like a Gentleman and a Gentlewoman, walking towards the Suburbs for their recreation: Well (saith he) go on, go on;

> You need not pay your Whore. for this is true,
> Although she be unpaid, she will pay you;
> For though that she your wanton Senses pleases,
> She'l pay you with repentance and diseases.

---

1. Diogenes, the Cynic, famed for his extreme asceticism and independence made an admirable cicerone for the vices of the times. The fact that he lived in a tub probably appealed to the popular imagination.

But Diogenes not willing to come neer, their infectious breath, went onward, and the next was a flourishing Ass, trapt[2] like Alexander's horse, with a great feather in his Head, and his pace seemed to imitate his trot, and his face swelled up with pride, to think himself the super-eminent Coxcomb of the City: Diogenes startled at the first sight, but when he came nearer, he took the wall[3] very stoutly of Diogenes, who thus replyed as he passed by him:

> Thou that takest the wall at noon,
> Wilt reel into the kennel[4] soon;
> Go on my precious Ass, go on,
> I know thou wilt be drunk anon.

[Vol. I, no. 55]

2. Trapped out, dolled up. Alexander was Diogenes's contemporary, and said that if he were not Alexander he would wish to be Diogenes. The latter was typically far from awed. 3. Barged past on the side farthest from the road. This precedence in keeping as far as possible from the filth in the roadway was a frequent source of hostility, even duels. 4. The channel or gutter usually running down the middle of streets.

V. JOKES AND JESTS

Canterbury Tales. by Chaucer Junior. 1687.

The Dedication to the Bakers, Smiths, Millers, and other Readers.[1]

You are presented here with a Choice Banquet of delightful Tales,[2] pleasant Stories, witty Jests, and merry Songs to divert the young Men and Maids when they come to the Bake-house, Forge or Mill; and by these you may encrease your Trade and call Customers to you: for be sure the merry Lasses will go where they can be furnished with Tales, Stories and Jests; therefore these are as necessary for you as a fair Wife for a fine Tavern, a young Hostess for an old Inn, or a Gazet[3] for a Coffee-House. It is fitted for all manner of Persons, therefore I hope you will all furnish your selves with it; for it will be a rare Companion for Old and Young upon many Occasions; especially at Christmas, Easter, VVhitsontide, or long Winter Evenings over a Cup of Nut-brown-Ale and Lambs-wool[4]. In a word, you will find it as comfortable as Matrimony, or as sweet as a Maiden-head at midnight, or a Sack-Posset[5] at the latter end of a Fire, what would you have more, the young Men and Maids may laugh till their Lungs ake, and the old and melancholy, will find Dr. Merryman the best Physitian. Farewel.[6]

(2)

An unlucky Boy in Canterbury, got a great many a Rams-horns together in a Basket, went up and down the streets in VVinter-

1. People who can read. 2. Itself a common title for jestbooks; five editions with similar titles appeared 1630–1660. 3. Newspaper. 4. Hot ale, with apple pulp, sugar and spice. 5. Eggs, sugar and dry white wine, supposedly an aphrodisiac. 6. There is an interesting mixture here between bourgeois salesmanship and off-duty merriment.

time; crying, here's choice of new Fruit. At length, an ancient Gentleman, that was Husband to a Beautiful young VVife, ask'd to see them, which as soon as he had, he replyed, you fool, do you think I want Horns? no says the Boy, tho' you are provided yet I may meet with some body that is not: at which several Spectators laught heartily.[7]

(4)

A Young Man and Maid living in Kent, being in Love together, but Marriage deferr'd by their Friends, by reason of the inequality in the Maidens Portion: they resolved to steal some private embraces, contrary to their Parents knowledge. And it fell out, they met together at Canterbury, that being a place pretty far from home, and not much acquainted. There they took Lodgings at a certain Inn: but the Man having some small business in the City, fell into Company, and night approaching, the young Maid waiting with patience, and no Lover came, ten a clock strikes, up stairs she goes, admiring[8] to the House, that her pretended Husband did not come; desiring to have a little Sack Posset, thinking he might eat some after his Journey. That was made, brought up, and set on the Cupboards head with a Candle lighted, she being tyred, goes to Bed and there waits[9] the happy hour, of her Lovers coming: Now you must understand, there comes a Bearheard[10], that had been newly landed in the Downs,[11] with three lusty Bears; which being late was plac'd in a Stable-Room, just under the floor where the Lovers was to enjoy themselves: but one of the Bears winding[12] the Sack Posset; begins to roar, when scratching the wall and finding it yield, made a large hole just in the stair-case, gets through and up stairs he comes into the Chamber, where the Maid was then fallen asleep; the Bear mounting his two fore-feet on the Cubbord, to get to the Sack-Posset his claws hung so in the Cubboard-cloath that he pulls down the Sack Posset, Candle and all, upon him

7. Archetypal cuckolding situation. 8. Surprised. 9. Awaits. 10. Keeper of bears for baiting or performing tricks. 11. Off the east coast of Kent, within the Goodwin Sands. 12. Scenting.

which noise awakened the young Maid, who thinking her Lover
was come, started up on a sudden, but seeing a hairy thing all on
fire as the Bear was, by the Candles falling upon him: she hid her
self under the Bed-cloaths, the Bear by rouling about, at length
put out the fire on his back, and falls to licking up the Posset;
which at length, so intoxicated his Brain, that being disposed to
sleep, he leaps on the bed, and their lyes; the fright whereof,
caused our young VVoman to let fly behind. In the interim comes
in her Lover, who ascending the stairs, half fluster'd, falls on the
Bed, hugging the Bear instead of his sweetheart; and begging her
Pardon for his long stay: but he scented such a smell of bak'd,
boyl'd, stew'd and Roasted, that he knew not what to think of it;
calling out, my Dear, my Dear, why doest not speak? when in
the midst of all this Freak, the Bearheard miss'd his Bear, and
looking for him, found the hole, where he had made his escape;
comes up stairs with a lighted Torch, and three or four belonging
to the Inn, discovered the whole intrigue, to the no small shame
of the two Amoretta's.

(5)

At a Coffee-house in Canterbury, several Gentlemen were together; one was asking what news they heard from London, why
reply'd, another; there was forty thousand Men rose[13] yesterday
morning; which made them all to wonder, and ask if he knew
for what, yes says he, only to goe to Bed when night came: which
occasion'd a great laughter.

(6)

In Canterbury, there was a Carpenter that had married a handsome
young wife; and he had a Gentleman that had boarded with him,
that pretended to study Astrology; but no otherwise than to gull
the Husband and lye with his VVife, who had promised him
that favour, if he could beguile the Carpenter. Now this Gentleman had a Rival, that had a months mind[14] to have a lick at her

13. Sc. in revolt. 14. Strong urge.

Honey-pot, but she hated him and loved her Boarder. It happened that the Carpenter miss'd his Boarder upon a time, and searching about, found him in a Cock-loft, looking up toward the Skie: what's the matter, quoth he? Oh says the Gentleman, I find by Astrology that on Monday next at quarter-night, there will fall such a Prodigious Rain that Noah's Flood was not half so great; therefore get quickly three Bucking-Tubs[15] that we may get into them, and tye them to the top of the Garret, that we may save our Lives: the Carpenter quak'd for fear, got three Tubs, and at night, he and his wife and the boarder, climb a Ladder and severally get in. After much sighing, the Carpenter falls asleep, and the Gentleman and the Landlady, merrily marches to their intended business: but while they were at it, the Rival knocks at the door and entreats her to grant him a Kiss; now, said she to the Boarder, you shall laugh your fill: my Dearest quoth she, come close to the window, and I will be with you immediately: the Rival wipes his mouth to receive the kiss. At length, she opens the VVindow, and desires what he does to do quickly: now the night was very dark, and she felt about till she found him, and to tell the Tale neither better nor worse; he very savourly kiss'd her bare Arse. The Rival cruelly vext; got a red hot iron, and comes again, tell her he had brought her a Ring, provided she would give him another kiss; and the Boarder thinking to encrease the sport, places his Arse out at the same window; which his Rival did singe and burn, that he cried out, water, water, water; at which, the poor Carpenter thinking that Noah's Flood was come, starts on a sudden, out of the Bucking-Tub, fell upon the floor, broke his noddle, bepiss'd his Breeches; and at length discovers all the intreague.[16]

(7)

A VVoman sitting with Fish in Canterbury Market, would always have a saying to Men when they came to buy any thing: As a

---

15. For bleaching, dyeing or washing. 16. *The Miller's Tale,* of course.

Man was cheapning[17] her Fish, says she to him, as you intend to have some of my Fish in your Belly, so I would fain have some of your Flesh in my Belly; no says he, I can't spare my Flesh to such an ugly Puss as you: No, No, reply'd she, I did not mean as you mean, I mean your nose in my Arse.[18]

(11)

A beautiful young Gentlewoman of Canterbury, being wedded to an old Man in respect of his Riches, he being as full of Ice, as she of Fire, had a mind to try the difference between young and old Flesh, shewed some Kindness more than ordinary to her Serving-man; which he perceiving, lays hold of all Opportunities to address himself to her by way of Love; but she would not yield to his Desire, unless he would contrive some way to cornute[19] her Husband in his presence and he not to believe it, this caused the Serving-man to stretch his Invention upon the Rack, who at last acquainted his Mistress that he had found an Experiment to do it, provided she would when her Husband and she was a walking in the Garden, pretend to Long for some Fruit on some of the highest Trees, and to leave to him the management of the rest, which accordingly she did: The old Man calling his Man to ascend the Tree to gather the Fruit; which, as soon as he had got up, cryed out with a loud Voice, Master, Master, leave off for shame, I never in all my life see so unseemly an Action, for shame disengage your self from my Mistress, or else some of the Neighbours will see you: the old Man amazed at this Language, asked if the Fellow was mad, and what he meant? O Sir, said the Man, the Tree is either bewitched, or else I cannot believe mine own Eyes; for I fancy I see you upon my Mistress. Come down, come down, and let me get up the Tree to know if, it seems so to me; the Fellow comes down and the old Man gets up: in the Interim, the young Fellow fell to work with his Mistress, the old Man looks down and sees it,

17. Deprecating, bringing down the price. 18. Displaying the deepest contempt. 19. Cuckold.

cries out, in good Faith says he, it seems to me just as it did to you, for methinks I see you upon your Mistress as perfectly as if it was really so: the old Man gets down and thinks the Tree bewitched; orders presently[20] to be cut down, for fear it should infect the rest. Thus was the old Man made a Cuckold to his own Face and would not believe it.[21]

15.

A married Gentleman coming through Canterbury, his Horse threw him, which a young Gentlewoman seeing, fell a laughing; the Man being terribly vext that she should laugh at his fall, angerly said, Madam, pray admire not at this, for my Horse always stumbles when he meets a Whore; she sharply reply'd, have a care then Sir, you do not meet your Wife, for then you will certainly break your neck.

[Vol. II, no. 12]

---

20. Immediately. 21. A variant of *The Merchant's Tale*.

THE *Sack-ful* OF NEWS.[1] 1685.

. . . Another.

THere was an old man that could not well see, who had a fair young Wife, and with them dwelt a young man, which had long wooed his Mistris to have his pleasure of her, who at last consented to him, but they knew not how to bring it to pass, for she did never go abroad, but in her husbands company, and lead him alwaies. At last she deviled a very fine shift,[2] and bid her servant that he should that night about midnight come into her chamber where her Husband and she lay, & she would find some device for him. Night came, and the old man and wife went to bed, but she slept not a wink, but thought still upon her pretended purpose, but a little before the time prefixed, she awakened her Husband, & said thus unto him: Sir, I will tell you a thing in secret, which your servant was purposed to do; when I am alone I can never be quiet for him, but he is always inticing me to have me at his will, and so at the last to be quiet with him, I consented to meet him in the Garden, but for mine Honesties[3] sake I will not. Wherefore I pray you put on my clothes and go meet him: so when he comes to you, beat him well, and chide him, for I know well he will not strike you, because you are his Master, and then he may amend himself & prove a good servant: & the man was well pleased therewith. So the good man put on his wives Cloaths, and took a good Cudgel in his hand, & went into the garden. At length there came the servant to his mistris, where she lay in bed, and did what he would with her, and she was content, & then she told him how she had sent her Husband into the garden in her apparel, & wherefore, and to what purpose. So her servant arose, and as she bade him, took a good staff with him, and went into the garden, as though he knew not it was his master, & said unto him: Nay you whore, I did this but only to

1. This title was first used in 1557. News is here used in the old sense of novelties, and is here a breach of the trades descriptions act. 2. Devise a very fine trick, stratagem. 3. Honour's.

prove thee whether thou wouldest be false to my good master, and not that I would do such a vile thing with thee: whereupon he fell upon his Master, giving him many sore stripes, & beating him most cruelly, still calling him nothing but, out you Whore, will you offer this abuse to my good Master: Alas, (qd. his Master) good John, I am thy Master, strike me no more I pray thee. Nay whore (qd. he) I know who thou are well enough, & so he strook him again, beating him most grievously. Good John (said his Master) feel, I have a Beard, Then the servant felt (knowing well who it was) who presently kneeled down and cryed his Master mercy. Now thanks be to God (qd. his Master) I have as good a servant of thee as a man can have, and I have as good a Wife as the World affords. Afterwards the Master went to bed, & his servant also. When the old man came to bed to his wife; she demanded of him how he sped: He answered and said, By my troth Wife, I have the trustiest servant in the world, & as faithful a Wife; for my Servant came thither with a great staff & did beat me right sore, thinking it had been you, wherefore I was well pleased therewith. But ever after the Servant was well beloved of his Master, but better of his Mistris: for his Master had no mistrust of him, though he had made him a Cuckold. so the poor man was cruelly beaten, and made a Summers Bird[4] nevertheless. . . .[5]

. . . Another.

THere was a Priest in the Country which had christened a Child, and when he had christened it, he & the Clerk were biden to the drinking that should be there, and thither they went with other people, and being there, the Priest drank and made so merry, that he was quite foxed, and thought to go home before he laid him down to sleep; but having gone a little way, he grew so

4. Cuckoo, i.e. cuckold. 5. This jest, *Cocu battu et content* (Cuckolded, beaten, yet happy) is in the *Decameron*, seventh story, seventh day, other collections of facetiae and fabliaux and La Fontaine's *Contes*. It started the rounds in England in *A C. Mery Talyes* (A Hundred Merry Tales) printed by John Rastell in 1526.

drowsie, that he could go no further, but laid him down by a ditch-side so that his feet did hang in the water, & lying on his back, the Moon shined in his face: thus he lay till the rest of the company came from drinking, who as they came home found the Priest lying as aforesaid, and they thought to get him away, but do what they could he would no rise, but said, Do not meddle with me, for I lye very well, and will not stir hence before the morning, but I pray lay some more clothes on my feet, and blow out the Candle, and let me lye and take my rest.

Another.

THere was once a Country-man, which came to London, where he had never been before, and as he went over London bridge, he saw certain Ships sailing, being the first time he had seen any[6] & perceiving the Sails made of cloath, he thought to assay if his Plough would go so, and when he came home, he caused his Wife to give him a large new Sheet, and went and set it on the Plough like a Sail, thinking the Plough would go with the Wind, but it removed not. Which when he saw, he said what the Devil, have I spoiled my sheet about nothing? so set his Horses to the Plough again. . . .

[Vol. I, no. 6]

6. It would have been not at all uncommon for countrymen never to have seen the sea or sailing ships.

Humphry Frollicksome.

... Sir Humphrys Journey up to London; And his putting a Trick upon his Brother; And how he got himself reconciled again to his Father.

Sir Humphry having now raised his Fortune to so high a pitch in so short a time, was inclined to let himself loose to his accustomed Pleasures; and having heard much of the Fame of London, he had a longing desire to see that place, and to satisfie his Curiosity, he takes his Journey that way, and having eased himself of the burthen of Necessity, he resolved to travel like a Gentleman, and lay aside all his Politick Contrivances, till Poverty should oblige him to make use of them again: so up to the City of London he came, well mounted, and his Pockets lined with the best of Coyn; his Journey was very prosperous and pleasant, not meeting with any interruption[1] in all his passage, in which he found a great deal of satisfaction: When he had reach'd London, that Famous City, in which his desire was lodged, he was mightily pleased with the Noble Fabricks[2] and the many Grandeurs he had not before seen; and when he had taken up his Lodging and provided himself all things necessary to his Settlement, he walks about, and makes what enquiry he could after some that been formerly his Acquaintance at Oxford, that they might introduce him into a farther knowledge of the Town, to which he was a perfect stranger: He had not made this his business long, but Fortune so favoured him, that he met one by meer accident, who had been his intimate Friend and Acquaintance, who were both mightily surprized, and extremely glad to see each other; and after a kind salutation on both sides, they consented to carrouse one hearty Bottle to their happy meeting, and to laugh at old passages, in which they had been both concerned; and in their discourse Sir Humphrys Friend happened

1. Highwaymen or accidents, implying what a risky business travel was.
2. Buildings.

to inform, that his Father and his Brother was in Town, and that he had seen them not above two days ago; Sir Humphry replyed, he was very glad to hear it; and being both intimate together, and sufficiently assured of one anothers friendship, said, that he would lay hold of the first opportunity he could, to make himself amends for the Injury his Brother had done him, in being an Instrument in putting his Father and him at variance; and enquired of his Friend where it was he lodg'd, who gave him an account of every matter requisite for Sir Humphrys purpose; and when they had laughed and chatted three or four hours, it began to grow late, and the Wine had almost turned their Noddles top-side turvey, they thought it time to part, and to retire home to their respective Habitations; so they pay'd their Reckoning, and Sir Humphry desired his friend not to take notice to his Father of his being in Town, who assured he would not; and when they had appointed where to meet the next time, they took a kind leave of one another, and so parted.

And as Sir Humphry (in his Cups being a little more Frollicksome than ordinary) happened to ramble some way by a House that was new building, where he heard something rustle in the dark Cellar, and resolved to see what it was, steps in, and asks, Who's there? It happened to be a poor Beggar-wench, about Eighteen years of Age, who replyed, Nothing (Sir) but a poor Girl, who is forc'd to lye here, for want of a better habitation. Sir Humphry steps in and swore he would bear her company a little, before he went any further, and catched hold of the wench, and fell a tumbling and touzing[3] her, and askt her how she could make shift to lye in so cold a dwelling; she told him, she had made her a Bed of Shavings in the next Cellar, which was warmer; and Sir Humphry being desirous to see it, entreated the Wench to conduct him into her Bed-Chamber, which according to his request she did, and down she and Sir Humphry lay together, who began to be very brisk with her, and she being loth to deny him the Civility of a Female Bed-fellow, but receiv'd his close embraces as a courteous obligation. When the heat of Pastime began to be over, and Sir Humphry considering what he had

3. Kissing and cuddling.

done, resolved to contrive a way to lay this Action as a Scandal upon his Brother. By this time the Wench began to lay open her unfortunate Condition, and to desire some Charity from Sir Humphry, for her Relief, which Request put him in mind of the Outlandish[4] piece of money he had privately taken from his Brother, who never knew which way he had lost it, thinking That would be a good Instrument to make his Father really believe his Brother to be guilty of the thing which he designed to put upon him, which was the chief hopes of Sir Humphry, who told her, he had spent that day what money he had brought out with him, had and nothing left but an Outlandish piece of money, and that he gave her, and bid her come tomorrow to his Lodging, directing her to the place where his Father and Brother lay, and goes himself by his Brothers Name, and bids her ask for him, and bid her send up that piece of money, as a Token, by any of the Servants, and then he should know her business, and would send her down half a Piece;[5] the Wench was mighty thankful, and said, she would be sure to come: so Sir Humphry took his leave, and left her where he found her, and went home to Bed, hoping this design would work. The next day the Wench, according to his order, went to the place he had directed her, expecting it to be Sir Humphrys Lodging, where she knocks, and asks for Sir Humphry's Brother, expecting him to be the same man whom she had before seen; the Father being in the Entry, wondring what such a draggle-tail'd wench would have with his Son, goes to her, and enquires her business; the wench gives him the Token, and desires him to give the Gentleman that, and he would presently know her business: The Father knowing the piece of Coyn to be his Sons, that was given him as a Token by his Grandmother, wondered the more how such a Wench came by it; so he calls the Girl within the Doors, and there began to be mighty inquisitive, and examined her strictly how she came by that piece of money and what was the business she came to his Son about, and threatned the Girl with hard words into so many fears, that at last she told him the whole

4. Foreign. 5. Half a guinea, 10/6d, which at the going-rates for the period was extremely generous; 2/6d would have been normal.

circumstance of the matter; which put the Old Man into such a lamentable fury, that he coughed himself half dead with meer passion; his Son being not within all this time to vindicate himself before the wenches Face, who got away as soon as she could, and was glad to escape the old Gentlemans Rage. In this Agony of vexation the Old Man continued, exclaiming against his Son for a Reprobate-Rascal, who poor Gentleman, knew nothing of the matter; at last home he came, where he no sooner entred, but the old man met him with a lusty Cudgel, and fell to be-

Bissell's Sign.

labouring him with all the Vigour that fumbling old Age could lay upon him, crying out, Thou Villain, I'le teach you to have your draggle-tail'd Sluts come after you for Money, and you must give them Tokens, with a Pox to you; and i'le give you a Token to remember me too before I part with you. The Son cryed out for mercy, denying all his Father accused him with, but nothing could curb the Old mans passion; and when he thought he had bang'd him sufficiently, he turns him out of doors, not giving him the liberty to speak one word for himself, and vowed he would never see him more. The poor Gentleman thought the Devil was in his Father, to accuse him with what he knew nothing of, and to beat him so unmercifully, neither could he imagine what was the meaning of it. Sir Humphry hearing his design had took so effectually, resolved to take this opportunity of submitting himself to his Father, which he accordingly did, and by the endeavour of some Friends, got him throughly reconciled to him, and was placed again in the same splendid Station he had formerly lived in, leaving his Brother in the same condition that he himself was freed from.

FINIS.

[Vol. II, no. 25]

New London Drollery. 1687.

A new Song of Nanny and Jenny, two coy and scornful Maids; with half an hours chat on their Sweethearts; by way of Dialogue. Tune of, *My life and my death.*

Nanny.

I'm near Fifteen, and I have not seen
A man that I like where e'er I have been:
The finikin Taylor, who makes his address,
Is a lousy young Coxcomb, I needs must confess
And take away bodkin, his shreds,[1] & his goose,[2]
All the rest of his Tools are scarce worth a Louse.

Jenny.

And there is my Butcher, a bloody young knave,
A pretty spruce Lass he gladly would have;
With his Tool at his Arse,[3] & a dainty blew Frock,
And impudent language he has a great stock:
He often comes to me, but Foh, out I cry,
No butcherly Booby with Jenny shall lye.

Nanny.

And I have a Baker that busses[4] me oft,
His teeth are like Ivory, his lips they are soft,
But he stinks of sweat as bad as a Jaques;[5]
O that he smelt but so sweet as his Cakes,
I faith I could love him exceedingly well;
But his wife, I believe, may as well live in hell.[6]

1. Small pieces of cloth; also cant word for a tailor. 2. Smoothing iron. 3. Sharpening steel or stone worn on belt. 4. Kisses. 5. Privy; sweating from heat of his ovens. 6. Either because of oven-heat, or because of his night-work.

Jenny.

And there's an Ale-Draper[7] as spruce as a Prince,
And that he doth love me he does me convince;
He swears I shall shine like a new Morning-star,
And simper most sweetly each night in his Bar:
But thinks he i'le have him? not I by my troth,
For I from my Cradle abhor'd Nick and Froth.[8]

Nanny.

A Fop of a Barber comes early and late,
And thunders a March at my Master's old Gate;
He swears he will have me by all that is good,
And tells me a Story of bold Robin Hood:
But I let him know with a rap on his crown,
I'le marry with no Powder-Monkey[9] in town.

Jenny.

And a Pimp of St. Crispin's[10] that makes all my shooes
The making of many a pair he does lose,
He boasts of his Trade, comes so mighty and fast,
That often I ask him to court his Last,
And I tell him plainly, I'd rather be dead,
Than like a poor Cobler's wife, sit and spin thread.

Nanny.

A prodigal Pavier comes oft to our door,
I bid him be gone for a Son of a Wh - - -
He brags of his getting,[11] but I cannot see't,
I find he must live by the stones[12] in the street,
And therefore I bid him be gone from the gate,
Or else I will throw a large stone at his pate.

---

7. Alehouse-keeper. 8. False bottom in beer-cans and too much froth on top.
9. Pun on gunpowder carriers. 10. Patron saint of cobblers. 11. Pun on
begetting, i.e. virility, and his income. 12. Slang for testicles.

Jenny.

A weaver comes hobling to me e'ry night.
And swears he is sick when I'm out of his sight:
I ask him his Errand; he tells me it's love,
With tears in his eyes; my pitty he'd move,
But pitty and love they are now out of date,
Had he courted my Granam,[13] he'd sure come too late.

Nanny.

Well, but a Jockey came prancing to me
With a delicate Gelding as e're I did see:
He swore that he lov'd me much more than his life
And fain wou'd have had me to have been his wife.
But I told the Jockey his Oaths were all lost,
By none of that Crew I would ever be crost.[14]

Jenny.

No, no, let us live, and live in mans spight,
From all that fond Sex I'le ever take flight;
Unless a blind Usurer courts me with Gold,
No mortal shall ever touch my Copyhold;
A Pox upon all their dissembling tricks,
They'l lye from Sixteen till Sixty and Six. . . .

[Vol. II, no. 42]

13. Grandmother, grandam. 14. Bred with.

Strange and Wonderful Relation.[1]

It was last Sunday morning, at four a clock in the afternoon, before Sun-rise; going over High-Gate-hill in a Boat; I met with a man I overtook, I asked him, if the old woman was dead that was drowned at Ratcliff high way[2] a fortnight ago; He told me he could not tell? But if I went a little further, I should meet with two men a Horse-back upon a Mare, in a Blew Jerkin, and a pair of Freestone Breeches,[3] & they would give me true intelligence, so when I came up with the fellows, they thought I was a Hector[4] which came to rob them, and therefore ran from me, but I furiously pursued before them. Their horse for haste died under them, so that one of them for madness drew forth his sword and kill'd him, the horse for vexation seeing himself dead, ran away as fast as he could, leaving them to go a foot upon another horse back Forty miles. Friends said I, I mean you no harm, but pray inform me whether or no the old Woman be Dead that was drownd at Ratliff high-way a fortnight ago, they all told me they could not tell, but if I went a little further I should meet with two men driving of an empty Cart full of apples, & a millstone in the midst, and they would give me true Intelligence; but when I came up with them, they could not satisfie me neither, but told me if I went to the water side there livd one Sir Iohn Vangs that would give me intelligence. So going up to ye water side; I hoopt & hollowed,[5] but could make no body see: At last I heard six country lads & lasses fast asleep, playing at ninepins under a Haycock[6] made of Pease[7] straw, in the midst of the Thames, & eating of rost bag pudding[8] freezing hot: but at last I met with two she Watermen,[9] that carried me clean over the

1. This kind of nonsense had been used by Rabelais, *Gargantua,* I, vii, published for the first time in English, in Urquhart's brilliant translation, in 1653. 2. Mainroad running eastward out of London. 3. Sand or limestone easily sawn. 4. Bully. 5. Whooped and hollered; Vangs defeats me, though Sir John was slang for either a priest or a commode. 6. Conical heap of hay. 7. Pea. 8. Boiled in a bag. 9. Part of the play here is on she-men, and part on women in this exclusively male occupation.

water, and landed me up to the knees in mud, and when we were
in the midst of the Thames in Ratcliff High-way, one of the she-
watermen espied a swan, and swore if she had it at home, it
would make a brave Goose-Pye. . . .

[Vol. II, no. 27]

Riddles. By S.M. 1687.

... (2)

Q. While I do flourish here on Earth,
    By me young ones nourisht are;
    I have a thousand at a birth,
    And yet I take no thought nor care?

A. A Goose-berry-bush.

(3)

Q. This moment I was not at all,
    Then straight I in the World do fall,
    And if not careful I annoy,
    For where I come I do destroy?

A. Fire from a Flint and Steel, which before struck was nothing,
but when falling into Tender, without care will destroy.

(4)

Q. Though it be cold I wear no cloaths,
    The Frost and Snow I never fear,
    I value neither Shooes nor Hose,
    And yet I wander far and near,
    both meat and drink is always free,
    I drink no Syder, Mum[1] nor sack;[2]
    what providence doth send to me,
    I neither buy, nor sell, nor lack?

A. A Herring swimming in the Seas.

[Vol. I, no. 23]

1. Imported Brunswick beer. 2. Dry white wine.

Here Beginneth The first Riddle.

Two legs sat upon three legs, and had one leg in her hand,
then in came four legs and bare away one leg, then up starts
two legs and threw three legs at four legs, and brought
again one leg.

Solution.

That is a woman with two legs, sate on a stool with three legs,
and had a leg of Mutton in her hand, then came a Dog that hath
four legs, and bare away the leg of Mutton, then up starts the
woman and threw the stool with three legs at the Dog with four
legs, and brought away the leg of Mutton.

The second Riddle.

He went to the Wood and he caught it
He sat him down and he sought it,
Because he could not find it,
Home with him he brought it.

Solution.

That is a Thorn; for a man went to the wood and caught a thorn
in his foot, and then he sat him down, and thought to have
pulled it out, and because he could not find it out he must needs
bring it home.

The Third Riddle.

What work is that, the faster you work the longer it is e're you
have done, and the slower you work, the sooner ye make an end?

Solution.

That is the turning of a Spit; for if you turn fast, it will be long e're the meat be roasted, but if you turn slow, the sooner it is.

The Fourth Riddle.

What is that shineth bright all the day, and at night is raked up in the dirt?

Solution.

That is the fire that burneth bright all day, and at night is raked up in its ashes.

[Vol. I, no. 24]

Crossing of Proverbs. By B. R. Gent. 1683.

Proverb.

Every Tradesman knows his own ware best.

Cross.

Not if his female deceive him.

P. Most hast worst speed.
C. Not in the hast but lack of heed.

P. He that hath his eyes in his head will look about him.
C. Not so, he may be blindfold, and then he cannot.

P. Wanton Kisses are the keys of sin.
C. Not except the Devil keep the locks.

P. Pride is the greatest despoiling of a Kingdom.
C. Not so, a plague if it continued may be greater.[1]

P. Give give is a good fellow.
C. Not so, he is churl that hath no charity.

P. Love is the peace of the senses.
C. Not where it is joyned with jealousie.

P. Witty women are sweet companions.
C. Not but when they are pleased, for else they are froward.

P. Crabbed minds are pleased with nothing.
C. Not so, for nothing can give no pleasure.

P. Kind hearts are soonest wronged.
C. Not if they be careful.

P. There is no tree but beareth fruit.
C. Yes the Cycamour.

[Vol. I, no. 53]

1. This edition published only eighteen years after the last great plague in England.

The Five Strange Wonders. By L.P.[1] 1683.

. . . Five lessons fit for young Scholars to Learn.

To give honour to Age,
To be courteous in behaviour,
To be humble in condition,[2]
To be excellent in knowledge,
And to be charitable to the poor.

Five things too common in use.

Hateful pride in married women,
Wanton Lust in wilful Maids,
Deadly drunkenness in sinful women,
Griping greediness in covetous persons,
And dissimulation among fawning people.

There are five sorts of nimble pickers which
deserve to be punished.

A Pick-thank[3] for telling false tales,
A Pick-quarrel for making mischief,
A Pick-lock for robbing his neighbour,
A Pick-window to let in Rogues,
And they that pick pockets to purchase the Halter.[4]

1. Possibly Lawrence Price, famous chapbook and ballad writer, noticed in
D.N.B. 2. Mental disposition. 3. A sycophant. 4. Noosed rope.

. . . These five things offend the Eyes.

Taking too much Tobacco,
Standing too long in the cold,
Gazing too much upon painted drabs,[5]
To see others flourish with thy goods,
And to see thy friends want and cannot help them. . . .

Five sorts of Creatures most busie in hot weather.

A Bee in the Honey-pot, A Mole in a Park,
A Duck in a Fish-pond, A Lowse in a bosom,
And a Fox among Geese.

Five special good things in a winter season.

Wholesome diet for the belly,
Warm cloathing for the back,
Ale and Spice for the stomach,
A good fire to sit by,
And a soft bed to lie upon. . . .

[Vol. II, no. 2]

5. Whores.

The *Figure of Seaven*. By Poor Robin.[1]

... Seven marks to know a Man that is Hen-peckt,

1 He that lets his wife keep his Money and when he wants two pence to drink with a Friend, is forced to sue to her to borrow it, 2 He that is followed by his wife to the Alehouse, and dares not stay no longer when she comes for him, 3 He that warms the Childs Clous at the fire whilst his Maid is dressing it, and his wife boozing it at the Ale-house with her Companions, 4 He that goes to the Ale-house for a Pitcher of Bub.[2] and leaves another man at home with his wife, 5 He that lets his wife run to Conventicles,[3] whilst he stays at home to skim the Pot, 6 He that gives account to his wife what money he takes, what he spends at the Ale-house, and what he laies out for Goods, 7 He that stays at home to rock the Cradle whilst his wife rides in a hackny Coach to see a Play.

The Seven Properties belonging to an Host.

1 He must have the forehead of an Ox, 2 The Ears of an Ass, 3 The Back of a Nag, 4 The Belly of a Swine, 5 The Subtilty of a Fox, 6 Skip up and down like a Frog, 7 Fawn and lye like a Dog.

Seven sorts of people great in Title, but poor in Purse.

1 The Dons of Spain, 2 The Monsiers of France, 3 The Bishop of Italy, 4 The Nobility of Hungary, 5 The Lairds of Scotland, 6 The Earls of Germany, 7 The Knights of Naples.

---

1. Generic term, denoting a humble jester, like Robin Goodfellow. *Poor Robin's Almanack* (1664) parodying the efforts of such as Lilly had been a popular success. 2. Strong beer. 3. Sectarian religious meetings.

Seven things which the chast Romans did shun.

1 To talk much in Feasts and Assemblies, 2 To eat too much in Banquets, 3 To drink wine being in health, 4 To speak aside with other men; 5 To stay long at their windows, 6 To lift up their Eyes in the Temple, 7 To go out of their Houses without their Husbands.

He that seeketh after these seven things looseth his Labour.

1 Fat Hog among the Jews, 2 Loyalty in a Flatterer, 3 Soberness in a Drunkard, 4 Money in a prodigal mans Purse, 5 VVisdom in a Fool, 6 A fine wit in a fat Belly, 7 Vertue in evil Company.

Seven things against Nature.

1 A fair Maden without a Lover, 2 A merchant Town without Thieves, 3 An old Usurer without money, 4 An old Barn without Mice, 5 A scald Head without Lice,[4] 6 An old He-Goat without a Beard, 7 A sleeping man deckt with Learning. . . .

[Vol. I, no. 34]

---

4. Someone suffering with ringworm or tinea.

The Figure of Nine. (Samuel Smithson)

The Figure of Nine, Containing mirth, Wit and Pleasure.

Assist me now you Muses all Divine,
To write upon this Figure of Nine.

Nine Vertues Compleats and makes an honest Women: Patience, Modesty, Chastity, Loving moderately, Giving charitably, a Vice reprover, a Gospel lover, jealous in goodnesse, and to be faithfull in her promise.

Nine excellent treasures which will cause a Man to love a Maid: Beauty, Feature, Amity, Riches, Lands, Livings, Noble birth, gallant behaviour, and a tongue that is civil.

Nine sorts of heads much nominated[1] in these times:[2] a square head, a long head, rattle head, a round head, a Bulls head, calves head, a Rams head, a Cuckolds head, and a Maiden head.[3]

Nine pretty passages and pastimes cause mirth and laughter: a play with a clown in it, a Court with a fool in it, a changling and an antick:[4] a Lord and his master, a mad man in Bedlam,[5] Iack-pudding[6] in dancing, a song from a fidler, the politick Iugler, and the Hobby-horse Morris.

Nine sorts of wives and other things torment horn mad Cuckolds: wanton wives, avishing[7] wives, fighting wives, scolding wives, jeering wives, costly wives, handsome wives, sparks in their Beds, and themselves kickt out of service.

Nine ill conditions in a Married Man puts his wife out of temper: to be idle, to be a drunkard, to swear, lye and dissemble, to be a

1. Talked about. 2. First edition, 1662. 3. Square may be dons, some of whom were ejected in 1662 for refusing oaths of conformity; long may be witty; rattle was a fool; round a puritan; Bull may be Bull and Mouth, Quaker meeting; calves defeats me; Rams may be armorial. 4. A grotesque. 5. A Bethlehem hospital for lunatics, a frequent source of popular amusement. 6. Buffoon. 7. Misprint for ravishing.

At the afore-mentioned place, any Country Chapmen or others, may be Furnished with all sorts of Small Books and Ballads.

Joshua Deacon's Sign.

glutton, to pawn his clothes and bedding, to be dogged and full of Envy.

Nine things delight a Shepherd: The killing of Wolves, the destroying of Foxes, the barking of Cut,[8] his Crook, Bagpipes and tarbox, his bottle, a wench in the fold, when his wife is charming.

Nine sorts of common Dances always used: Salingers round, Bobbin-jo, Jingle-de-cut, Bodkins Galliard, the madmans Morris, Drunken Barnaby, the Bed full of bones, room for Cuckolds, and the Lankishire horn-pipe.

Nine sorts of foolish things are unseemly: to eat pottage with a Ladle, to blow ones Nose at supper, to Fart before a Justice, to slabber in eating, to laugh at prayer, to Kiss like a clown, to stand like a fool, to jeer continually, and to laugh at a dogs tail wagging. . . .

Vol. I, no. 20]

8. His dog.

A
Hundred Notabe Things,
And
MERRY CONCEITS FOR A PENNY.
Wherein is shewed

1. To make a Candle burn under Water.
2. How to make beans grow up in an hours space.
3. How to make a good Bait to catch fish.
4. A rare Art to know whether a Man or Woman shall marry or not.
5. To know whether a Person sick is bewitched.
6. How to drive away all Inchantments or Witchcraft.
7. How to know precious Stones from Counterfeit.
8. How to know whether a Woman be with Child of a Boy or a Girl.
9. How to know whether a sick Party will live or die.
10. How to make a Thief afraid to come into your House.
11. How to make a Varnish upon Iron to shine like Gold.
12. How to make Ink that will shew like Gold.

With abundance of Pleasant Histories of the Wonderful things of Art and Nature, shewing the Mistery of the Loadstone.

By JOSH CROYNES Gent.[1]

Licensed according to Order.

LONDON,

Printed for J. Conyers at the Black Raven in
Duck Lane, 1680.

---

1. An anagram of the publisher's name. This, misprints and all, is the title-page.

How to make a flame pass suddenly out of a Pot of water, a
rare Secret.

1. This is done by taking an Egg & make an hole in the head,
and draw out all the substance out of it, then fill it with the
powder of brimstone and unslacked Lime mixed together,
then seal it up with wax, then let to the bottome a pot full of
water taking your hands suddenly away, & presently a flame
will issue out of the pot.

2. To for[2] any birds that you may take them with your hands,
is by seething barley or seeds in Lees of wine, & when they
have eaten it twill make them drunk, so that you may take them
up with your hands, or turmentil[3] boiled in wine steeping your
seeds will do the same.

3. A fish in all parts like a man, was taken near Oxford[4] in
Suffolk, and for six months was kept in the Castle: whence
afterwards he escaped and got into the Sea again.

4. Near the same place, in the Year 555. in a time of great
Dearth, a Crop of Pease grew in the Rocks without Tillage or
Sowing, so that in August there had been 100 Quarters gathered,
and as many more left blossoming.[5]

5. There dyed in the year 1348. in Norwich of the Plague,
15504.

6. Breakspear an Englishman, born in Langley in Hartford-
shire, known by the name of Pope Adrian the 4th, whose Sturrup
was held up by Frederick the Emperour, was kill'd by a fly.[6]

7. Before the civil Wars of Lancaster & York, the River Owse
near Harwood in Bedfordshire, stood stone still.

2. Misprint for fox? 3. Low-growing herb, septfoil. 4. Orford; mermen were
staples of books of wonders. 5. John Ray, the botanist, noted these in 1662
when he was staying at nearby Friston. 6. Frederick I Barbarossa. Adrian
died 1159, of a quinsy.

8. In Salisbury Cathedral Church, there are as many Windows as days, as many Marble Pillars as hours, and Doors as months in the Year.

9. An Egg laid in white wine Vinegar three days, will become so soft that you may draw it through a Ring: Cast it for the same time into warm water, and it will be hard again.

10. Take Oyl of Tartar made of the Lees of good Wine, and it will both take the spots out of your Iron, and keep it from rusting.

11. If you would make any stones soft, you must put them all night in the fat of a Weather,[7] and blood of an Ox, and strong Vinegar.

12. Sir Francis Drake, in two Years and ten months, went round the world.

13. At Dunstar on Sommerset shire, a virtuous Lady beg'd as much Common ground for the town, as she could incompass in one day barefoot.

14. At Mottingham in Kent, in the Year 1586 the ground began to sink, and three great Elms growing thereon sunk, & let a hole eighty yards in compass, of which could be found no bottom.

15. If you would make a Glew that will glew up your broken glasses; you must take Quick-Lime mixed with old Cheese, which being well beaten together will accomplish your desire.

16. To hatch Chickens without the help of a hen, if you take an Egg and keep it in your arm-hole, it will hatch them as well as a Hen.

17. To make a candle burn under water, take Wax, Brimstone, and Vinegar, of each a little quantity, boyl all these together till the Vinegar appear quite consumed, & then of that wax which remains, make a Candle which will burn under water.

18. If you would make beans grow up in an hours space, take the beans & put them into boyling hot Oyl, let them there remain for eleven days, & then dry them; & when you would make your proof of them, set them & go to dinner, and by that time you have din'd, you shall find them grown up near a span[8] high.

7. Castrated ram. 8. Nine inches.

19. To make a good bait for fish, that will serve all seasons of the year; take white flower and tallow of a new slein sheep, and the glair[9] of an Egg, and beat them all together, and bait them all therewith.

20. A neat Conclusion, whether a Man or woman shall marry or not? take the number of the mans name and 3 and likewise of the womans, and divide them asunder by 9. if the mans name exceed the womans they shall marry, or otherwise not.

21. Aurelianus the Emperour, being about to sign an Edict against the Christians, a Thunder bolt from heaven struck so near him, that all conceited him a dead man; but he recovering and not taking that for a warning, was after slain by his own servants.

22. London was built 356 years before Rome in the time of Eli the High Priest.

23. In the year of our Lord 1552 a Child was born at Middlestone with two bodies, two heads, four Arms and hands, one Belly and navel: it lived four dayes & one side dyed before the other,[10]

24. Lopez[11] being Executed for Treason against Queen Elizabeth, at Tyburn professed that he loved the Queen as well as he did Jesus Christ, for which he was railed at by some, but laught at by others who knew him to be a Jew.

25. How to serve a Tapster a trick so that he shall not be able to froth his Cans; which is done by only rubing the inside of his Pot or Can with the skin of a Red Herring.

[Vol. I, no. 52]

9. White. 10. Appears to have been Siamese twins. 11. Roderigo Lopez, executed for conspiring to poison the Queen in 1594; a victim of Essex.

VI. PRACTICAL.

The *Queens Royal Closet, Newly Opened.*
By that most Famous Physitian, Dr. Boules.[1] 1682.

... *For Hearing.*

Take four drops of the juyce of Bettony,[2] and warm it in a Saucer, then drop two drops into each ear when you go to bed, then stop them up close with black wool, and it will recover your hearing.

To *take away Freckles in the face.*

Anoint your face often with Oyl of Almonds, and it will take it away.

For *the pain at the heart or stomach.*

Take four grains of Mastick[3] at Evening going to bed, and it will take away the pain thereof.

For *a Sinew strained.*

Take Nerve Oyl,[4] Pompilion,[5] and Oyl of Exeter,[6] of each two penniworth, then mix them together, and warm it in a Saucer: then anoint the joynt therewith, and bind it up close, and it cureth.

---

1. Probably George Bowles, FRCP in 1664, of Chislehurst, Kent. 2. Plant with spiked purple flowers. 3. Gum or resin from pistacio tree. 4. Oil for soothing nerves. 5. Grapefruit. 6. Herbs, seeds and flowers digested in wine and oil.

For the taking away Warts.

Take Fig-tree leaves, & rub your Warts therewith, and bury the said leaves in the ground, and the Warts will consume away as the leaves do rot.

For Convulsion Fits.

Take black-cherry-water, and the sirrop of violets, and three drops of the oyl of amber, then mix them together, and take three or four spoonfuls of it at a time, just as the fit begins to come upon you, and you shall find present remedy, *probatum*.[7]

For the Cough or stopping of the breath.

Take the Sirrop of Hysop, the sirrop of Liquorish, the sirrop of Maiden-hair,[8] of each an ounce, and take thereof every morning a spoonful or two.

For the Head-ache.

Take a handful of Spere-mint, and shred it small, then grate some Nutmeg into it, with some Rose-water, and bind it close to your forehead, and it will take away the pain thereof.

For the Worms in Children.

Take two ounces of Purslain-seed,[9] and boyl it a pint of white-wine, then give it the Child fasting three mornings together, and it will kill the Worms. . . .

[Vol. I, no. 12]

7. Proved (effective). 8. A fern. 9. Kitchen-garden herb.

How to Roast a Hare the newest way.

The Hare being flea'd,[1] Lard her with small slips of Bacon-lard: stick her over with Cloves, the Ears being stripped and left on: then make a Pudding of grated Bread, beaten Cinamon, grated Nutmeg, Currans, Cream, Sugar and Salt: make it up with White-wine or Claret-wine, and put it into the Belly; when tying the Hare to the Spit, Roast it by a gentle fire: which done, make Sawce of Cinamon, Ginger, Nutmegs, Pruens, grated Bread and Sugar: boil them up to a thickness, and laying the divided Pudden on either side the Hare, serve it up with the Sawce.

To Roast a Haunch of Venison after the best fashion.

You must season it a little, then let it lye a while in warm water: after which sprig it with Rosemary, Roast it well by a soft fire, and make up your Sawce of Claret-wine, grated Bread, Ginger, Cinamon, Sugar and Verjuice,[2] or Lemonjuice: boil them to a thickness of melted Butter, put it into your Dish, and lay the Venison on it, and so serve it up.

To Stew a Leg of Lamb the best way.

Slice it and lay it in order in your Stewing-pan, seasoned with Salt and Nutmeg, adding a pound of Butter, and half a pint of Clarret, with a handful of sliced Dates, and the like quantity of Currans, and make the Sawce with the yolk of two Eggs, a quarter of a pint of Verjuice,[2] and two ounces of Sugar: boil them up, and put them to the meat, serving all up hot together.

1. Skinned. 2. Acid juice from sour or unripe fruit.

To make Collups[3] of Veal the best way.

Slice your Veal fat and lean, beat half a dozen Eggs with Salt, grate a Nutmeg, and stamp or cop[4] a handful of Thyme: add a pint of Stewing-Oysters, and stew them together with a pound of sweet Butter: make Anchovy-sawce, and strew the Dish over with Capers, and so serve it up.

Kitchen Scenes.

3. Slices. 4. Misprint for chop.

To Roast a Shoulder of Mutton with Oysters the best way.

Take one not too fat nor too lean, open it in divers places, stuff your Oysters in with a little chopt Peny-royal,[5] baste it with Butter and Claret-wine, then serve it up with grated Nutmeg, yolks of Eggs, Ginger, Cinamon, Butter and Red-wine Vinegar.

To stew a Rump of Beef in the best order.

Sason it with Nutmeg, Salt and Sugar, lay the boney side downward, slice a dozen Shalots, cast in a bunch of Rosemary, Elder, Vinegar and Water, of each three pints; suffer it to stew over a gentle fire in a close Stew-pan two hours, and then with the Gravy dish it up with Sippits.[6] . . .

The Art of Beautifying the Hands, Neck, Breast and Face: Harmless and Approved, with other Rare Curiosities.

To make the Hands and Arms white, clear and smooth.
Take a quarter of a pound of sweet Almonds, blanch and bruise them, with a quarter of a pint of Oyl of Roses, and the like quantity of Betony-water: heat them over a gentle fire; and then press out the liquid part, and it will serve for either Hands or Face anointed therewith.

To make the Face fair and fresh-coloured.

Take Lineament and dip it in Oyl of Mirrh, often anointing your Face therewith, and it will effect it.

---

5. Mint or basil. 6. Croutons; small pieces of fried bread.

To make your Face clear and white.

Take the distilled water of Rosemary-flower Bean-blossoms, and wash your Hand and Neck morning and evening, and you will be fair.

To take away Freckles, Morphew[7] or Sun burn.[8]

Steep a piece of Copper in the Juice of Lemon till it be dissolved, and anoint the place with a feather morning and evening, washing it off with White-wine.

To take off any Scurf from the Hands and Face.

Take Water of Tartar, that is, such wherein Calcined[9] Tartar has been infused, anoint the place, and wash it as the former.

To sweeten the Breath, and preserve the Teeth and Gums.

Boil a handful of Juniper-berrys, a handful of Sage, and an ounce of Carraway-seeds in a quart of White-wine, till a third part be consumed: strain it and wash your mouth with it morning and evening, suffering a small quantity to pass down: You may whiten the Teeth by rubbing them with a Pumice-stone. . . .

[Vol. I, no. 39]

7. Scurfy skin. 8. Not considered an enhancement of female beauty until this century; women working in the fields in the last century used to wear capacious head scarves to keep their faces white. 9. Burnt to a powder.

To make Rice-milk.

Take a quart of good Milk, two handfulls of Rice-flower, beaten very small, and a quarter of a pound of Sugar, & put them into the Milk; then take the yolk of an Egg, beat it with a spoonful or two of Rose-water, then put it into the Milk, and stir all these together, and put it over a quick fire, keeping it continually stirring till it be as thick as water-pap.[1]

To make Fritters.

Take nine Eggs, yelks and whites, beat them very well, and take half a pint of sack a Pint of Ale, some Ale-Yest;[2] put these to the Eggs, and beat them all together, put in some Spice and salt, and fine flower, then shred in your apples, & let them be well tempered,[3] and fry them with Beef-Suet, or half Beef and half Hogs-suet dryed out of the Leaf.[4]

To make a good Cake.

Take half a peck of Flower, three pound of Butter, some Nutmeg, Cloves and mace, Cinnamon, Ginger and a pound of Sugar; mingle these well together with the Flower, then take four pound of Currants well washed, picked, and dryed in a warm cloath, a little Ale-yest,[2] twelve Eggs, a quart of Cream, or good Milk warm'd, half a pint of Sack, a quartern of Rose-water; knead it well, and let it be very lith, lay it in a warm cloath, and let it lye half an hour against the fire, then make it up with the White of an Egg beaten with a little Butter, rose-water, and Sugar; put it into the Oven, and let it stand an hour and a half.

1. Gruel. 2. Yeast. 3. Soaked. 4. Round the kidneys

To Pickle Cowcumbers.

Take an Earthen Vessel, and lay therein first a lay of Salt and Dill, then a lay of Cowcumbers, and so till they all be laid; then put in some cloves and whole Pepper, and some Fennel-seeds, then fill it up with Beer-Vinegar, and lay a clean board with a stone upon it, to keep them in the Pickle, and so keep them close covered, and when the Vinegar looks black, pour it out and put in fresh. . . .

[Vol. II, no. 5]

The Country-Mans
COUNSELLOR:
OR,
Every Man made his own Lawyer.

Plainly shewing the Nature and Offices of
all Courts, as Kings-Bench, Common-pleas,
Chancery, Exchequer, Marshalsey, etc. With the just
Fees for all Writs and Proceedings in each Court;
Allowed and established by Act of Parliament.

As ALSO

How to sue a Man to the Outlawry, or to
    Reverse the same.
    To Pass a Fine or Recovery.
    To sue an Attorney or Clerk.
    To get an Injunction in Chancery to
        stop your Adversaries Proceed-
        ings at LAW.
    To Sue in *Forma Pauperis,* etc.

With approved Presidents,[1] and easie Di-
    rections for all Persons, how to make
    according to Law, Bonds, Bills, Acquittan-
    ces, General Releases, Letters of Attor-
    ney, Bills of Sale, Wills, etc.

A WORK most useful to all Persons, the like not Extant,
and now published for a General Good.

With Allowance.[2]   By H.R.

Printed for J. Clark in West-Smithfield.

1. Precedents. 2. Sc. of the Licensers of the Press. This is, of course, the
title-page, and like many, promises more than it delivers.

A Bill of Sale for any Goods.

Know all men by these Presents, that I T. Downs of, etc. for and in consideration of the summ of, etc. to me in hand, paid by W. Harris of, etc. at and before the sealing hereof, have bargained and sold, and by these Presents do bargain and sell fully, clearly and absolutely, unto the said W. H. in plain and open Market, the Goods and Chattels following; *viz*. One Feather-Bed, two Dozen of Turkey-work Chairs,[3] etc. (As the Case is) to have and to hold the same Feather-bed, etc. to the said W.H. his Executors and Assings,[4] to his and their own proper use and uses, for ever. And I the said T.D. my Executors and Administrators, and every of us, the said Feather-bed, etc. unto the said W.H. his Executors and Administrators, against all people, shall and will forever acquit and defend by these presents: Provided always, That if I the said T.D. my Executors or Administrators, or any of us, do well and truly pay unto the said W.H. his Executors or Administrators, the full sum of 8l.[5] on the 24th of June next ensuing the date hereof, without Fraud or Covin:[6] Then this present Bill of Sale, and the Bargain and Sale of the said Feather-bed, etc. shall be utterly void and of none effect; or else to stand and be in full force and vertue.

> Sealed and delivered, together with the said
> Goods above-mentioned in the presence of

[Vol. II, no. 33]

---

3. Upholstered with Turkish tapestry. 4. Assigns. 5. £8; it appears from this provision that the goods are being used in settlement of a debt. 6. Conspiracy.

VII. ROGUES AND FOOLS.

The Life and Death of Sheffery ap Morgan.

CHAP. I.

Of Sheffery's Birth and Education.

The Person we intend to insist upon[1] in this following Discourse, is one Sheffery Morgan, who was born near Denby, a place eminently known in Wales, His Father being a Man of no small account, kept two or three Hoggs, and Brewed week for week the Year round, half a peck of Malt;[2] Her[3] being a Man so well to pass in the world, resolved to bring up her Son Sheffery Scolar-like; and in order thereunto put him to the greatest school in those parts, where he improved his time so well, that in six or seven Years he was able to Spell his own Name with a small matter of help. But not long after, her fond Father supposed her fit for the University, and disposed of her accordingly; but Jeffry grew negligent, unknown to her Father, and minded more her Waggish Pastimes then her serious Studdy; and her Father supposing her to be capable to manage a Parsons place, took a Fatherly care of her, and went to the Bishop of that Diocess, making sute for a Benefice for her, which was granted, provided that her should preach a Sermon of Approbation.[4] Did Shon ap Morgan being joyful of this answer from the Bishop, writ Post to her Son Sheffry, wishing her with all speed to come, for her was likely to become a Welsh Parson, and have a Benifice of 40 l. per annum.[5] These good Tydings so tickled the Ear of our young Parson, that her omitted no opportunity, but took Horse and rid full speed to her Fathers House in Wales, who told her all the matter

1. Dwell upon. 2. Heavy sarcasm here; self-inflation was commonly held to be a Welsh disease. 3. Meaning 'his', a common parody of Welsh speech. 4. Passable sermon. 5. A rather meagre stipend.

in hand; but when her heard that her was to preach before her could have her money, her knew not what to think on't.

The day appointed drawing nigh when Sheffery was to Preach, being sensible of her inability, her knew not what course to take, or how her should perform her Task imposed upon her; sometimes her thought to fly from the presence of the Bishop and her Father both, and then contradicted that thought with this Resolution, That if he could not do as well as he should, that he would do as well as he could. So the day being come, Sheffery lay somewhat long a Bed, and seemed to have small stomach to his new Concern; which her Father perceiving, stept up to give her a call, telling her the Saints Bell had rung in: O Father, said her, I am in a brown Study, look Father upon the top of Mr. Quibus his[6] House, and behold a Cow-Curd[7] that lyes there; and I have been studying how it might be; whether the top of the House came down to the Cow, or whether the Cow went up to the top of the House! O fie Son, this is idle discourse, come make hast, for it draws near ten a Clock, the Bishop and the people begin to think you long. Well Father I have but a short Sermon to make, but it is such a Tickler as has not been Preached at your Church, since you came to the Parish, well Son, I shall leave that to your Judgment. Sheffery no sooner enters the Church, but he steps into the Pulpit; and begins as followeth.

Good people all, her knows there is something expected from her by way of Discourse, and seeing we are all met together, take this following matter as an undeniable Truth.

There are some Things that I know and you know not; and there are some Things that you know, and I know not; and there are some Things that neither I nor you know.

For thus, As I went over a stile I tore my Breeches, that I know and you know not; but what you will give me towards the mending of them, that you know, and I know not, but what the Knave the Taylor will have for mending them, that neither you nor I know.

The Bishop hearing such a strange Welsh Discourse delivered

6. Old form of genitive, thus Quibus's. 7. It could be curd as in curds and whey, or it could, more probably given the tone, be turd.

as a Sermon, fell into such a laughter, that he laughed himself into a Looseness,[8] that he was forced to carry his Arse under his Arm ever after;[9] and Old Shon ap Morgan fell into such a passion, that her solemnly protested, her would Dis-inherit her Son Sheffery. . . .

CHAP. III.

How Sheffery being weary of London, and short of Money, took a Journey toward the North; and how he got the good Will of a Sow, which prov'd the first rise of Sheffery's Fortune.

Sheffery being forsaken of her Countrymen, & allmost mony-less, wandred to and fro feasting her Eyes, but starving her Belly, resolved to travel farther towards the North: her had not gone above 20 miles, but her was surprized by the dismal night, and being unacquainted with the way, lost her self, and wandred up and down, till at last her hapned upon a small Cottage, and knocking at the door, her asked how far it might be to the next Town? the old Man answered: he was far from any Town or House except his: them Sheffery craved for Entertainment for that night; but the old Man reply'd, he had no convenience,[10] but her pressed hard for Lodging; so the old Man said, I have no place for you, except you will lye with our old Sow, with all her heart, quoth Sheffery. This being agreed, on they went to their Bed, and Sheffery to the Hogg-Stye, which joyned to the House, near the old Man and Womans Beds-head: Sheffery having but a sorry Lodging and a turbulent Bed-fellow, took no rest at all: the old Man and Woman waking about midnight, fell in discourse, quoth the old Woman, Husband, what if the young man should fall in love with our Sow, and forthwith get her good will to be Married? Who, quoth the old Man, should be against her Preferment, if they like each other? Ah! but Hus-

8. Of the bowels. 9. I cannot discover the meaning of this alliterative phrase. 10. Nowhere convenient.

band, she hath been a good Old Servant[11] to us, and if ever she goes, I hope you will bestow something with her: Well, well, Wife, I shan't be backward, but ten or twenty pound I will bestow[12] if the Man be deserving. Sheffery minding their Discourse, arose and went into a Carrot field near by, and pull'd some up, and brought them to the Sow, giving her plentifully to eat, then tyed the rest about his middle, underneath his Coat: & going into the house to return thanks for his nights Lodging, the Sow having tasted the sweetness of the Carrots, rav'd as though she would have torn down the stye, longing for more Carrots, the old Woman hearing the Sow to rave, cry'd out to her Husband, What is the matter with our Sow? Quoth Sheffery, her can tell best what is the matter; for her and I have made a match to be Marry'd and now she finding me to be gone without her, causeth her to rave in this sort? The old Woman runs with speed to her Husband, and said, Cuts hobby[13] Husband, I told you our Sow is in Love with the Young Man. Ah! but quoth her, that must be farther try'd, i'le see first whether she will follow him sooner than another; and letting her out, she ran directly at him, and taking hold on him, as if she loved him above others; the Old Man seeing this, was much satisfied, and call'd Sheffery in, and laid him down 20 pound, wishing them much joy together: This being done, Sheffery took her leave of the old people and went her way, by the smell of the Carrots the Sow followed him, which the Old Woman spying, she cry'd out, Come hither Mistris Bride, pray stay and take my best hat with you, which she did, and look'd like Mother Shipton[14] with her long Nose. . . .

[Vol. I, no. 45]

11. As a producer of piglets; many small-holders and labourers kept a pig or two as a valuable sideline. 12. As a dowry. 13. Another weird Welsh oath: possibly God help me? 14. Long-nosed cunning woman, see Section II.

The *Welch Traveller*. By Humphry Crouch.[1]

. . . At last her[2] legs began to fail
which wrought her discontent.
And then into an hedge her crept:
thinking to take a nap,
And then her sate her down and wept,
lamenting her mishap:
At last a handsome man came by,
with him a pretty Lass,
These Lovers did not her espie
but set them on the grass,
He to this Maid a Ring did give
which she did well accept:
And with a kiss did her relieve,
and close unto her crept:
This ring it seems did prove too wide,
which gallantly did shine,
From off her finger it did slide
and so at last was mine.
This Ring her much did think upon,
they minded more their play,
So when these Lovers they were gone,
her found it where it lay:
Her put it up into her poke,[3]
away her went amain:[4]
For why? her was afraid those folks
would quick return again,
Now her had got a gay gold Ring,
her knew not where to bide,
But Fortune often plays the Jade,
she's seldome constant known,
For why? at last her was betray'd
her could not keep her own,

1. Fl. 1635–1671; noticed in *D.N.B.* 2. Meaning 'his' throughout. 3. Pocket.
4. At full speed.

For going through a town God wot,
amongst some ill-bred Curs,
Her shew'd it to a cheating trot[5]
who said the Ring was hers.
Cuts plutteranails[6] was tell a lie,
her found it as her went:
But she used such extremity,
which wrought her discontent.
Before a Justice brought her then,
and there her kept such stirs,
The Justice said before all men
that sure the Ring was hers:
Her called the Justice great Boobee,
then her receiv'd some knocks,
The Justice made no more ado
but sent her to the stocks:
The boys did jear her to her face,
and call'd her thief and knave,
O was it not a great disgrace
that boys should her out-brave?
Now her hath mark'd what hath been past
now mark but this one thing,
The man and maid came by at last
that lost this gay gold Ring:
How glad was her then in the end
though her was but a thief,
Her hop'd that her would stand her friend
to ease her of her grief:
Hoe shentleman, her pray her stay
and likewise her fair maid,
Did not her lose her ring to day,
regard her what her said;
They wondred how he came to know
how she should lose the ring,
Nor did they know what they should do
for to regain this thing.

5. Old hag. 6. God's blood and nails, Welshified.

Have you any Ring kind man, quoth they
tell us if that you took it?
Her had the Ring as her may say,
but now her may go look it:
A woman cheated her of it,
her kept such grievous stirs,
For want of honesty or wit,
her Justice said 'twas hers.
And can you tell where he doth dwell
that wrought us this despight.
For ought her knows her lives in hell,
she's such a wicked wight.[7]
A little boy now standing by,
told them where he did live,
The author of their villany
a groat to him they give.
Unto this womans house they go.
before a Justice bring her,
Where she was cast[8] with much ado,
and in the Stocks they fling her:
Now Taffie had his hearts desire,
he had her company,
But when he did begin to jear,
she in his face did fly,
She claw'd him so with her nails
she made him almost mad,
He was not used so in Wales,
his luck was then so bad:
Moreover as I understand
to add to his disgrace,
The quean[9] she pissed in her hand
and cast it in her face. . . .

7. Person. 8. Convicted. 9. Whore.

Taffies Indictment.

Imprimis, for troubling the Shepherd to help him out of the pit.

Item, for selling the lowsie Jerkin for a groat, which was borrowed of his country-man Pinkin.

Item, for casting stinking fish and roten eggs into his Hostess face.

Item, for casting dung into his Hostess sons face.

Item, for casting Apples at the countryman from the tree, when he had the worst himself.

Item, for going away with the gold ring.

Item, for calling the Justice Boobee.

Item, for sitting in the stocks with an old woman.

Item, for creeping up into the smoak-loft, and then falling down into the fire with a packsaddle at his back.

Item, for acting the Devils part when he put all the house into a bodily fear.

A Man pelted in the Pillory.

Item, for scaring all the children in the town.

Item, for scaring the sexton in the Church, for which loose behaviour he was adjudged to stand in the Pillory, where I leave him till the next mad prank he shall play.

[Vol. I, no. 40]

Black Tom.[1] 1686

... CHAP. II.

How this Young Tom came to be known, and how he went by
the Name of Black Tom; and what befell.

When Tom was grown to be a Man, as lusty and as strong a
Thief as his Father, he told his Father he would now set up for
himself; and when they were both agreed, Tom took his leave in
the Evening, and went for Wapping, where he goes to a House
standing nigh to the Thames: There he enter'd, and call'd for a
Pot of Ale; and as he sat drinking his Ale, in the next room were
sitting very merrily over a Bowl of Punch, a Company of jovial
Drunken Sea-men, which Tom observed to make a noise, he
also falls to singing as well as they. The Sea-men observing him
to be so merry a Fellow, call'd him in amongst them; and after
he had saluted the Company, and drank a dish of Punch or two,
they ask'd him to sing them a merry Song to pass the time away:
But he cryed no, let's rather drink while we are by land, for you
are always hard employ'd upon the Sea; which Proposal pleas'd
the Sea-men so well, that they oblieg'd themselves to follow
Tom's example; who thereupon began so many Healths one
after another, that the Sea-men not being so fresh[2] as he, by
degrees fell fast asleep. Now Tom minding his opportunity,
insensibly creeps to their Pockets, and takes away all the Money
they had, and when he had discharg'd the Reckoning, took his
leave of his Hostess and went off: but the Sea-men waking, and
missing their Money, began to curse and swear at the Black
Dog most bitterly; and one of them remembering that his name
was Tom, resolved to put him in the Gazette by the name of
Black Tom, but they being almost Drunk, when he came first
amongst them, that they could not remember what sort of

1. A negro; we learn in Chapter I that his grandfather was a black brought
to Venice, where his father was born. 2. Had done more drinking.

Cloaths he wore, or whether his Visage was round or long, or
his Body by stature tall or short. So that one of them coming one
day by Charing-Cross, saw a Black[3] behind a Gentlemans Coach,
cryed out very eagerly to the Coach-man to stop his Horses: and
then eagerly running to the Foot-man behind the Coach, lay'd
hold on him, and causing a Constable to be call'd, had the poor
Man before a Justice, and swore against him, That he was the
very Man that Rob'd him at such a time, and such a place; But the
Youth making it appear[4] that he was not there, but was employed
on some business for his Lady, was clear'd, and the Man look'd
upon as Mad.

CHAP. III.

How Black Tom committed a Robbery at St. Katherines, and how he came off.

After Tom and the Sea-men had parted, Tom takes a Boat, and
Rows to St. Katherines,[5] where he lay three days before he heard
of any thing fit for his purpose: At last entring into Discourse
with his Landlady, Lord, Landlady, (says he) I admire[6] some
People that are Rich, and but few in Family, are not afraid to
stay out of their Houses, especially by Night, so many loitering
idle Fellows as lie here about! Indeed Sir, says she) I wonder as
much as you do; but above all People in St. Katherines, I admire
at my next Neighbour, that hath always good store of Plate, and
Coin of Gold and Silver always by her, that she dares lye alone,
or with none but a poor simple Girl, that is her Servant; especially having such a weak Old House, and by my truly, sometimes
they both go out; and one perhaps has got the Key of the Door,
and the other coming home, wanting the Key, will lift the Door
off the Hinges: Which hath been done so often, that it comes off
now without any noise. Indeed Landlady, (says Tom) 'tis a great
Miracle to me, that they escape so well.

3. Negro. 4. Clearly demonstrated. 5. About a mile upstream from Wapping,
by the Tower of London. 6. I am amazed at.

Now Tom being very glad of this News, after a small meditation what to do, tells his Landlady, That he was invited out, and should be pretty late before he could come in that Night, and therefore desires her not to sit up late for him, and so departed till toward Night[7], which time he imployed in viewing the House, to see how or where he might break in most easily. At last considering that his Landladys way was the best, he would stay[8] till Night, and venture at the Door, therefore he goes to an Ale-house hard by, to spend his time. But not long after the Watch had passed by, crying the time of the Night, out goes Tom; who coming to the Door, and gently renches it off the Hinges, goes up the Stairs, and finding every body fast,[9] opens a Coffer, in which was a Till or Drawer, from whence Tom takes an Hundred pounds, besides Jewels and Rings; so being very well contented with his prize, was preparing to go off, but the Watch was passing by, whose custome is to knock at the Doors, and if they be open, to call upon the People to shut them; but Tom was got withoutside the Door endeavouring to fasten it again. Now the Watch-men finding the Door off the Hinges, began to think that Mr. Thomas had committed a fault, and therefore took him into examination.[10] Now Tom told them that it was his own House, and he had some occasion to go out, and could not find his Key until he had lifted the Door off the Hinges; and if they would not believe it was his House, they might come in, and he would make them drink for their pains. Now as 'tis not the custome of Watch-men to deny drink at any time, they entered into the House: Now Tom taking down a Mug from the Shelf, and going to the Door, praying them not to make any noise, under pretension of going to fetch drink, ran quite away. Now the Constable having a Drunken Man that was scarce able to go with him, commanded one of the Watch-men to stay there with him, until Mr. Black Thomas should come in, and because the poor Man look'd like a Gentleman, should beg Mr. Black Thomas to lend him a Bed, so the Constable and part of the Watch departed. Now Mr. Black Thomas not returning, the Gentleman that was o'recome with drink fell fast asleep, and

7. Dusk. 8. Wait. 9. Sc. asleep. 10. Began to question him.

likewise the Watch-man being in the dark, and no body left to
talk to, fell fast asleep also; and slept soundly until the Morning,
that the woman of the House finding her Coffer open, and her
Money gone, came happily[11] down, and caused them to be seized,
as Men guilty of Burglary and Robbery, and had them before
the Justice, and he had committed them, had not the Constable
and Watch come and cleared them. Thus Black Tom came off.[12]

CHAP. IV.

How Black Tom served an Old Miser.

Black Tom had not lain long still, but he deviseth a new Project
to take him a Lodging at the Horse-Ferry in Westminster; he
had not been above two days, but his Fingers itch'd to be at
work. Now, there liv'd a certain watch-man hard by, that had
gotten a considerable quantity of wealth, who was an old dry
Batchelor that liv'd alone, and one that liv'd more upon looking
on his Coin, than making use on it; for he had at any time rather
beg, then part with a Farthing of Money. Now Tom was plotting
how he might get this Money from this old Miser; So Tom lay a
bed most part of that morning, contriving on his Pillar,[13] but
getting up, walks towards the Watch-mans House, where he
found him standing at the door, makes several bows and cringes,
and afterwards made him this Speech.

Gwide Maystre, Me non Inglant by mine Phace, none Inglant
by mine Twang: Me de grecat strawnger of Aphric, me de
pherry phull of Maney; me sa have van Hundred Poonds in
mine Phocquet, no phlace to put it shafe, you have de gwide
Logings; let me de gwide me give gwide Maney.[14]

The old Miser lik'd this speech very well, and was resolved
(as he was a Stranger) to make him pay dearly for his Lodging; so
Black Tom gave him twenty shillings before-hand, and was to

11. Perchance, haply. 12. Escaped. 13. Pillow, either a misprint or a prov
erb. 14. Grecat defeats me; the last sentence means rent me a good room
and I will give you good money.

pay him twenty shillings[15] every Saturday Night. But Black Tom
had not been long there before the old Man was to go out upon
the Watch, and that Night Black Tom conveyed a Coffer out of
his House, wherein the Old Man's Treasure lay, and ne'r return'd
to his Lodging more. The poor old Miser returning home to
his House, and missing his Lodger and his Money, made a sad
lamentation, telling all his neighbours that Black Tom had
Rob'd him, and he knew not where to find him, nor what to do.
Now this old Man had a Friend that liv'd down in Whitechappel,
that he was resolved to complain to, thinking, that he being
a Thief-catcher,[16] might inform him of him that had wronged
him; but as he went, who should encounter him but Mr. Black
Thomas, who he presently[17] commands to be laid hold on, and
has him before a Justice. Now it hapned that this Justice had a
Black-a-moor in his House that had not been long in England,
and did not speak good English; and it hapned that this Black-a-
moor comes to the door, of whom the Constable as'd, if the
Justice were within? Who answered, Dat he was at team, put
note at leeberdy,[18] but dat he vill be if you stay but de little. So
they stay'd a little time: now Black Tom was meditating how to
come off,[19] for he knew himself Guilty of what was laid to his
charge, but remembring that he had acted or imitated the Speech
of a Barbarian, so he being an Englinsh-man, was resolved how
to come off. Now the Justice being come to them, the Miser made
his Complaint thus: Sir, not much above five days since, this
Black came to be my lodger, & the third night, he carried away
my Coffer with two hundred Pounds in Gold; he is one that
cannot well be understood, for he is an Out-landish Man,[20] and
speaks no English, and therefore hard to be understood. I, an
out-landish man! says Tom, I was never out of England in my
days, my Mother is an English Woman, but indeed my Father
was a Black Born at Venice; but as for me, I speak nothing but
English, nor never could.

15. Twice or three times the going-rate. 16. Private entrepreneur who worked
for a fee for those who had been robbed. Often shady customers, members of the underworld, receivers of stolen goods, etc. 17. There and then.
18. He was at home, but not free to see them. 19. Escape. 20. Foreigner.

The old Miser hearing these Words, knew not what to think, whether this was the Man or no. But however, he remembering that the Justices Man that let him in was a Black, and spake but bad English, he told the Justice, that he could not be very positive, whether Tom was the Man or not, for since he came there, he fancied that it was his Black that did him that mischief. Now the Justice observing that the Miser accused both, and did not know if either were Guilty, freed them both. So Tom came very well off with this Watch-man also.[21]

[Vol. II, no. 17]

21. Plainly negro slaves were still something of a rarity in London, but the vogue for owning a black servant was growing.

The True Portrai-
cture of Captain
James Hind, the
Robber, who dyed
for *TREASON*.

I·D

CHAP. I.

Containing Hind's birth, and how he first came to be a High-way-man.

Captain James Hind (the subject of our ensuing discourse) was born at Chiping-Norton in Oxfordshire: His Father having no more Children but he, put him to School, intending to make him a Scholar, but he minded his wagish Pastimes more then his Book, which his Father perceiving, bound him Prentice to a Butcher, but he having a Running Pate,[1] soon grew weary of that also, and in conclusion ran away from his Master, comes up to London, there grows acquainted with a Company of Roaring deboyst[2] Blades, who by their evil examples made him as bad as themselves. To be short, as they seldom abounded with Money, so they scorned to be long in want. When their stock grew short, they rode a Cutting[3] for more. At last the Knot[4] was discovered, the Chief of them Hanged, and Hind (only) escaped, with the loss of his horse; & now he sets up for himself.

CHAP. III.

How Hind was betrayed by Two whores, who sent Two High-way-men to take his Money, and how he Rob'd them.

Hind having gotten a good purchase of gold, past away the day very merrily, and then towards Night he rides to an Inn which stood in the private rode, where it seems some High-way-men

1. Roving disposition. 2. Debauched. 3. Cant for robbing. 4. Gang, conspiracy, group. The most famous anti-Cromwellian royalists were known as The Sealed Knot.

did use: after he had seen his Horse carefully drest[5] and fed he came into the House, where were two handsome Ladies by the Fire, he bespoke a good supper, and invited them unto it, when supper was ready he called for Wine, and made them merry. They seemed very coy to him, but he knowing their humours, pulled out of his Pocket a handful of Gold: singing, *Maids, where are your hearts become, look you what here is.* And after much mirth, to Bed he went, & presently after came in the two men which kept these two Whores, to whom they related all the courtesie of Hind, and that he had abundance of gold about him: they resolve to watch his going & to follow him in the morn: but Hind being wakeful, was up and mounted before the 2 Ladies were stirring: when they[6] heard his horse prance they look out of the window, and seeing he had so good a horse, were ready to fall out who should have him. I will have the horse, says one, & you shall have his money, nay, i'le have his horse says the other: in conclusion they quickly made themselves ready, & rode after Hind, when they had overtook him, they askt him which way he rode, he answers them towards Cambridge; they tell him they would be glad of his company: Now riding in a place where no people were nigh, one of the thieves sings, *Maids where are your hearts become? look you what here is:* Hind seeing there intent, and knowing he was betrayed, answered them in the same tune. *Now you rogues you are both undone, look you what here is,* and drawing forth his Pistol, and firing at one of them, by chance shot his horse in the head, who presently fell down with his masters leg under him, the other seeing this, betook himself to flight, but Hind quickly overtook him, and made him deliver such money as he had, and cutting his girts[7] and his bridle, made him work enough to catch his horse again: hind now rides to the other thief, who lay but in little ease, he alights and pulls the horse from his Leg, and then helps him up, and takes away his Money also, saying is there but one Master Thief in England, and would you venture to rob him? verily, were you not of my Profession, neither of you should have lived, but seeing you ventured hard for it, thou deservest something. So Hind gave

5. Rubbed down and groomed. 6. The whoremasters. 7. Saddle-girths.

him his money back again to buy him another horse, saying unto him, disgrace not your selves with small sums but aim high, and for great ones: for the least will bring you to the Gallows. So Hind shaking the poor thief by the hand, left him to his partner to catch the Horse, and bid him farewel.

CHAP. VII.

How Hind robbed a Gentleman of 30 pound, that would give twenty pound to see him.

Hind overtook a Gentleman as he rid on the Rode, and they fell in discourse. So the Gentleman was saying he would give twenty pound to see Hind, but as they were Riding the Gentleman fancied Hinds horse, Sir, said the Gentleman, what money shall I give you to exchange horses with me? Forty Pounds, said Hind, I will give you 30 pounds in Gold said the Gentleman. Hind said, Sir, ride him, so the Gentleman gave thirty pounds in Gold and his Horse. But as they rode along, there was a ditch, sir, says Hind, leap him over this ditch, I cannot says the Gentleman, Hind desired the Gentleman to alight, so he got on his own horse and leapt over the ditch, and when he was on the other side he said, Sir you would give 20 pounds to see Hind, and now you have seen him, the other ten pound was for Riding of my horse. So now I think you have seen enough of him, and so farewel.

CHAP. XV.

How Hind went into Scotland to the Scotch King at Sterling, and how he was apprehended in London.

Hind being ever weary of staying long in a place, shipt himself for Scotland, when he was landed he went and presented his service to the King[8] at Sterlin, the King being informed who it was, had some discourse with him, and commended him to the Duke of Buckingham,[9] then present to ride in his troop because his life-guard was full, he came into England with the same troop, was in the ingagement at Warington, came into the fight at Worcester,[10] and staid till the K. was fled. Hind being in the City, seeing the gates full of dying persons, leapt over the wall on foot by himself, travelled the country, and lay three days under bushes & hedges because of the souldiery, afterwards he came to sir Io. Pickingtons wood where he lay 5 days, from thence he come to London and lodged five weeks very securely: but on Nov. 9. 1651. a discovery was made of Captain Hinds frequenting one Denzies a Barber over-against St. Dunstans Church in Fleet-Street, who went by the name of Brown, this information was communicated to certain Gentlemen belonging to the Right Honourable Mr. Speaker,[11] who with great care so ordered the business that there was no suspition at all: to his chamber door they went, forc'd it open, and immediately with their Pistols cockt, seized on his person, carried him to Mr. Speakers house in Chancery-Lane, and so secured him for that night. The next day being munday, by order from the Right Honourable the Counsel of State, the said Captain Hind was brought to Whitehall, who was examined before a Committee, and divers questions put to him concerning his late ingagement with Charles Stuart,[12] and whether he accompanied the Scotch King, to the furtherance of his escape, to which he answered, That he never saw the King since the fight at Woster, neither knew he of his getting[13] the field, but was glad that he had made so happy an escape[14] after some time spent about his examination, 'twas ordered he should be sent Prisoner to the Gate house till the next day. So the next day by special order from the Counsel of State,

8. This was during Charles II's unfortunate Presbyterian phase after his father's execution. His trip to Scotland would have been in 1650 or 1651. 9. The second duke. 10. September 3, 1651, precipitating Charles II's famous flight back to the continent. 11. During the Commonwealth period, the Speaker was of prime importance in state affairs. The Speaker was William Lenthall. 12. The Republic's designation of the exiled king. 13. Sc. away from. 14. A full stop missing here.

he was brought from thence in a Coach, with Iron bolts on his legs, Cap. Compton, and two other Messengers belonging to the State, guarding him, and about two of the Clock in the afternoon he was put into Newgate, where he lay till the next Sessions. . . .

CHAP. XVI.

Containing the conclusion of the story, and Captain Hinds last farewel to VVorcester.

on Munday the 1. of March 1651[15] he was arraigned before the Right Honourable Judge Warberton for killing one Pool his Companion at Knowl, a little Village in that Country; after evidence given in against him, he was found guilty of Manslaughter, and condemned to dye, but on the next morning the Act of Oblivion[16] being sent acquitted all former offences, only the Indictment of High-Treason against the State, and for that fact he was carried Worcester, and there hang'd & quartered on Friday, Sep. 24 1652.

> Thus Fate the great Derider did Deride,
> Who liv'd by Robberry, yet for Treason Dy'd.

[Vol. II, no. 3]

15. 1652; by the Gregorian calendar the year began on March 25. 16. Ordinance of Pardon and Oblivion, 1652, for offences against the state prior to the Battle of Worcester.

John Frank.

The Epistle to the READER.

John Frank, the reputed Son of John Ward, was Born in Much Easton Parish in Essex, within three miles of Dunmow: He had no Friends to take care of him, his being a Fool was the cause of his well-being; for every one was in love with the sport which he made, and the unexpected answers which he would give, did much amaze all people. When he was grown to be of Mans stature, there was a worthy Knight who took him to keep, where he did many pretty and strange pranks, he was a comly person, and had a good Complexion: his Hair of a dark flaxen: he was of a middle stature, and good countenance; if his Tongue had not betrayed his Foolery, no one would ever think, but that he had been a Wise man.

... Here follows many pritty Sayings and Jests of Jack, which are very witty and worth observing.

Jack's Lord and Lady going forth one day in the Coach, Jack had obtained the favour to run by the Coach side and upon the way they met another Lords Coach, whose Gentleman riding by the Coach, and seeing Jack, puts off his Hat in derision, and bows himself, saying, I pray whose Fool are you? The Fool presently pulls off his Calves-skin Cap, and shakes his Ears, saying, I am my Lord M's Fool: pray whose Fool are you: The Gentleman being thus answered was much ashamed, and rode away, and Jack went his way.

Jack standing by one time where some Gentlemen were talking, and hearing 'em talk of Round-heads, Round-heads said Jack to himself, I Jack, said one of them, what is a round-Head? (now this Gentleman who askt him was a round Head, but would not be thought one) what's a round-Head, says Jack, a round-Head is one that has no wit at all; give me your hand Sir, says Jack, the Gentleman did so, ha, ha, ha, and shaked it, saying, there I mumpt you:[1] the rest laughing, he laughed, though he were vexed.

One Night his Lady being at Supper, Jack came into the room, bawling aloud, that he could not get the Coach-man to buy him a Chamber-pot; Madam, saith he, the Coach-man wont buy me a Pot, and I am fain to rise in the night, to make water in the yard, in my shirt, and I have got a Cough, must I not have some Sugar Candy Madam? the Lady laughed to think how seasonable he was in his request, but gave order to the Coach-man to buy him what he wanted.

In the time of the Ladies Lying-Inn, Jack found that he carried up more wood than at other times to the Chamber door, he having his Arms full of wood, throws it down, making a great noise therewith, saying to himself aloud, Pox take my Lady, I think she burns more wood then her body is worth.

One time Jack coming late to dinner in the Hall, and seeing there was no room for him at the table, he runs forth, and comes presently in again, saying, do you hear sirs, the King is come into the back yard, with his Coach and six Horses, and a great many men; they not knowing what to think, ran all out to see; in the meantime Jack sets him down and carves for himself, they coming into the yard could see no body there, but laughed to think how the Fool had out-witted them.

He being asked one day what would become of him when he was dead, I shall lye in the ground saith he, till Gods Trumpet sounds, and then shall I rise again and go into Heaven. I but what will you say, said one to him, when Gods Trumpet sounds to call you before him? he answer'd, God will not require more then he hath given me: which words so unexpected, did much amaze all that heard him.

He was duly morning and evening at prayers in the Chappel, though he had no understanding, and every night in his Chamber he would pray thus by himself.

Lord, said he, thou knowest I can do nothing of my self, Lord

1. Worsted.

thou knowest I can do nothing; Lord have mercy upon me, and help me.

He lived till about fourscore years, and died at a Knights house in Enfield-Parish, where he was handsomely buried, all that knew him being very sorry for his death (poor innocent soul) who did no evil, than[2] by evil examples.

There might be more said of him, but that may serve for a second part, these Stories I hope will be the more pleasing, because they are true.

[Vol. II, no. 20]

2. Except.

. . . . Jack was sent unto the Wood,
on purpose to fell Oaks,
He shewed his endeavour good,
and laid on lusty stroaks;
He cut a mighty Oak in two,
his Cart and Team stood by,
The Tree fell down, and there it slew
his Horses presently.
What course to take he did not know,
his Horses being slain,
Unto his Father-in-Law to go,
he thought it was in vain.
Jack went o're bogs and sandy Shelves,
at last he spy'd a pool,
Where a flock of wild-geese shew'd themselves,
too wise for this poor fool.
Quoth he, sure I may kill with ease,
one of these Fowls so fell,
My Father-in-Law then shall I please,
and all things shall be well.
His Hatchet at them he did fling,
hoping to strike one dead,
But they were all too light of wing,
and from him straight they fled.
His Hatchet sunk immediately,
it could not swim to shore,
Alas, quoth he, why now am I
in worse case then before.
I will not loose my Hatchet so,
although my luck be ill,
But I will have it e're I go,
or I will want my will.
He stript off his Cloaths some say,
and so to diving went,

A Knave came by and stole away
his Cloaths incontinent:[1]
Why now (quoth Jack) I am undone,
alas, who can assure me,[2]
My Dad will own me for his son,
or eke my Wife endure me. . . .

Jack naked was, the wind blew cold,
he could no longer stay,
But in the Hogstye he made bold,
and there full close[3] he lay.
The churlish Hogs so hoggish were,
to this their Masters Son,
Small manners in them did appear,
for o're him they did run.
And some upon his head did tread,
and some full sore did bite him,
And they with him so quarrelled,
he fear'd they would indite[4] him. . . .

Until at last his Wife did hear
thy cry of this rude Cattel,[5]
And out o'th door she came in fear,
to end this sudden battel.
Jack heard her coming, and began
with speed to stand upright,
She seeing there a naked man,
was in a grievous fright.
She gave a shriek, and leapt i'th dirt,
so greatly she was moved,
But she was more afraid then hurt,
for it was her beloved . . . .

Into the Buttery I will go,
and there I shall be sure,
A pot of Butter-milk I know,
for you I can procure.

1. Quickly. 2. Sc. whether. 3. Hidden. 4. Give him away. 5. Livestock.

And 'cause it is a dark night,
that you may not forget it,
I'le cover it with a cloth that's white,
and on the Dunghill set it.
Whilst she went into the Buttery,
a great white Dog came out,
And on the Dunghill down did lye,
to bring the Jest about:
Poor Jack out of the Hogstye peeps,
the great white Dog he spies,
With joy and gladness out he creeps,
his hunger to suffice.
The Dog he took to be a Clout[6]
that the Butter-milk did cover,
But he did find it was a flout,[7]
before that he gave over.
The Dog was white, as he might see,
the night was dark and black,
And sure a wiser man then he,
might very well mistake.
Fast by the back Jack took the Dog,
instead of the Butter-milk pot,
And being naked as a Frog,
pray judge you what he got.
The Dog took Jack fast by the toe,
and Jack with him did strive,
Quoth Jack, I ne'r before did know
that Butter-milk was alive. . . .

[Vol. I, no. 27]

6. Cloth. 7. A mockery, illusion.

The second part of Unfortunate Jack. 1681.

. . . He'l be a Husband-man[1] again,
to plow and cart will go,
And likewise thrash all kind of grain,
this he's resolv'd to do.
A Country man a daughter had,
and she was pretty trim,
Jack did dwell with her good Dad,
her Father hired him.[2]
He set him for to thrash his corn
and he great pains did take,
For he rose early in the morn,
wrought till his bones did ake.
His breeches 'twixt his legs were torn
his whim-whams[3] they hung out,
And Jack he spoke these words in scorn,
gep,[4] are you grown so stout?
No marvel sure, and pray wherefore
doth provender prick you so[5]
That you have broke the stable door,
        ho Bal ho.
Now still when he to threshing fell
his whim-whams bobbed out,
Just like the clapper of a bell,
so strong was he and stout.
Mean while his Masters daughter came
to see their servants work.
But Jack was senseless of his shame
and desperate as a Turk.
What things are they kind friend quoth she
that dingle dangle hang.

1. Farmer or farm-labourer. 2. Farm-workers often lived in. 3. Testicles.
4. Go along with you! 5. Proverb, usually applied to horses, meaning does
good feed stimulate and strengthen you so?

My marking irons[6] Maid quoth he,
as good as ere did twang.
Your marking irons said the Maid,
what do you do with them?
Mark maids with them then Jack he said
and answered with a hem:
What will you take for marking me,
it must be understood,
Five shillings is the least quoth he
my irons are very good.
Five shillings he had, which made him glad
and he was pleased also:
It was the best money she said
that ever she did bestow.
I pray quoth she mark me again,
five shillings more i'le give,
Jack makes a trade of marking them
and bravely he did live:
But what with marking and thrashing too
poor Jack so weary grows,
He able was no more to do
but streight to bed he goes.
Now Jack a Gentleman may be
if fortune on him smile,
But she that was both frank and free,
at last did him beguile.
For when as Jack in bed doth sleep,
his pockets then she picks,
And down the stairs she softly creep,
so these were her sly tricks.
So that was hers, was his by grant,
and hers again by cheat,
O may they never thrive but want,
who useth such deceit.
Next morning when as Jack awakes,
and found his money gone,

6. For branding animals?

Although his heart a little akes
his grief was quickly done.
For though he did not know the thief
which now had made him poor,
He knew she would yield him relief,
and he desir'd no more.
Now five mile off there was a Fair
and Jack with her must go,
Because she knew he had good ware
for she had found it so.
A horse they have, the dogs they barkt,
away with speed they ride,
But she must light still to be markt
and must not be deny'd:
Forty shillings he got out-right,
he must be at her call,
He got by day, and lost by night
she couzen'd him of all.
But Jack was so tyred God wot
with marking her that day,
A stone[7] into his pocket got,
as I did hear some say:
And riding by a little brook
he let the stone fall down,
Whereat she angry then did look
and on him she did frown,
What's that that's fallen from you qd. she
some thing from you did fall,
It was my marking irons quoth he,
with that she then did braul;[8]
Your marking irons I would not lose
for fourty pound I say;
Lets light, and pull off our hose and shoos
and look them while we may;
He lights then to give her content
and they a wading fall,

7. Also slang for testicle. 8. Cried, shrieked.

And in the brook much time they spent
to no puprose at all.
Mean while a labouring man came by,
and askt them what they sought,
Quoth she my marking-irons truly,
which I so dear have bought:
I'le help to seek for them quoth he,
if yo'l give me content:
I will give thee a groat[9] quoth she,
so he a wading went;
So now a wading did they go,
with feet, and hands, and eyes,
And whatsoever they did do
the woman she was wise.
For though her marking-irons was spent,
she found another pair,
Which might give her as good content
but 'twas the poor mans ware:
Fast hold at last she took thereon,
the poor mans case was bad,
Hold, hold quoth he, I am undone,
what mistris are you mad?
They are my marking-irons quoth he,
let go if you be wise;
For if my wife should come and see,
she'd claw out both your eyes.
He pul'd and she pul'd to and fro
which when to Jack 'twas known,
Quoth he, give over, now let go
for I have found my own.
Now Jack did stand the poor mans friend
let no man at him scoff.
Had he not been sure in the end
she would have pul'd them off:
Here is a groat quoth she for thee
why are you discontent,

9. Fourpence.

Pox take you and your groat quoth he,
and so away he went.
Well now she must be markt again
since he his irons have found,
But Jack did tell her flat and plain
the water did them confound:
And they had lost their vertue quite,
so homewards then they went,
But she was vexed all that night
and slept in discontent.
But now she prov'd with Child
which fil'd Jacks heart with fear,
For now poor Jack went to the pot[10]
as you shall shortly hear.
Her Father kept a mighty stir,
and she to him did say
That it was Jack that marked her
and offered her fair play,
His marking-irons I found were good,
he never urged me,
Then if the case be understood
the fault lies all in me.
You Quean[11] quoth he, I'l knock you down
if that you take his part,
Father quoth she pray do not frown
for he is my sweet-heart.
His marking irons were good quoth she,
no wench can better have,
I'le spoil his marking irons, quoth he,
and mark him for a knave:
With that he fell upon Jacks bones,
and curst all ill-bred bores,[12]

---

10. To pot. 11. Whore. 12. The modern sense of someone who is tedious was not coined until mid-eighteenth century, according to *O.E.D.* This could be a variant spelling of boar, or bor, short for neighbour, or the borer of his daughter.

He with a knife cut out his stones,
then turn'd him out of doors . . .

And for all these things underwritten
Jack was ordered to be banished.

Item, For asking service at a Baudyhouse.
Item, For losing his Ears.
Item, For falling into the house of office.
Item, For scaring the Bear.
Item, For scaring the Priest.
Item, For losing the ten pound found in the tomb.
Item, For losing his Mark-irons.
Item, For scaring the Usurer his master.
Item, For throwing the blind man his master into the River.
Item, For scaring the people of the town with his Bears skin,
which was the cause of his banishment into the isle of Fools
and Knaves.[13]

                    FINIS.

[Vol. I, no. 28]

---

13. Summaries of this kind were common, especially at the end of fool stories.

Tom Ladle.

CHAP. I.

How Peter the Plow-man wooed Betty,[1] Tom Ladle's Mother, with what happened.

In the Country lived with a worthy Lady a Maid-servant, who was more handsome than rich, her Fortune consisting only of a good Face, and such small moneys and cloaths as she had gained in service; The premises considered, and also well knowing that it is but slippery holding by Holly Branches, she resolved to accept the proffers of Peter the Plow-man (who had long suited her) the next time he should ask her the question. Peter had somewhat more than she, but not much; yet rather than she would run the hazard of losing her Teeming time,[2] she would venture that manner of living (which amongst Love-toys is but little considered.) The Business was not long deferred, but upon the first opportunity he renewed his old suit, and in short time gained what he long had pursued with little hopes. They having thus far proceeded, nothing was wanting but the consent of the Lady, (who was noble to her Servants that matched with her consent,) but who should ask that question was the question, for she was loth, and he resolved rather to break off the Match, that to go about to speak to the Lady upon any such Errand; for her part she was in long doubt, but recalling to mind all the before-mention'd Considerations, she pluc'kd up a good heart, early one Morning in her Ladies Chamber, who then was a dressing, where after some pauses, and fluttering of words, she broke the matter to her Lady, who at first seemed amazed (for she judged the Wench to deserve a better Fortune) but recovering her Judgment, she answered her with words suitable to the occasion: But the Wench persisting in the suit with much earnestness, her

1. A name with sexual connotations in the seventeenth century, not unlike Fanny nowadays. 2. Child-bearing years.

Lady bid her go forward, and feel the smart of her folly; the Wench hasting out of the Chamber, said, That she could better endure both the smart and pain all her life long, then she could endure the present itching: which being spoken with a dry simplicity, caused all present to laugh.

> The flye fed Sow little knows
> What for the Meat she eats she ows:[3]
> Even so, pamper'd Wenches will be Wives,
> To leave plenteous quiet for sorry lives.

CHAP. II.

How Tom's Mother went to Market, where she met with a Gallant, and what happened with Peter's and Betty's Marriage.

Leave being granted, the day of Marriage was soon appointed, and they both judged what was necessary for the solemnizing of that ensuing Feast, saving some small matter that was to be bought at Market, whither she went; as she travelled the Road, it was her Fortune to meet with a neighbouring Gentleman, with whom she falling into discourse, it was agreed to go to his Inn; where they being Arrived, and Chambered, he freely calls for burnt[4] Claret, she not acquainted with its strength, swallowed it down hastily, she thinking the sweetness thereof had been the worst,[5] became thereby so mettled[6] in discourse, and so enflamed in colour, that it added much to her natural parts, and so much to his courage, that at last he began to move her to yield to his desires; at first she seems coy, but he Firing some Chase Guns[7] at her Honesty, she but weakly try'd to defend her self against a Man of War, of his Force; in conclusion she was forced to tack a Stern, and strike Sail, and enter into so amorous an Encounter,

---

3. The debt, i.e. slaughter, she will pay in return for her food. 4. Mulled, spiced and heated. 5. Sc. thing about it. 6. Mettlesome, lively, skittish. 7. Naval guns fired forward and aft.

that the furious Youth well nigh had sunk her in the Ocean of delight. In the end of this Rancounter he became an alter'd Man, for he who but now, even now went on like a Lyon, became more tame than an Ass; then recollecting all the folly past, and that for one moments pleasure, he had run the hazard of losing his Father's Affection who had disinherited his Eldest Brother, for getting a Wench with Child; and he well foresaw, that he must not expect more favour from him on the self same occasion.

> The eager Youth with heat pursues
> What he no sooner gain'd, but rues . . .

but all parties concerned hast forward to solemnize the Bridal Feast to which the youngster hastens amongst the rest; to Church they go, Sir John[8] opens his Book, proceeds to the half, then calls for moneys,[9] saing he could not trust; some Peter gave him, but not enough, which he refuses, whereat the Bride being angry told him, that the greatest of his labour being wind, if he grudged it so much, he might keep it to cool his Pottage, and let so many words be omitted as countervailed the wanting part;[10] whereupon the covetous Parson being ashamed, and heartily laughed at, proceeded to the conclusion, and all content, home they went to Dinner.

Table being taken away, some fell to drinking, some to dancing, and others to courting the Maids; of which he was one of the formost, giving slip to the company, he got the opportunity to be led into the Brides Room; who pretending not to be well, was laid down; the Room was dark, and they thought the freelier to pass the time without suspicion, for her Mother had taken the task upon her to answer all demands.

> But when Danger's least our fear,
> Then is danger oft most near.

For so then it came to pass; for Peter longing to have a kiss of his Bride (unknown to the mother) steals in, whose sudden

8. The parson. 9. Fees for marrying them. 10. Equivalent to the amount they were short of money.

arrival made the Gamesters begin to shift;[11] but as ill Fortune
would have it, a short Board being carelessly laid over an empty
broken-headed Barrel, upon which he unadvisedly stept, and so
fell in, with so hideous a noise, that Peter was almost frightned
out of the Room, but the care of his Bride so encouraged him,
that laying all danger aside, he boldly came to the Bed side, where
he found poor Love in a Tub,[12] and his wife half dead, through
the surprizal and fear; he soon knew him, and spared no threatning
Language, though in such secret wise, that none else knew ought
thereof; the young Man excused her, and generously underook
all the blame, giving the Cuckold some Guinea's, which so eased
his mind, that he had almost forgot to keep the Amorous Gallant
out of the Trap,[13] who was not a little overjoy'd that he had past
so eminent a danger, and brought her out of that fear with so little
charge and trouble.

> Few that this Reads, but well doth know,
> That Love will creep where it cannot go:
> And Women with rich Men may be bold,
> For Cuckold's Sight are dim with Gold.

CHAP. III.

How Tom was born, his Mother lost her first Gallant, and how
she entertained Cut-beard the Barber, with what happened.

Endeavours, and Time swell'd Betty's Belly, who shortly after
was delivered of a brave Boy, to whom the Gallant was God
Father, and as became his quality, he gave the Gifts of a well-bred
Gentleman; which so endeared Betty's Affections towards him,
that they were in all respects so indulging, that she never doubted[14]

11. The young gallant and Betty shift for themselves, i.e. try to escape.
12. Pun on love in a cottage idea, i.e. with insufficient material means.
13. I take keep to be a misprint for help, the Trap being the tub. Alternatively,
the trap could refer to getting Betty with child. 14. She doubted that they
would ever change.

their change. But alas! the Sun that shone yesterday, this day is Set, and he to his grief must not only be married, but also live far from the Jewel of his heart, which happen'd so suddenly, that he had not the least opportunity to give Betty notice thereof; of which she was sometime ignorant, but no sooner heard thereof but like a mad woman, she endangered the running out of her wits. But Cut-beard the Barber being a Smell-Smock,[15] and handsom, who all along tendred her his Service, so handled the matter (who under the notice of giving of Physick)[16] had the recourse unto her, that he not only perswades her out of her sorrow, but also got her good will, which he freely possessed with all she had, till Tom grew up and went to School.

Tom being one day come from School, perceived the Barber and his Mother doing something, but what he knew not, nevertheless supposed the thing to be to the disadvantage of his Mother, she being undermost, and contrary to her will, caught up a new mended Ladle, out of which stuck a sharp piece of Wyer with which he let drive at the Barber's Posteriors, and not only wounded him, but made leave his sport to see what enemy gave him that back blow, when he least dreamed of more Battels to fight, then what he was engaged in; the hasty Barber (not dreaming of ensuing Evil) struck the Boy such a blow on the Ear, that he felled him; which his Mother espying, so foully fell upon the Barber, that with the noise Peter came in, who seeing the fray, and the boy crying, made without further examination, the fourth Person, and so belaboured poor Cut-beard, that with Breeches in hand, he was forced to betake himself homeward both through thick and thin. The Barber gone, and Peter return'd, he ask'd the reason of the Quarrel, to whom she said, that he out of his kindness, starting upon a Joint-stool[17] to take down a Cheese, fell, hurt himself and broke down his Breeches, and in the fall hurt the Child, for which they were then at Wars; he no sooner hearing that, but said, She did ill to abuse, and cause to be abus'd, a man that was in no fault, for hastning out of doors,

15. Womaniser. 16. Barbers, especially in the country, were still barber-surgeons. 17. A properly joined stool, rather than a home-made one. Chairs were an unusual luxury for cottagers.

posted after his Neighbour, who having but even now got up
his Breeches, and seeing Peter coming after him (fraught with a
guilty Conscience) fled like a Hare before the Dog; for he only
considered the danger that was behind, and not minding a low
Hedge just before him, which he to his sorrow fell over, breaking
his Shins, and to amend the matter, he fell unto a Pond half full
of Water, and half full of Puddle,[18] which was just behind the
Hedge, in which he doubtless had been drown'd, had not the
most charitable Cuckold alive helped him out, home, and to bed,
where he lay some time in a bad posture. But in the mean time,
many of Tom's Play-fellows hearing his Out-cry, asked the
question what the matter was, to which as the time would serve,
she answered that he had shit in the Ladle, for which he was
whipped; whereat all laughing, called him Tom Ladle; which
name Winter and Summer he retained all the days of his Life.

> Old love rak'd up, and though in Embers hid,
> Will nevertheless all equal power forbid.

[Vol. I, no. 58]

18. Mire.

Tom Tram

The Mad Pranks of Tom Tram Mother Winters Son-in-Law.[1]

There was an Old Woman named Mother Winter, that had but one Son-in-Law, whose Name was Tom, and though he were at Mans Estate, yet would he do what he list,[2] which grieved his old Mother to the Heart: Upon a time being in the Market she heard a Proclamation, That those that would not Work should be Whipped: At which the old Woman leaped, and with great joy home she comes, meets with her Son, and tells him that the Mayor of the Town had made a Decree, that those that would not work should be Whipp'd: Has he so? says Tom; Marry Gods blessing on his heart for my part I will not break the Decree: so the old woman left her Son, and went again to the Market, she being no sooner gone, but her Son looks into the great Stone Pots, which his Mother kept small Beer in, and when he saw the Beer did not work,[3] he taketh the Pots and setteth them in the midst of the street, and strips off his Doublet, and with a Carters whip, he lays on the pots as hard as he could drive: the people seeing him so earnest, told his Mother what he was doing, which made the old Woman cry out, O that young knave will be hang'd: In that tone home she goeth: her Son Tom seeing his Mother come running, foaming at the mouth, laid on as hard as he could drive, that he broke both the Pots, which made the old woman cry out: O thou Villain, what hast thou done? O Mother, quoth he, you told me that it was Proclaimed, That those that would not work should be whipped; and I've often seen our pots work so hard, that they have foamed so much at the Mouth, that they befouled all the House where they stood; but these two lazy Knaves, said he, told me that they did never work, nor never meant to work, and therefore, quoth he, I have whipped them to death, to teach the rest of their fellows to work, or never look me in the face again.

1. Often used for step-son. 2. Wished. 3. Ferment.

Another Jest of old Mother Winter and her Son Tom.

Upon a time Mother Winter sent her Son Tom into the Market to buy her a pennyworth of Soap, and gave him twelve pence, and charged him to bring it home safe, Tom told her it should be so; & to the end it should be safe brought home, according to his Mothers charge, he goes and buys one pennyworth of Soap, and hired two men with a Hand-barrow to carry the Soap, & four men with brown Bills[4] to guard it along to his Mother, giving them the Eleven-pence for their pains, which made his Mother in great fury to go to the Mayor of the Town and complain: the Mayor committed him to Prison: Now the Prison Window joyned close to the Mayors Chamber-window. Tom and some other merry Prisoners like himself, getting a Cup of good Liquor, in their heads, began to sing and roar, and domineer,[5] insomuch that the Mayor heard them that night and charged them that they should leave off drinking and singing of bawdy songs, & sing good Psalms; Tom told him that he should hear he would amend his Life, if he would pardon his fault: the Mayor said, that for their misdemeanours, they should be that night in Prison and upon amendment, being Neighbours, he would release them in the morning; they thanked the Mayor, but Tom Winter prevailed so far with a friend of his, that he borrowed three shillings the which three shillings he spent upon his fellow Prisoners, which made the poor men be ruled by him, to do whatsoever he enjoyned them to do, so that when the Mayor was gone to bed, the Prison-window being close to his Chamber-Window, they began to sing Psalms so loud, that the Mayor could take no rest, which made him to cause one of his Servants to bid them to leave singing: Tom Winter said, That it was, the Mayors good Crunsel,[6] that they should sing Psalms, and sing they would as long as they lived there; which made the Mayor to bid the Jaylor turn them out of Prison without paying any Fees.[7]

---

4. Staffs. 5. Revel, roister. 6. Misprint for counsel. 7. To the gaoler for food etc.

Another merry Jest, how Tom served his Hostiss
and a Tobacco-seller.

It fortuned that Tom was sent of an Errand forty Miles from his
abode, over Heaths and plains, where having dispatched his
business, he chanced to be lodged in a Room that opened into a
yard, where his Hostiss kept many Turkies, which Tom seeing,
he thrust pins into two of their heads, which in the night dyed:
The woman in the morning wondring how the Fowl should come
to dye. Tom perswaded her that there was a great sickness where
he dwelt among all manner of Fowl, and wished his Hostess to
fling them away, the which she did: Tom watcht where she flung
them, and when he took his leave of his Hostess, it was at such a
time when she was busie in setting Bread into the Oven, so that
he was sure she should not look after him: so he goeth and wraps
the two Turkies in his coat, and away he goes: but finding his two
Turkies very heavy, he seeth a Man that sold Tobacco up and
down the Country, at the foot of a Hill, where he a'lighted to
lead the Horse down the Hill: at the foot of the Hill Tom falls
down, and lyes crying as if he had broke one of his Leggs: and
maketh to the Man a most piteous lamentation, that he was six
or seven miles from any town, there being no houses near, and
that he was like to perish for want of succour: the man asked
where he dwelt? he said with such a Knight, to whom Tom did
live as Jester; the Man knowing the Knight, and thinking Toms
legg had been broken, as he said, with much ado he lifted Tom
upon his Horse, when Tom was on the Hors s back, he prayed
the Man to give him his Masters Turkies, which were sent him
for a Present: but as the man stooped for the Turkies, Tom made
the Horse to gallop away, crying out: I shall be kill'd, I shall be
kill'd, O my Leg, O my Leg, what shall I do, my Leg? The Man
seeing him gone stood a while in amaze, and knew not what to
think; nevertheless he durst not leave his Turkies behind him,
for displeasing the Kt. but carryed them lugging along, fretting
& sweating in his Boots, until he came to the next Town, where
he hired a Horse to over-take Tom, but could not until he came
to the Knights House, where Tom stood to attend his coming,

looking out at a Window, where the man being alighted, Tom called to him so loud, that most of the House heard him: O (said he) now I see thou art an honest man, I had thought you had set me upon your head-strong Horse on purpose to deceive me of my Turkies: The man replyed; A Pox take you and your Turkies, for I never was so played the Knave withal in my life; I hope that thou wilt pay for the hire of the Horse, which I was driven to hire to follow you withal? That I will with all my heart, said Tom. . . .

[Vol. I, no. 41]

THE
Merry TALES
Of the Mad-Men
OF
GOTAM.

By A. B. Dr. of Physick.

Printed for J. Clarke, W. Thackeray,
and L. Passinger.

Mad-Men of Gotam.[1] By A.B.[2] Dr. of Physick.

. . . The Second Tale.

There was a Man of Gotam did ride to the Market with two
bushels of wheat, and because his Horse should not bear heavy, he
carried his Corn upon his own neck, and did ride upon his horse
because his Horse should not carry too heavy a Burden Judge
you which was the wisest, his Horse or himself.

The Third Tale.

On a time the Men of Gotam would have pinned in the Cuckoo,
whereby she should sing all the year, and in the middle of the
Town they made a Hedge, round in compass, and they got a
Cuckoo and put her into it, and said, Sing here all the year, and
thou shalt want neither meat nor drink. The Cuckoo as soon as
she see herself incompassed within the Hedge, flew away.
A vengeance on her, said they, we made not our Hedge high
enough.

. . . The Sixth Tale.

There dwelt a Smith in Gotam, who had a Wasps-Nest in Straw
in the end of his Forge, there did come one of his Neighbours
to have his Horse shooed, and the Wasps were so base, that the
Fellow was stung with a Wasp: he being angry, said; Art thou
worthy to keep a Forge or no? to have men here stung with
Wasps. O Neighbour, said the Smith, be content, and I will put
them from their Nests by and by; immediately he took a Coulter,[3]
and het[4] it in his Forge glowing hot, and he thrust it into the
Straw at the end of his Forge, and set his Forge on fire, and burnt

1. Village in Nottinghamshire; the stories are medieval in origin. 2. Andrew
Borde, 1490–1549, who also recorded *The Jests of Scoggin*. See Wardroper,
Jest, pp. 5–8, 198–199. 3. Iron blade. 4. Heated.

it up. Then said the Smith, I told thee I would fire them out of their Nest.

. . . The Ninth Tale.

On a time there was one of Gotam Mowing in the Meads,[5] and found a great Grashopper; so casts down his Sith, and did run home to his Neighbors, and said that there was a Devil in the Field, that hoppeth in the Grass: then there was every Man ready with Clubs, and Staves, with Halberts, and other Weapons, to go to kill the Grashopper: when they did come to the place where the Grashopper should be, said the one to the other; Let every Man Cross himself from the Devil; for we will not meddle with him. And so they returned again, and said, We were blest this day, that we went no further. Ah! Cowards, said he that had the Sithe in the Mead, help me to fetch my Sithe: No, said they, it is good to sleep in a whole Skin, better loose the Sithe then to marr us all.

. . . The Twelfth Tale.

There was a Man of Gotam and he did not love his wife; and she having a fair Hair,[6] her Husband said divers times that he would cut it off, and he durst not do it when she was waking, but when she was asleep: So one night he took up a pair of Sheers, and did lay them under his Bedshead, the which when his wife perceived, she called to her one of her Maids, and said; Go to bed to my Husband, for he is minded to cut off my Hair this very night; let him cut off thy Hair, and I will give thee as good a Kirtle[7] as ever thou did'st wear: the Maid did so, and feigned her self asleep, the which the Man perceiving, cut off the Maids Hair, and did wrap it about his Sheers, and laid it about his Beds-head, and fell asleep. The Wife made her Maid rise, and took the Hair and Sheers, and went into the Hall, and there burnt the Hair. The man had a Horse, the which he did love above all things, (as she did well know) the good Wife went unto her Husbands Stable and cut the Horse-tail, and laid them under her Husbands head.

5. Meadows. 6. Being fair, blonde. 7. Gown, or outer petticoat.

In the morning she did arise betimes, and did sit by the fire
Combing of her head, at last the Man did come to the fire, and
seeing his Wife Combing of her head, marvelled much thereat.
The Maid seeing her Master in a brown study said, What a Devil
ails the Horse in the Stable, for he bleedeth sore? The good man
ran into the Stable, and found that this horse tail was cut off,
he went to the Beds-head and found his Sheers wrapt up his
Horse tail, and did come to his Wife, saying, I cry thee mercy,[8]
for I had thought that I had cut off thy hair to night, and I have
cut off my Horse-tail. (Said she) self do, self have;[9] Many a Man
thinketh to do another Man a shrewd[10] turn, and turneth oftentimes to his own self.

. . . The Thirteenth Tale.

There was a Man of Gotam that laid a Wager with his Wife, that
she should not make him a Cuckold; No said she, but I can:
Spare not (quoth he) do what thou canst. On a time she hid all
the Spiggots and Fausets[11] in the house, and she went into her
Buttery, and set a Barrel abroach,[12] and cryed out to her Husband,
and said, I pray thee bring me hither a Spiggot and a Fauset, or
else all the Ale will run out: the good Man sought up and down
and could find none; Come hither then, said she, and hold your
finger in the Tap-hole, she pulled out her finger and the good
Man put in his; She then called unto her Taylor, which did then
dwell at the next door, with whom she made a blind Bargain:
and within a while after, she came to her Husband, and did bring
a Spiggot and a Fauset with her, saying, pull out thy finger out
of the Tap-hole, gentle Cuckold, for you have lost your Bargain;
I beshrew[13] your heart for your labour, said the good Man:[14]
make no such Bargains then, said she, with me.

[Vol. II, no. 21]

8. A somewhat formal mode of address. 9. One gets one's just desserts, an
old proverb. 10. Malicious. 11. Wooden implements for tapping beer out of a
barrel. 12. Pierced, here, by knocking out the bung. 13. Curse. 14. Husband,
or mode of address, as Goodman Brown.

VIII. MARITAL AND EXTRAMARITAL.

The Womans Brawl.

Jack.

Never was poor Man so perplexed with a wife as I am; if there be a destiny in Marriage and Hanging, would I had married the three-leged Bride at Hide-Park-corner,[1] when I married her: for I never enjoyed a happy hour since. They say she was made of a crooked thing called a Rib,[2] but she hath rib'd me with a vengeance. A Woman, for no man indeed, tribulation & anguish, I must needs (like a pittiful Coxcomb) Marry her to take off her ill Name, and make an honest woman of her forsooth, but what hath she made of me? Booh; but since 'twas my own seeking, I must patiently bear the Cuckolds Badge, as well as my next Neighbours: as soon as she is up in a morning, away to the Ale-house, and there spend all that I can get, and when she hath liquored her tongue with Oyl of Barley,[3] she either quarrels with her Neighbours, and goes to Law, pawns Gown, Petticoat, Smock and all, or else comes home as bubby[4] as a drunken Tubb-woman; calls me not Lord and Master, but Rogue and Rascal, makes Horns at me, bids me seek under the Candlestick.[5] But Mum,[6] stand clear, and give attention, and you shall hear her speak for her self.

Doll.

I have a good Beast on ye, have I not? other womens husbands can rise in a morning and make their wives a fire, fetch them in water, wash shitten Clouts, sweep the house, scour the Andirons, make the Bed, scrape Trenchers, make clean chooes,[7] rub Stockings, air Apparel, and empty the Pot; but I have a Drone good for nothing but to be set in a Chimney-corner, to dry pist Clouts

---

1. Gallows at Tyburn. 2. Adam's Rib. 3. Beer. 4. Inebriated. 5. This piece of abuse defeats me. 6. Hush, as in Keep mum or Mum's the word. 7. Shoes.

upon his Horns:[8] When I would have ye do any thing for me, then your back akes with a P – – – r to ye, you are sick then: then you can turn your Leaden Breech and lye like a Log by me all night, and when you rise turn your backside to me, as though I should kiss that.

Out thou Unnatural Clown, thou feeble Dick thou: As I am an Honest Woman Neighbour (I went like a fool) and made him a Caudle[9] with Turkey-Eggs, and afterwards a Tanzey[10] with new-laid eggs, from a Hen trod[11] by a Game Cock, put in Cumfrey[12] and Clary,[13] and fed him with Lamb-stones,[14] Cavior, and Potato-Pies: yet he could do no more good to a Woman then a Boy of a year old; but let him be at his old Pye-house in Turnmill-street,[15] then who but Jack Hold-my-staff: his Pye-Mobs are stark mad for him: one-ey'd Kate, Bristow Bess, Black Jug, half-breech'd Moll, the Devils Trumpeter, long-sided Nell, Nan Tickle-tail of the Hemp-stamp,[16] and a hundred Whores, more than the Devil ever gave name to: then you are a Town-Bull, ready to run over them all, though you come like a Suck-Egg Rascal home, with a pair Weezle Chops, looking like one that would rob a Hen-roost, rather than give a Wanton Woman content: such a feeble Doe-little as thou, makes many an honest woman go astray as they do, but as the Song saith, A Cuckold is a good mans fellow, and a Bastard hath not always the worst fortune. Peter Grievous must be a contended man; and sit in the Chimney-corner, and dry his wives Dish-clouts on his Horns, and sometimes get a Groat or Sixpence by going of an errand, for to fetch his wives Friend to come to her, and he must wait below Stairs, while she is earning a little Money of her Culley,[17] and he must write Letters to his wives Friend to meet her in Wood-street,[18] or any where else: the Grazier hath been a Rum Culley.[19]

---

8. Diapers on his cuckold's horns. 9. Medicinal gruel. 10. Pudding. 11. Mated by. 12. Medicinal plant. 13. Sweetened wine. 14. Testicles; all ingredients considered aphrodisiac. 15. Brothel in red-light district, near Saffron Hill. 16. Convicted prostitutes proverbially beat hemp in Bridewells. 17. Prostitute's dupe. 18. Tavern. 19. Country bumpkin paid through the nose.

Jack.

Yes, yes, they are very honest[20] women that Cuckold their Husbands, and beget Bastards.

Doll. As Honest as thy Mother, thou Rascal, as honest as the skin between the brows of thee:[21] It is both honest and honourable, and to the advancement, as well as Exaltation of your heads: Are not many men made men when that they are made Cuckolds?[22] and preferred by their wives friends into high places, and Offices of great Concernment: Doth not the courtesie of the Wife many times utter her Husbands ill Commodities, or unsaleable Wares, that we can grace forth, and put off at pleasure, (to our Friends) for a Good round Price too? Well, well, let men say what they will, it is we women that cause Trading: Your poor Citizens would be in a falling Condition else, did not we Women hold up their Occupation.[23] Is not a handsome Woman in a Shop attractive, and a very Load-stone for to draw in Customers? I pray what Gentleman would not gladly be a trading with her? Yes, I warrant ye, and they had rather be dealing with her, then with her Husband, or with any Fore-man or any Smock-fac'd[24] Prentice of them all: What think you of Jane Shore? was she not a Goldsmiths Wife in Lumbard-street, that got the Custome of a King[25] by her Beauty? Well, well, a handsome Shop-keepers Wife is a thing of an unknown price. I my self, as simple as I stand here, was once a Dame y'faith, that would not have given my face for washing,[26] and as stately a Dame as ever walkt round the Exchange: though now I am but a simple Halter-makers Wife, yet you may thank me Rascal, for getting you Squire Catch[27] the Hang-mans custome; for though it be but little, tis constant, and sure pay: besides, he is my good friend.

Iack. Am I a Cuckold by the Hangman? the Devil take take[28] your trade no marvel but ye must go into Turn-mill-street, with a Pox t'ye, to speak with a Gentleman about some work, if Catch the Hangman be your Master.

20. Honourable, faithful. 21. I.e. between the horns. 22. Either by wives of impotent men bearing children, or because of a new-found manliness against the horner. 23. Slang for intercourse. 24. Effeminate looking. 25. Edward III. 26. Disdainful, proud. 27. Jack Ketch, hangman 1663–1686, of barbarous reputation. 28. Misprint.

Doll. How now foul manners, plain Catch, you might have an M under your Girdle,[29] he was a Squire the first day he came to his place, and is a good companion, and a true friend to a Woman i'le warrant him.

Iack. I believe he loves women indeed, he marks so many of them for his own, and deals so kindly with them at the Gallows.

Doll. Out thou Wittally Knave, thou Cuckoldly Hedge-Sparrow,[30] thou Foul-mouth'd Knave; because some few women offend, must the blame lye on their whole Sex? no, thou Rascal, one of them that was hang'd was thy Mother, thou Rascal, thou Nitty-breech'd[31] Knave, thou had'st not a shirt to thy back when I married thee; no, thou drunken Knave, all the Neighbours can tell that I was well enough before I married with such a Wittal as thou art, I was taken for an understanding woman, and though I say it, an honest woman.

Iack. Yes, the whole Parish knows your Honesty, when you were brought to Bed in a Cage on Tower-Hill, with three Bastards one after another, where one brought thee Clouts, another a Caudle, a third a Smock to shift[32] your Whores Hide, you have forgotten that, 'twas a little before ye had been at Mount-Mill, a Knocking with a Rat-catcher,[33] when you were drunk at the Three Tuns in Bedlam,[34] and coming home staggered, and fell down in the Dirt, and to blind the people, told them ye were troubled with the Falling-sickness.

Doll.

No marvel that thou twitest me with having three Bastards in the Cage; when thy Mother had lain in with half a dozen Bastards, thou thy self art one of those precious Cage-Birds, like a foul-mouth'd Knave as thou art, to disparage an honest woman so.

Jack.

You were very honest indeed, when you down on your Mary-bones,[35] and beg'd at my feet, crying, sweet Iohn, do but marry

29. Call him *Mister*. 30. Wittally, hedge-sparrow both symbolise impotence. 31. Lousy. 32. Clothe. 33. Despised profession. 34. Beside Moorfields, red-light area. 35. Marrow-bones, knees.

me and make me an honest Woman, and i'le prove the best Wife to thee in all the World: believe ye and hang ye.

Doll.

Too Honest for such a Knave as thou art: When I came up first to London all the whole Parish where I lived, can tell that I was an honest Woman, and a well-bred Woman, and a good Woman (though I say't) as any belonging to the Tower-Liberty.[36] My Husband was Warden of the Gun-Smiths: Besides, he had born all Offices in the parish where he liv'd, yet by over-shooting himself by his own kind heart, and passing his word,[37] he was undone and flung into the Gaol, where he dyed, and I his poor Wife turned out of house and home, having all my goods and cloaths taken from me by the Varlets: then was poor I glad to take a house in Ratcliff High-way, where I sold a cup of good Ale, kept two Beds going;[38] and had as much resort to my house early and late, as the best Trader of them all, and I had as good sweet conditioned souls under me: no Trugmullians,[39] but Gentle-women born: that knew how to entertain men of fashion: From the Earl to the Esquire, and from the Esquire so the Yeoman, and from the Yeoman to the Plow-jogger: I had good Citizens,[40] no Broken Companions came after me, and for Gallant Seamen, from the Captain to the Bowson, and from the Bowson to the Swabber: not a Tar-Pawling that Plowed over the Rugged Bosome of Curled Neptunes Waves, but paid Custome of my house, and found such sweet entertainment, that so long as one Penny was left, they'd be hang'd e're they'd step one foot to Sea again: But when I had by my fine allurements pumped them dry, I bid them turn out, told them I had my Rent to pay, and the Brewer and Baker were come for Money: No. no, No money, no Coney,[41] if they would not be packing, I had a Chamber-pot for to wash them out, or else a Winchester Goose[42] for them to

36. Outside the city wall, by the Tower. 37. Giving a pledge, or guarantee for somebody else, who failed. 38. On a main road into London, and near the Thames and docks. 39. Whores. 40. This could refer to female citizens; broken companions, to ladies, are female. 41. Common saying: no money, no rabbit, often with double meaning, as here. 42. Venereal disorder.

pull; I learnt that Trick of my Neighbours, Mrs. Damrose Page,[43] Mistris Smite, and the rest of my Worshipful Occupation.

    Iack. A Worshipful Occupation indeed, to keep a Bawdy-house, and be as common as a Barbers Chair, for every Rake-shame to clap his breech in.[44]

[Vol. II, no. 1]

43. Damaris Page, along with Mother Creswell, the most famous bawd in Restoration London. James II, as Duke of York, once platonically visited her establishment. She specialised in sailors. 44. One of the corniest puns of the period, though the play on clap is less threadbare.

THE
Parliament of women;

With the Merry Laws by them newly Enacted;
To live in more Ease, Pomp, and Wantonness; But especially that they may Domineer
over their Husbands. With a new way found
out by them to cure any old or new Cuckolds;
and how both parties may recover their
Credit and Honesty again.

Printed for *T. Paſſinger*, *I. Deacon*, and *G. Conyers*, and are to
be Sold at their Shops on *London Bridge*, in *Guiltſpurſtreet*,
and on *Ludgate Hill*.

Parliament of Women.[1]

... To you, as well of the Manufacture, as the matronship, I speak to all in general, I have known a Lord contented with one Lackey, a Master with one man, a Tennant with one Landlord, a Bird with one mate, a Cow with one Milk-maid; and shall a man desire to have two Wives, that (alas) when all he can do, can hardly please one: Nay, grant them two, in time they will grow to Ten, from ten to twenty: and then what a racket would there be who should rule the roast? Nay, I have heard of one that had once a thousand Wives and Concubines.[2] Now out upon him for a Jew, (said a second) and taking the Tale out of her mouth,[3] thus proceeded; Methinks they should rather have consulted, that Women might have had two strings to their Bow, that if one slip, the other might hold, one for week-days, to drudge within doors, another for holy-days, to walk abroad with her, & usher her in her best cloaths: keeping one for delight, the other for drudgery. To which motion, they with an unanimous voice consented. Then up starts a third, and said; our sex is of late grown cowards, carpit, & curtain-hearted:[4] where be those Magnanimous and masculine spirited Matrons? those valiant Viragoes? those lusty Ladies, those daring Amozonian Damosels, Orithena, Penthisiliaea, Thalestres[5] and the rest? who made Coxcombs of Keysars,[6] Puppits of Princes, Captives of Captains, Fools of Philosophers, and henchmen of their husbands? but though we want Weapons, and are abridged of their Arms,[7] yet they shall know that we have the law in our own hands & in our own cases we will be our own Lawyers, & plead our own rights, for we have tongues to tell our own tales, & our tales[8] shall be heard and handled, when some of theirs shall not: What! let

1. Aristophanes originated this well-worked idea. This piece is modelled on a broadside of 1640, and two parts of *The Parliament of Ladies*, by Henry Neville, 1647. The extract opens with the first female speech; the scene is Rome. 2. Solomon. 3. Interrupting her, taking up the running. 4. Armchair campaigners, indoor strategists, faint-hearted. 5. All queens of the Amazons. 6. Caesars. 7. Common phallic symbol. 8. Slang term for female pudend.

these Cocks crow, and we shall have the Ravens follow after.[9]

These words were spoke with such an emphasis, that there was a general hum throughout all the Parliament parlor: then there was a motion made, that every one for the present should put in a particular of their grievances; 1. Up starts one Mrs. Rattle, a Taylors wife, and said, I think the Proverb may be very well verified in my Husband, which is, That many Taylors go to the making up of one Man;[10] for he hath no more metal in him than a Mouse, he works altogether with hot Needle and burnt Thread, for nothing he doth prospers with me, I think the reason is because he uses an unlawful Yard,[11] and wants that handful which belongs to the City-Measure, or else because he sits cross-leg'd on his Shop-board like a Dead Hare on a Poulterers Stall, and no good work can be done that way: if at any time he makes me a new Petticoat, he will threaten to sit upon my Skirts,[12] and that's all: He will sow, and sow,[13] yet when he hath done all he can, proves but so and so, with that she put finger in Eye an wept.

Nay, said another Gossip, seeing and pittying the poor puleing Creature: I think your best course Mrs. Rattle, is to acquaint your self with some Courtier his Customer, and when any Mask[14] or show is to be presented at Court, he may help you to a good standing. Then another starts up and said, My name is Frank[15] Falldown, a Felmakers Wife, and know no more from my Husband of the 3 parts that belong to a Noun-Substantive but the first, and their is felt, and nothing else worthy to be heard or understood.[16] Sisly[17] the Sadlers Wife sat next. Nay, you may take me too in your number, for my Case is as much to be condoled as any's, who have a very Pea-Goose, and Patch-Pannel to my good-man;[18] well, his girts or latches may pass for currant but could never see a good stir-rup[19] from him since he was my

9. Proverb, roughly pride comes before a fall. 10. Nine; a traditionally effeminate trade. 11. Illegally short measure, and slang for penis. 12. Cuddles. 13. Cliché, seed planting. 14. Masque. 15. Common female abbreviation for Frances; feltmaker's wife. 16. Feeling, hearing and understanding were the three parts. 17. Cicely. 18. Peak-goose, a ninny; patch-pannel, scraps of stuff fit only for a patchwork. 19. The pun on girts and latches, girths and thongs, suggests mere embracing.

Husband; I confess he is saddle nosed & saddle back't too,[20] but could never set the saddle on the right horse since I knew him; to whom the Horse-coursers[21] wife, called Hair-brain reply'd, My good-man is his Customer, who keeps the Saddle to himself, but gives me the Bit and the Bridle; he can teach his horse to pace as he list, but for himself, he hath neither good Amble, Trot, nor Gallop. After them, Grace the Gold-smiths Wife Sarah the Silkmans, Kate the Comfit-makers,[22] Beatrice the Braisiers, Parnal the Apothecaries, Maudlin the Masons, Wenifred the wire-drawers, Dorithy the drapers, etc. Every one laid down their several grievances, which as they were attentively heard, so they were much to be commisecrated. I am loath to insist on too many, therefore for brevity sake let these suffice for the rest.) Then consultation was had now to rectifie what was amiss, for the general good of their Sex, how to wrest the power in men from wronging their wives, that henceforward they might live in the more ease, pride, pomp, and liberty: for which they thought fit that good and wholsome Laws should be Enacted. . . .

I put the case to you, suppose a handsome Lass marries a Seafaring man, perchance his occasions calls him to go a long Voyage to Sea, as to the East or West Endies, or to the Streights Magdalen,[23] Reed or Red Sea, or to the Persian-Gulph, he is bound to stay a year, two, or three, before he can return? . . . do you think it convenient such a pretty soul should lye alone, having been wedded so short a time, and only tasted of you know what, and having been a fellow-feeler, and helper in most cases, for the commonwealths good, that she can be content to lye alone tumbling and tossing in a good Feather-bed, sometimes on one side, and sometimes on the other: sighing and groaning, as if her very twatling-strings[24] would break, makeing her moan to the Curtains, fumbling, and biting, and tearing the Sheets, and by no means ease her oppressed body and mind. Nay, I should not say oppressed body, for there I was mistaken, there my

20. Snub-nosed and concave backed. 21. Trainer. 22. Sweet jam or jelly. 23. Magellan; English sea-borne trade had expanded enormously since 1600. 24. Vocal chords, but twat already a slang term.

Tongue went too fast, I should have said, her troubled and perplexed spirit, heart, or what you term it. Ought not I say, such women to have two or three husbands; Yes yes, said they, being alwayes provided, and for the good of the Commonwealth.[25] . . .

Yet, saith she, my husband is a Gamester, and as he games abroad, so I play at home; if he be at Bowls and kiss the Mistris, I can for recreation play at Rubbers with his Man: when he hath been all the day at Passage and Hazard, at night he comes home and plays with me at Dublets, Barams-Ace, and Back-Gammon:[26] but yet I am sometimes even with him, for when he with his Sweethearts ventures his Estate at the Hole,[27] I with his Servant can pass away the time at Inn and Inn.[28]

After spake Mrs. Rachel Rattle-apace, and said, As I hold Mistris Dorcas that lawful which you do, so I hope that I bringing my Sack to the Mill, it may be ground among the rest; that is, when our Husbands trouble us, we may likewise torment them: if they fret, we frown; they grudge, we grumble: they prate, we glout:[29] they cross, we curse: if they bend their brows, we may bend our fists: and be they never so outragious, we to carry no Coals in any case.[30]

But let it then be added (said she that sat next) that there be no Reconcilement without some Reward, and no Pardon may be granted without a new Gown and Petticoat, which if demurr'd upon at the first or second Demand, it shall be in her choice to ask him the third, and if he cog[31] and offer to Kiss you, and tell you that he will Kiss you, bid him take you about the middle and Kiss the heaviest end:[32] or if he fail, she may read him a Juniper Lectar[33] as far as the scope of her invention, or the scarcity of breath will give her leave. Or, if he notwithstanding all this, be peevish and perverse, she may also continue proud and peremtory, till she rail him into reconcilement, and make him provide a

25. Typical wording of provision in a statute. 26. These puns on card and dice games were far from original. 27. Intended as inn-name. 28. Also a card game. 29. Sulk. 30. Be put upon. 31. Persuade, wheedle. 32. Highly disdainful and insulting. 33 Pungent or prickly.

Feast to entertain her Gossips, and make his peace that way.

And then (said another, taking the Tale out of her mouth) or if she have a mind to take the air, or walk to Green-Goose Fair,[34] or any merry Meeting, or Market, if she desire his company, that he new black his shooes, and put on his best Hat and Cloak to wait on her thither, ushering her before to take her gently by the arm, and lovingly to lead her, of if (for some reasons best known to her self) she would have his absence, that he patiently put Money in her Purse and that he stay at home without grumbling. . . .

But one thing we have forgot, said they, which is a main matter: that is, to seek out cure for any old or young Cuckolds. Then spake Mrs. Dorithy Doe-little, and said, My good Man came home Drunk the other day, and because I should not see him in that manner, he hid himself in the House of special Office,[35] and there he began to ease his stomach, and lay about him like a Hog, when he had eaten so much that he was ready to burst: and because I should not hear him, he trust his head into the hole: and whether it were his large Asses Ears, or his Bull Neck I cannot tell but he could not get his Neck out again, and needs must pull up the seat about his Neck, so that he looked as if he had been in the Pillory. Upon which Relation they all fell into a great laughter, and withal concluded, that it was his horns, for Acteon,[36] said they, put his head out of the Window well enough, but could not get it back again, which was long of his hornes: this, said they, is your husbands case. . . .

The chief Heads of the Womens LAWS.

First, That instead of allowing Men two Wives, women, especially the strongest, and greatest Vessels,[37] shall have two or three Husbands.

That Women might vex, perplex, and any ways torment their Husbands.

34. Goose fairs, like that still held at Nottingham, were common; a green goose was a whore. 35. Privy; it was not unknown for food to be kept in there. 36. Horned by Diana as a punishment. 37. Double meaning, cliché.

That Women may twattle[38] it as well as their Husbands.

That Women may feast, Banquet, and Gossip, when, and where they please.

Likewise it is thought fit and convenient by us, that all rich and stale Batchelors do forthwith Marry poor Widdows that have no means to live on, and so become Fathers the first day.

Item. That it is thought meet, that rich Widdows shall marry Gentlemens youngest Sons, that have no means to maintain themselves.[39]

Item. It is concluded, and fully agreed upon, that all Women should have their Husbands Tenants at will, and that they should do them Night-Service, and have their homage[40] paid before every Sun-rising, or at every Weeks end, or at utmost between the Quarters,[41] and not a day longer to be deferr'd, unless it be in the Dog-days.[42]

Item. Let our Husbands remember, though it be a trick of them to forsake our beds in the Dog-days, yet let them take notice there is no Dog-nights, and that it was at first but a trick of their own invention to save their labour and money too, which Act we disallow for ever.

Item. That no Yeoman or Husbandman shall keep, or suffer to be kept in the House, Barn, or Stable, any Cock or Cocks, that will not tread his Hens, especially when the Hens thrust their heads under the Cocks-neck, etc.

Item. That Man which promises a pretty Maid a good turn and doth not perform it in three Months, shall loose his what de ye call 'em.

FINIS.

[Vol. II, no. 34]

38. Chatter, etc. 39. Truism; because of primogeniture and entail, and the strict settlement of estates on the eldest son. 40. All terms of feudal fealty. 41. Quarter-days were debt-settling days. There may be an intentional innuendo. 42. Days of great heat.

Fumblers[1]-Hall, KEPT And holden in Feeble[2]-Court, at the sign of the Labour-in-vain, in Doe-little-lane.

... The females of Cornucopia, being a great number of agrieved Mortals that a long time have Languished: gnaw Sheets, eat Oatmeal, and licked Walls for satisfaction of their longing desires, & finding none to pitty their cases, but growing worse and worse in their desired faculty, resolved with one consent to draw up their agrievances; and present them to the Masters of the Corporation of Fumblers-Hall. ...

Alice. An't please this Honourable Table, I have been his obedient Creature, waking and sleeping, these 3 long years, and yet am as pure a Virgin, as ever lay by the side of a young Bride-groom; & so am like to continue for him, whereby I receive many taunts and jeers of my Neighbours, who call me Barren-Doe, & a thousand such names: when 'tis known, Gentlemen, the fault is not mine in the least: I have done my endeavour up and down, ever since I was his Wife, fed him with Anchovis, Caviarre, bought bottles of Muskadine, Montefisco Frontimack:[3] nay, he has wanted nothing that the industery of Woman could invent, to make him capable of doing his duty: Yet he is no more to me, Gentlemen, than a straw in the Nostrils of a cow, a very slug, a meer frible,[4] an it please ye, Gentlemen hear what he can alledge for himself.

Mast. Sir Nicholas answer for your self, what can you alledge against the accusation of the Woman?

Sir Nicholas. So please your Grave Worships to consider of the Impudence of this woman, who is more insatiate then the Grave, nay, Hell it self: no man though never so lusty, being able to give her satisfaction: besides, one sluttish nasty trick she hath, that every night she Farts in her sleep, which above all the rest of her bad qualities, is most hateful to me.

1. Impotents. 2. The same; used of one of the inadequate recruits in *2 Henry IV*, III, ii. 3. Frontignac, a muscat wine, supposedly aphrodisiac. 4. Ridiculous trifle.

Sir Fardinañdo Fumbler, Clerk of the Company

Mast. That is but a weak infirmity Sir Nicholas; you know he that refuseth a wife for a Fart, a Horse for a start, and a Groat for a crack,[5] shall never be well wiv'd, well Hors'd, nor well money'd; come, come, Sir Nicholas, you must bear with her weakness, she is a woman, and your wife.

Alice. I, and will be a woman too in spight of his teeth, or else i'le want of my will,[6] cannot I break wind when I catch cold, but you must mouth it?

Mast. A Womans will indeed, is a resolute beast, and deserves a strong kirb; if they once get a bit in their mouth they'l run to the devil.

Sir Nick. Therefore ile flye them, as I flye from evil.
　　　　And shun bad women, as i'de shun the Devil.
　　　　　　　　(Exit, Sir Nick and Alice.)

Mast. Clerk; Call in Jone Wood hav-more and Daniel Doe-little, to answer what shall be objected each by other.

Clerk. Jone Wood-have-more, and Daniel Doe-little appear in the Court, and bring your Summons with you,

　　　Enter Jone Wood-have-more, and Daniel Doe-little.

Mast. Jone, What canst thou say against Daniel? is he not a loving husband to thee?

Ione. I cannot say but he is loving enough, but love is not all that pleaseth a Woman, will love beget such beautiful Children as my neighbour K. or my neighbour B. hath; no, no, Love will not do it alone: I must confess he is a Musitian, and as timber-some[7] a man as any lives in Cock-Lane, yet has but a meer Gut, a Chitterling,[8] a Fiddle-string, that will make no musick to a Womans Instrument; yet when I tell him on't, he pulls it out and shakes it, and puts up his Fiddle-stick again, falls a kissing of me, & with a few other Jack-Puddings[9] tricks, thinks that sufficient satisfaction; but this is the short & the long of the business, I have been his wife long enough, and have found his performances to be meer fooling, and no real performance at all: a fine speech to a rotten Puppit-play; but I look for Reality Gentlemen, and to

5. Proverb; start is a nervous movement; groat is fourpence. 6. Despite him, or else my wishes will be unfulfilled. 7. Well-built. 8. Smaller intestine. 9. Buffoon's.

have Children as Well as my Neighbours: 'tis not now and then a Hoop-ring[10] will please me, No, no, i'le get a Cooper i'le warrant him, that shall not want an Addze[11] to labour withal.

No Woman can indure so vile a wrong,
As too too short, or have it too too long.

Mast. Daniel, what say'st for thy self?

Daniel. Will ye please to see, and if here be not enough to content any Woman in England ile —

Mast. Fie on him uncivil beast, kick him out of the Court, and commit him close prisoner to his own Horn-Pipe, and grant Jone liscence of freedom, to use and occupy[12] for a year and a day, and then this business to be called over again.

Ione. I humble thank your good Worships, I shall not be unthankful to you.

D. This is a doom I little thought to have.
For natures gifts to be a womans slave.

Exit Jone and Daniel. . . .

[Vol. I, no. 7]

10. Holding together staves of a barrel. 11. Cutting tool to shape wood. 12. This often has sexual connotations.

Worm-wood[1] *Lectures*. (translated by Martin Parker.[2] 1682.)

... Dialogue 5.

A Woman to her Husband finding him at the Tavern or Ale-house.

So, so now 'tis as it should be, this is your good Husbandry, is it not? Now the work goes well forward, doth't not? This is the way to maintain your Wife and Children, wilt not? ifaith you drunken Rascal, I'm glad I have (at the last) found out your haunt, this way your Money goes; 'tis no marvel you are so sparing at home, there you grudge a penny to fetch milk for your Children; nay, you'l hardly allow Soap and Candle, but every thing is too much; this groat is grumbled at, that twopence is pin'd at. But here among your pot-companions, twelve or eighteen pence is not thought much of; but ifaith i'le take an order with you, i'le ferret you out in all your holes: come, will you come away, Sir? I protest if you come not altogether the sooner, mark the end on't, if I come again and find you here, i'le break all the juggs, classes,[3] pots, and pipes that I can find upon the Table, I will in troth; and now I think on't, i'le have you with me, or i'le ne're go away alive, you shall not put me off with your whimsies, you shall not, you drunken beast, you shall not, etc. .

His Answer.

I.

I Prethee good Wife,
Leave making of strife,
And sit down by me if thou pleasest,
But if thou wilt not,

---

1. Along with gall, traditionally associated with bitterness. 2. Most famous ballad-writer of seventeenth century, ob. c. 1656. 3. Glasses.

Then be gon like a Trot,[4]
For my company much thou displeasest.

2.

What comest thou for,
Knowing I abhor
To be thus pursu'd and reproved?
Then leave off thy prate,
For I tell thee old Kate,
My patience is very much moved.[5]

3.

'Tis invain to resist,
For i'le come when I list,
Then drink and be gone without scolding;
I'm sure what I spend,
I get,[6] there's an end,
To thee I am nothing beholding.

4.

When she did perceive
That he would not leave
His company to go home with her;
She sate to him close,
And fudled her nose,[7]
And both went home reeling together. . . .[8]

[Vol. I, no. 16]

---

4. Old hag, scold, bitch. 5. Nearly exhausted. 6. Earn. 7. Got drunk. 8. The husbands always win the arguments in this set of lectures. Cf. *Sir John Barley-corn*, Section IV.

A merry Dialogue between
TOM the TAYLOR,
and His Maid *Jone*.

The Taylor was old, and his Maid she was young,
She pays his old scores with her tail & her tongue
For like an old fool he must make her his Wife,
She makes him a Cuckold all days of his life :
She could not long tarry, so great was her spight,
That she made him a Cuckold the very first night.

tom ỹ taler & his · wife · Ione

Printed for, *I. Clarke*, at the Bible and Harp,
in West-Smithfield. 1684.

Tom the Taylor. 1684.

A Merry Dialogue between
Tom the Taylor, and his Maid Joan.

Tom. Hark ye Joan, what a Clock is it? is not dinner ready yet, methinks I begin to be hungry?

Joan. Marry come up, be you hungry already? it is not yet eleven a Clock, and instead of one half-penny Loaf, you have eaten two; and instead of one pint of Ale, you have had a quart, and all this you have had to day already, I think the Devil is in your Guts, that I do.

Tom. Why how now Huswife, do you snap at me? do you grudge me my Victuals? Pray Madam Joan, what is it to you how much I eat and drink, do I not provide it? be it known to you Joan, that your Mistris when she was living, would not have said so much to me poor Soul.

Joan. No truly Master, no more would not I if I was your Wife, but as I am your Maid, I am not bound to you, and therefore I take the greater priviledge, but if you'd Marry me, I know what I know.

Tom. Why, what do you know Joan? suppose I should Marry thee:

Ione. Indeed Sir, I'de be the lovingest Wife that ever was made of flesh and blood, i'le be so kind.

Tom. How kind wouldst thou be?

Ione. Ah master, so kind as my mistris us'd to be to you, if not kinder, you may remember Sir that in her days I us'e to lye in the Truckle bed;[1] O then master.

Tom. Why what then Jone.

Ione. Oh dear master, ask me no more questions, I dare talk no more of those things, methinks I find strange alterations in me already, strange motions, strange qualms, Oh how could I

1. A low bed that rolled under the four-poster in day-time. Kind here has often a sexual connotation.

stretch my self, but (alas) to what purpose poor Maid that I am?

Tom. Well Jone, upon good terms, and upon good considerations, and upon divers causes moving me thereunto, I say Jone
I could find in my heart to make thee Mistriss of my household,
and Lady of my family, all which you know Ione is honour in
abundance, but first I say you must subscribe and consent to my
divers causes and considerations.

Ione. Pray master, what be those causes & considerations, i'le
do any thing rather then lose my longing.

Tom. Why then in brief these they are. First, you shall kiss my
hand and swear that you will acknowledge me to be your Lord
and Master.

Ione. I will Sir.

Tom. Secondly, when I come home drunk a nights, you shall be
diligent to make me unready[2] and get me to bed, and if I chance
to befoul my self, you are to make me clean without chiding me.

Ione. Why must I not keep a maid to do these things for me?

Tom. Yes, you must keep a Maid, but it is not fit she should
know of her Masters privicies. I say you must do these things
your self.[3]

Ione. Well if it must be so, it must.

Tom. Thirdly, if any Gentle Woman comes to have me take
measure of her, you must forthwith go out of the Room, and
leave us together and not be jealous.

Ione. All this I will observe.

Tom. Fourthly you must not let any man kiss you but your
Husband, but if any should offer any such thing to you, you must
be sure to let me know what they say or do to you.

Ione. You shall be sure to know all Sir.

Tom. Fiftly and lastly, you must Promise not to spend nor
waste your husbands Money nor Goods, and observe alwaies in
Cow-cumber-time,[4] to put less meat in the Pot than at other times,
because you know that then we have always a Bad Trade: And
one thing I had almost forgot, which is, that you shall be sure

---

2. Undress me. 3. These conditions are not dissimilar to the proviso scenes
in Restoration comedy. 4. Summer; proverbially used in tailoring trade for
time when best customers were out of town.

every day once or twice in the day to muster the Flees and the Lice that have taken possession in our Bedding and wearing Apparel: I say once again (and be sure you remember this last Article of our agreement) you must destroy, kill, and slay them all, if possible.

Ioan. If possible (as you say Master) I will, but i fear they have inhabited and dwelt with you so long, that now they will be sturdy and begin to plead custome,[5] but hoever I'le do my honest endeavour.

Tom. Well, do you consent to all these things, and will you be sure hereafter to observe and keep them all?

Ioan. I will Sir upon this condition, that you will grant me two things that I shall ask you.

Tom. Ay, ay, Joan, any thing I say, any thing, prithee speak quickly, for I begin to be in haste now.

Ioan. Thus it is then, First you shall give me leave to chuse what Maid-servant I please, and secondly, because you shall not be jealous after marriage, I must let you know that I have a young man that is kin to me, he is my Cozen; this young man I say, will often come to see me, you shall not be jealous of him will ye?

Tom. No, no, Wench, God forbid that I should be against thy Relations comming to see thee. No, no, I say, he shall be welcome; is this all you have to say Girl, prithee let's make an end of this Discourse, for I begin to be a little in haste.

Ioan. And so methinks am I, for I care not how soon I am married, and afterward how soon I go to bed, nor afterward how soon you.

Tom. Well, well honest Jone, I know thy meaning, come give me thy hand, let us to Church and be married with speed but now I think on't, what Church shall we go to Ione?

Jone. Why I think that Mr. Cornue[6] had best to marry us, for I am well acquainted with him.[7]

Tom. With all my heart, come on Girl.

---

5. Custom of the manor was a traditional defence against incursions and innovations by landlords. 6. 'Cornue' was a common term for cuckolder. 7. Possibly he was a solemniser of Fleet marriages, outside episcopal jurisdiction, because otherwise law required banns to be called.

Then merrily, with hand in hand
they merrily trip it away,
They scorn'd for to make any stop or stand,
but rejoyced at their Wedding-day:
Jone couzen'd her Master of his dearest delight,
For she made him a Cuckold the very first night.

No sooner the Parson this couple had wed,
and the day being pritty well spent,
Jone long'd till the women had put her to bed,
that she might have a little content:
But Tom in the corner (being drunk) fell asleep,
The Parson into bed with sweet Joan did creep.

Jone got her a Maid, whose name it was Nan,
a bouncing brisk Girl of the Game,[8]
She'l do't as well as her Mistris can,
as for that they were both the same:
Jone was young and handsome in every degree,
Poor Tom what a sneaking old Cuckold was he?

Tom. Oh sad, how Drunk was I last night, I could hang my self for being such a sot; especially the very first night after I was Married, and not to go to bed to my bride: well I must make her amends to night for this great fault, in the mean time i'le go and kiss her a little, perhaps that may stop her mouth for the present. Why wife, why Jone, why wife Jone, Jone, I say, where art thou?

Nan. Who's that bawls and makes such a noise to disturb my Mistris this morning so early, poor woman, she has had very little sleep this night.

Tom. What impudent Jades this that says I bawl in my own house, Hussy who are you that speaks to me thus?

Nan. Why Sir, I am a Servant to the Gentlewoman of this house.

Tom. Be you so, and pray how long have you been her servant?

Nan. Ever since last night.

8. A prostitute.

Tom. Have you so, then pray acknowledge me to be your Master: where is your Mistris?

Nan. Where is she? why she is a bed, and just gone to sleep, if you be her Husband, you have almost broke her heart in not comming to bed to her last night, especially being her Wedding-night, poor soul, she is like to have much good of you, is she not do you think?

Tom. Prithee good Wench hold thy tongue, and do not thou scold at me too, for I must expect a Lesson from her, and a thundring one, for in faith I deserve it: good Nan go up to her, and acquaint her that I am awake, and would very fain come up to her, and be reconciled to her again.

Nan. Well, stay you here, and I will go up stairs, and see what I can do with her, I'le do my best.

Ione. Who is that you are talking to below Nan, that there was such a noise among you?

Nan. Who do you think it was? why it was my Master, he says he will come up to you and beg his pardon for being so drunk last night therefore pray let the Parson make haste away out of Bed if you love your own quiet.

Ione. Yes, yes, Nan, I'le send him away presently, in the mean time till he makes ready, prithee go down and keep thy master in discourse.

Nan. Well forsooth, I go, but pray make haste.

Tom. Well wench, what says thy Mistris? is she willing to forgive me my fault, and to let me go up Stairs to her.

Nan. You may presently, but not yet, for she is not awake, and being disturb'd, will be more froward.

> Tom bears with patience till his wife doth call,
> Then in haste up he runs, thereby t' appease all:
> But at the stairs head she gave him such a rattle
> As if there had been ten thousand men it battle.

Tom. Nay pray wife be not angry, i'le swear to thee wife that i'le make thee amends tonight.

Ione. You shall be hang'd first, but if ever you expect that I shall be friends with you, there must be two things granted.

Tom. Any thing good wife, good wife I say any thing.

Ione. Why then thus it is; you shall give me leave to make void all those promises I made you before marriage, and next that you shall not lye with me, nor desire to lye with me at any time but when I please.

Tom. This is something a hard Chapter[9] I confess, but rather then loose my wifes favour I will grant it, I will do any thing to make her amends. I hope thou wilt not make me a Cuckold, sweetheart, wilt thou? . . .

[Vol. II, no. 4]

9. Hard lines, a painful lesson.

The Female Ramblers. 1683.

The Female Ramblers: or, A Fairing for Cuckolds.

Margery Wiseakers.[1]

Ha! Neighbour Doelittle, well met, I'faith, this is a pleasant morning, what think you of ganging[2] to the Fair today – Come, come for once Neighbours, let's take a Fegary to handsel[3] the Fair – Oh how we Firk it, Caper and jerk it,[4] under the Green-wood-tree.

Cisly Doelittle.) Truly Neighbour Wiseakers, I have had a months mind[5] to take a Ramble thither, but alas! you know how the Case stands with me, I am Marryed, and must be subject to the higher Powers, and I know Neighbour, you are not Ignorant to what a Jealous-pated Fumbling Coxcomb I have inslaved my self.

M.W. Ha-ha-ha, I'faith this is pritty—How! stand in fear of your Husband! as I hope to be well done betwixt this and Midnight, thou art not fit to be one of the Members of our Society: Why Neighbour, hast thou not read the many good Laws and Statutes by us Enacted,[6] for the better Regulating half-witted Fopps, Jealous-pated Coxcombs, and insufferable Fumblers, who long after fluttering like Cock-Sparrows, tire themselves and us with doing e'ne nothing. . . .

Enters Tom Doelittle.

T.D. Wife, Wife – ha – what are you a doing here Gossip[7] – why how now Baggage, did not I send you to call our Neighbour Clodpate, that we might take a walk to Islington?[8]

C.D. Yes truly Husband, but meeting my Neighbour Wiseakers by the way, she has made a motion worthy ten of it.

T.D. A motion, I think—pox of your motions, you'l

---

1. Fool pretending to be wise; refers to her husband. 2. Going. 3. Follow our whim to taste the Fair. 4. Common saying, all dance terms; firk means to jig. Oh what a ball we'll have. 5. Strong desire. 6. Cf. *Parliament of Women.* 7. Wife's companion. 8. Then, a village outside London.

never be good for any thing so long as you keep that Baggage Company.

C.D. Nay, pray Husband be angry if it don't please you, I am ready to be ruled by your directions, you know Husband, I have been always a loving, dutiful, and obedient Wife, by these Tears I have.

T.D. It may be so, that's more than i'le swear – But what's the motion pray – pray what motion? speak.

Enters Margery Wiseakers.

M.W. Pray Mr. Doelittle, what makes you so hasty with your Wife? I faith she's but e'ne too good for ye, and that makes you use her as you do; but Ud'sfoot and nines,[9] if I was as she I'de make you turn over a new Leaf I'faith, I wou'd –

T.D. Hey-day – Pray Mrs. Wiseakers, meddle you with your own Business, and let me and my Wife alone to our selves; don't come, don't I say, come to preach your Doctrine here, to make my Wife, I say, to make my Wife as bad as your self, I say, don't you.

M.W. How do you mean, you Old jealous-pated, Ram-headed – what shall I call you – How do you mean as bad as my self?

T.D. Oh! I shall be worryed to death, – nay, nay, nothing, nothing Neighbour. . . .

> They all go out, and the Sceene changes to the Fair, full of all manner of Toys,[10] etc. at which Doelittle, Wiseakers, and their Wives do arrive and gaze about.

C.D. Now Husband, is not this better a thousand times then creeping under a Hedge, to prick ones fingers in gathering May-boughs.

T.D. Ay, ay, and for ought I know, may prove a thousand times mor Chargeable before we get home again.

M.W. How chear you Neighbour Doelittle? how like you this? is it not wondrous pleasant.

9. God's foot; nines could mean perfection. 10. Fripperies.

T.D. Ay, ay, woundy[11] pleasant, but I don't like that the Gallants in Starched Breeches should look so pleasant upon my Wife, for all that.

The Fair Folks) See what you want Ladys, what you buy? Gloves, Scarves, Ribbons, Combs, Knives, Sizzars, or Lace? will you buy any Ginger-bread, Sugar-plumbs, or Sugar-Almons, a cool Can of good Beer or Ale, pray walk in Gentlemen, see what you want, what you buy –

C.D. Ha! is not this pritty Neighbour?

Comes up to them Horner[12] and Doewell.

1 Gallant) Wondrous pritty Ladies, pray won't you obliege us so far as to give you a Fairing[13] or two e're we part.

2 Gallant) Come Ladies, pray let us obliege you.

C.D. Alas Gentlemen, our Husbands are with us, what do you think they'l say if we should take Fairings of strange Gentlemen?

1 Gal. Damn your Husbands for Insipped Sots, we'l give you fairings Ladies, that shall content you to your hearts desire.

T.D. Ha! law[14] you there Neighbour, see, see whilst we have been gaping up and down, two Gentlemen are pratling to our Wives, – Nay, nay, this was it I feared, this is the fruits of coming to Fairs. . . .

C.D. Alas! our Husbands have drunk whilst they can hardly keep their eyes open, why Husband.

1 Gal. Nay, sweet Lady, don't wake him, let them take their natural rest, whilst we take our sweet repose.

M.W. What mean you Gentlemen? pray – nay – Oh.

2 Gal. Only Ladies, now all is whist[15] and still, your drousie Argus[16] is locked in Slumbers Arms, let us retire and daliance in the Charms of Love, all things Conspire for mutual Bliss; nay Ladies blush not, we are acquainted with the longing of all your Sex; come Madam, I'le take you as the sweet pledge of future joy.

11. Very. 12. Cuckold-maker, as in Wycherley's *Country Wife*. 13. Present, esp. cakes or sweets sold at the fair. 14. Variant of Look 15. Silence. 16. Jealous watcher with a hundred eyes of Greek myth.

1 Gal. And I you, sweet Lady.

C.D. O Sir! nay Sir! pray Sir; what mean you Sir? O fie Sir! nay i'le cry out.

2 Gal. Not so dear Lady, for mighty Loves sake, come, blush not, let's retire into the next Room, whilst your dear Husbands are Dreaming of the other world.

M.W. Come Neighbour, let's see what Fairings the Gentlemen will bestow upon us, I'm sure, nay, I'le pass my word they won't hurt us.

C.D. Well Neighbour, I'le be ruled by you for you'r most experienced in these Affairs, but O if my Husband should wake! and O if I would be tempted to make him a Cuckold.

1 Gal. Along, along, sweet Lady, fear nothing, we'l use you as gently as Swans brood their young ones beneath their Downey Wings, nothing but Love and strong desires shall be at this time our attendants.

> They withdraw, leaving their Husbands, asleep,
> soon after return with Fairings, the Gallants
> pay the Reckoning and depart.

C.D. Well, they are gone, Adads they were pritty Men; O who would not transgress for such Transporting pleasure; well, my Husband never made half so good Musick.

M.W. Nor mine, if we could be so served every time we came to the Fair, and it lasted forty days, I'd make hard shift[17] but I'de come to 'um; but see it grows late, and our Husbands begin to rouse. . . . .

[Vol. I, no. 26]

17. Persistent efforts.

John & his Mistris.

. . . Mr.[1] Well wife prethee see my man minds his business, for I must go meet a friend, as I have appointed this afternoon.

Mrs.[2] Is it a man friend or a woman friend Husband?

Mr. A Gentleman wife, a Gentleman, thou knowest I don't use to meet women alone.

Mrs. I hope you don't Husband; well you may thank God you have so careful a Servant, should you lose him you'l never have such another.

Mr. VVell, well, I know as well as you I think what he is, well I must go.

Mrs. Fare you well, but I think I shall know better then you e're it be long[3] what he is, but that's to my self: Now for to make an end[4] of my discourse with my man, I suppose he has din'd by this time, i'le call him down, John, why John I say come down stairs.

Ioh. I am coming forsooth.

Mrs. Do you remember the last question I ask'd you before Dinner Iohn, when your Master came and hindred our discourse.

Ioh. Truly forsooth I think I have forgot, pray be pleas'd to let me hear it again.

Mrs. Why then this it was: Suppose you should be the young-man I love above all other men in the world, would you be kind to me, and keep my Council, you know my meaning?

If you deny

Alas I dye.

Ioh. All that I can do forsooth, is but too little to serve so good a Mistris; you may command me at any time forsooth.

Mrs. Then I am the happiest woman in the World. But what do young people use to do when they love each other Iohn?

Ioh. Why they use to tell them they love them, do they not Mistris?

Mrs. Yes Iohn, but that's not all.

1. Abbreviation of Master. 2. Mistress. 3. E're long, before long. 4. Finish.

Ioh. Why what do they use to do then Mistris?

Mrs. Why they use to kiss one another, and stroke one anothers faces, and chock their Mistris under the chin, and –

Ioh. And what else forsooth?

Mrs. Away, away, I vow I am asham'd, what are you so dull[5] Iohn?

Ioh. What must I kiss you Mistris, and chock you under the chin, and stroke you for sooth?

Mrs. Nay e'en do what you please with me now.

Ioh. Oh God, I'le swear I am asham'd, but if I do you will not tell my Master, will you forsooth?

Mrs. No, no, you may swear it fool; come I see I must shew you the way, go up stairs, Iohn, and turn them Cheeses[6] that lye in the Garret where your bed stands, the Maid shall look to the shop, and I'le go up along with you and tell you what I would have you do.

Ioh. Yes, I will go forsooth.

SONG.

Then up stairs they did go,
Where she taught him to wooe,
The bashful Young-man she outfac'd,[7]
   Come Iohnny she said,
   Prethee be not afraid,
By me thou shalt ne'r be disgrac'd.

She taught him to bill,[8]
And to kiss her his fill,
Till his Courage began for to move,
   Oh then she did cry,
   Sweet Iohnny I dye,
These these are the pleasures of Love.

5. Slow, dim-witted. 6. Large round cheeses; this, of course, is an excuse to get him to his garret.
7. Overcame. 8. As in bill and coo.

Sweet Mistris, said John,
I'le never lye alone,
'Tis so sweet and so pleasant a pain,
Thus panting to lye,
Dear Mistris let's try,
For I long till I dye once again.

Her Johnny and she,
Very well did agree,
But now he begun to be cloy'd,
The maid cal'd him down,
And he left her alone,
But he thank'd her for what he enjoy'd.

Mrs. Well John, what do you think of Love now? is it not a
pleasant thing? . . .

[Vol. I, no. 35]

CHAP. I.

Of Tom Stitch's Parentage and Birth.

In Thred-Needle-street, at the upper end of Thimble-Alley, lived one William Stitch by Profession a Taylor, who was Married to Nan Needle,

> Whom many Men did often Thred,
> When they could gain her to their Bed.

She keeping company with many Men, to gain custom, at length she gained the French disease,[1] which increasing, she Burnt her Husbands thred, this being known among their Customers, they used to jeer her, and say, She was a hot Needle indeed to burn her Husbands Thred; and when her Husband asked them for Work, they answered, No, no, do you think we will let you be our Taylor, who sows with a hot Needle and a burning Thred. In a short time after they were Marry'd, there arose a great contention between him and his Wife, concerning their Names, she would not have hers buried in forgetfulness, and such a one as his to flourish: Her Husband, to save contention, yielded to let her Name be joyned to his, and so was called Stitch-Needle. Soon after that, she lived a more chaste life than heretofore, so that she proved with Child,[2] but her husband in a quarter of a year after dy'd. He being dead, and she very poor, could not tell whether to go for relief,[3] having scarcely any Friend living, that would regard her; the time soon slipt away, and the day of her delivery drew nigh; but she not thinking it so nigh as it was, caused her to neglect the getting such necessaries as one in her

1. V.D. 2. The medical theory of the time was that frequent 'occupation' inhibited conception. 3. Whither to go for help for the poor.

condition required; so one day (unexpectedly) she fell in Travel,[4] no one being with her but only one Maid, who first ran to call the Neighbours, and then the Midwife, but being delivered before she came, a poor Neighbour had dressed the new-born Babe, which was a Boy: Then a Minister was sent for to Baptize him, who having order, Named him Tom Stitch. . . .

Tom and his Mistris being glad of the opportunity thinking themselves safe, at night she went to Bed, and he to her as soon as his fellow Prentice was asleep, and there enjoy'd their wish'd desires. But what should prove their mishap, at twelve of the Clock her Husband knocked at the Door, and being let in by the Maid, went directly up stairs to his Wives Bed-side, draw'd the Curtains,[5] and there beheld his Wife and his Man Tom circled in one anothers Arms, both being fast asleep; when he beheld them lying so lovingly, could scarce contain himself in the bounds of reason, but was ready to pull them out of the Bed, yet pausing a while upon it, resolved to make an example of them both, and first of Tom; when he had called his Maid up to see, and bear witness of it, left the room, and left them both asleep; so about 2 or 3 of the Clock in the afternoon the next day, he came home, taking no notice of what he had seen in the night. The next day in order to Toms punishment, had him warned before the Chamberlain,[6] which started him and his Mistris when they heard it, she wondring that she did not know it; neither of them mistrusting it was for that. But she (that morning as he was to appear before the Chamberlain) asked her Husband what Tom had done that he should be had before the Chamberlain; to which he replyed, You shall know before night. When the time came, that Tom appeared before the Chamberlain, his Master made this complaint of him, Worshipful Sir, I have warned[7] my man before you, to have him severely punished for being so impudent and sawcy as to lye with my Wife; and to prove the truth of it, I have brought my Maid to Witness it, therefore I entreat your Worship to have him punished with all the severity

4. Travail. 5. Round the four-poster bed. 6. Official of the city with jurisdiction over apprentices. 7. Ordered to appear, summoned.

the Law can inflict. The Chamberlain hearing what a fool he was, to proclaim himself a Cuckold, smiled in Conceit, then called Tom and asked him whether that were true which his Master objected against him? To which he answered, If it please your Worship, I cannot deny it; You are, said the Chamberlain, an impudent Rogue; not, said Tom, such an impudent Rogue as your Worship ———— takes me to be; Come Sirrah, said the Chamberlain, I'le teach you to set your words closer together. He perceiving Tom to be very Arch,[8] reproved him for lying with his Mistris, telling him what a great sin it was, bidding him Fly the Embraces of his Mistris, as Joseph did: May it please your Worship, said Tom, if his Mistris had been so fair as mine, he would not have forborn her: When the Chamberlain heard this Jest he fell a laughing, (as likewise all that then were present) and dismist him without any Punishment.

Tom's Master seeing him dismist so, made what haste he could home, and told his Wife, if ever she let Tom lye with her again he would turn them both out of doors; but if she would promise never to lye with him again, he would forgive all that was past; yet for all her promises, she could not but love and steal some sweet Embraces of her pretty Tom. . . .

[Vol. I, no. 13]

8. Waggish, saucy.

Poor Robin.[1]

...CHAP. 6.

Of a very sad disaster that befel unto poor Robin.

It hapned on a time during these late unhappy Warrs,[2] that all the Essex Train-Bands[3] were assembled at Walden, to Resist the Kings Forces, who in a Bravado had made their Excursions as far as unto Huntingdon: amongst other Military Weapons of Destruction, they brought with them a Drake,[4] which they planted just under poor Robin's Chamber window, to be shot off at nine of the Clock in the night, for a warning to all people to repair home. Poor Robin and his wife were at that time newly gone to Bed: now it is to be understood, that the Chamber where

Pipe and Drum.

---

1. Generic name for jolly fellow. This one was a saddler. 2. Civil Wars. 3. Militia. 4. Small cannon.

they lay went but half way over the Room below, a Rail of about some four foot high being set up by the side to keep them from falling, close by which Rail was poor Robins Bed: the season then being indifferent warm, and poor Robin apt for Venerial Exercises, he would needs have a touch upon Cracket[5] with his Wife, but whilst they were busie at their port,[6] the Drake was shot off, which poor Sarah his wife hearing, in a marvellous fright, gave a sudden start, and threw poor Robin quite over the Rail into the Room below, and very fouly bewrayed[7] the bed, poor Robin himself much bruised in body, and half dead, at length got up, but his Courage was so cooled with the greatness of the fall, that he had more mind to go to a Chyrurgion[8] than a wench. . . .

CHAP. 8.

How poor Robin kist his Wifes Back-side instead of her Mouth.

Poor Robin having been out very late one night, his understanding being Eclips'd, he mistook himself, and went in at the Beds-feet instead of the head of it: where remembring how by his ill husbandry he had offended his Wife, to appease her anger, he falls to kissing her posteriors, imagining it had been her Mouth, but finding the platform[9] bigger than his face, he asks her the question if her Cheeks were swell'd: she for answer returns him a Foist,[10] which made him to ask her again, if her breath did stink: whereupon she bursting out in a very great laughter, let fly such a crack,[10] that the grains flew about his face: whereupon in a great rage turning him on the other side, You beastly quean[11] (quoth he) must you spit in my face, the Devil himself shall kiss you, e're I will kiss you again. . . .

5. Crack is slang for female pudendum. 6. Probably misprint for sport .7. With excrement. 8. Surgeon. 9. Surface area. 10. Both slang for fart. 11. Whore.

CHAP. X.

A witty Jest that poor Robin gave to a Serjeant.

The Bleu Regiment of Train Souldiers[12] being on a time at Walden, one of the Serjeants to show his bravery, had gotten a great Bleu Scarf about his middle, being as much or more than the Ensign[13] had in his Colours. Poor Robin thinking him to be too fine to fight, would venture to put a jeer upon him: and calling him, asked if he wanted any work, why, quoth the Serjeant, what makes you ask? O, cry you mercy, quoth poor Robin, I was mistaken in you, I took you at first for a Shoomaker, because you had gotten your Bleu Apron before you.

CHAP. XI.

How poor Robin won five shillings by kissing his Hostess.

Poor Robin with some other of his Mates, being drinking in an Ale-house where was an exceeding tall Hostess, one of them proffered to lay five shillings, (because poor Robin was low)[14] that he should not kiss her as he stood upon the ground: Poor Robin nothing daunted at his words, accepted the challenge and covered the Money: but when he went to kiss her, his mouth would not reach much higher than her Apron strings: Whereupon proffering as though he would put his hand under her Coats,[15] he made her stoop to put it by; then he clasping his Arms about her neck, gave her a kiss, and so won the wager. . . .

[Vol. I, no. 19]

12. County militia. 13. Junior commissioned officer. 14. Short. 15. Skirts.

Golden Garland.

The Barber fitted by a Wanton Miss of the Town.
To the Tune of, *The Country Farmer*.

O Did you not hear of a Barber of late,
When walking abroad how he pickt up a mate
It was I must tell you a Girl of the Game,
But yet I declare it, I know not her name.

As she was a ranging along in the street,
With this jolly Barber she chanced to meet,
He freely did proffer to give her a treat,
But now you shall hear how he met with a cheat.

Away to the Tavern they went in all hast,
A glass of good Wine he resolved to taste,
The Miss was array'd in her Silks and perfume,
The Drawer[1] he shew'd them a large upper room.

The Barber he then with a noble grace,
Began then to call for Canary[2] a pace,
Likewise his kind Miss he began to embrace,
But yet he was soon in a sorrowful case.

The Barber resolving to show himself great
He call'd up the Drawer to bring up some Plate,
A tankard was brought, and they fill'd it with Wine,
Then, then they went on in their jovial design;

For this was a Liquor which he did adore,
The Barber began for to rant and to rore,
His Miss she did ply him with brimmers good store,
And when all was out she still call'd for more.

The Wine was so strong it got into his head,
Before it was night he must needs go to bed,

1. Tapster, waiter. 2. Light, sweet wine from the Canary Islands.

With his precious jewel, the joy of his life,
He freely declard they were husband and Wife.

Therefore to his Lodging he posted away,
Which was the next Chamber most gallant & gay,
To sleep with his Miss till the Morning broad day,
But she had another fine project to play.

The Barber no sooner was laid in his bed,
But all his whole sences was perfectly fled,
Now, now is the time, to replenish my stock
While he is sleeping as fast as a Rock;

Then out of the bed she straightways arose,
Resolving to take all the best of his Cloaths
His Money, the Tankard, then down stairs she goes,
And where she is gone now there's no body knows.

Next Morning he finding himself all alone,
He sigh'd and lamenting made pittiful moan,
He found he had lost all the best of his suit,
His Money and likewise the Tankard to boot:

The Shaver was then in a pittiful fear,
For now he was rifled it well did appear.
He knew not what course in the World he should steer,
For sorrow must certainly bring up the rear.

He never before was so serv'd in his life,
Alas, he was forced to send for his Wife,
To bring him some money to pay for the loss,
And thus the poor Barber he met with a cross
The barber was noble, both gallant & great,
But now he hath paid for his Drinking in plate;
Let all other Shavers be warn'd by his fate
Lest you should be sorry when it is too late.[3]

[Vol. II, no. 43]

3. A common topic for ballads.

Vinegar and Muſtard:

OR,

Wormwood Lectures for every day in the week.

Being exerciſed and delivered in ſeveral Pa-
riſhes both of Town and City, on ſeveral days.

A diſh of tongues here's for a feaſt,
Sowre ſauce for ſweet meat is the beſt.

Taken Verbatim in ſhort writing by J. W.

Printed by J. B. for J. Clark, W. Thackeray,
and T. Paſſinger: 1686.

Vinegar and Mustard. By J.W.[1] 1686.

. . . 4. Thursdays Lecture.

Exercised and expressed by Mistris Seeming Wise
in her Chamber to her Husband, sitting in
her Chair, but he would not be edified by her.

Verily, verily, thou art a very Reprobate, idolater, and one that
is not worthy to enter in at the wicket or door, nay not to stir
over the threshold where the Elect doth dwell, thou are worthy
to be chastised and beaten with many stripes. You (forsooth)
will go no where to be edified, but to your Steeple-houses,[2] upon
your Heathenish daies, there where they teach nothing almost
but the language of the beast, the common Strumpet, Harlot,
and Whore of Babylon;[3] away thou unsanctified wretch, thy
blind eyes are not opened, but you will walk still in the dark
pains of iniquity and ignorance, that in the end you shall fall
into the pit of perdition. And you and the rest of the tribe of the
wicked, when you are at your unsanctified Tipling inns, your
Ale-houses or your Taverns, and are drunken with the dregs of
prophaneness, where your noses are smoaking like the gulph of
Sodom & Gomorrahs the Henbane[4] of your Heathen Tobacco.
I there there, I say, is the place where you utter and vent forth
your despightful reproaches against us, which are the immaculate
vessels: I profess, I profess, and that in sincerity, that the Righteous may have their fallings, and their failings, & may rise again,
but for you that are not called, but persevere in your old superstitious polatry,[5] which is but meer popery: you say again, and
again, your learned teachers, as they that built up the walls of
Babylon, but you can deride at our sincere teachers, although

1. The subtitle claims these lectures were 'taken verbatim in short writing'.
Short-hand was used by zealots to make notes of sermons. 2. Dismissive
Quaker phrase for churches. 3. Phrases used by puritans to describe Rome,
extended by Quakers to the Church of England. 4. Narcotic plant. 5. Quaker
nonce word, possibly meaning repetition of set forms of service.

they propagate, and are men of sanctity, therefore let us say or
teach what we will, you are like the Adder that stops her ears and
will hear nothing at all, therefore you will not edifie, but still
run on in your profane course of life: seeing so, I conclude as I
began, thou art a very reprobate.[6]

Her Husbands Answer.

Now I am glad your learned Lectures done,
And have concluded just as you begun,
Being with reverence, as you may say,
Unto your Husband, whom you should obey.
is this the Doctrine which you there do teach,
Where Ananias[7] unto you doth preach?
These same to you methinks are wondrous kind,
That open'd have your eyes were lately blind,
Surely unto the Papists they are kin,
But I thought Miracles had ceased bin,
They hate a whore, and on high points do ston,[8]
But 'tis none but the whore of Babylon:
They have their goodly gifts of countenance
True, before folks they will not kiss a wench,
it is the Spirit that doth move them to it,[9]
And therefore he must not refuse to do it.
To fail and fall it is sometimes your lot,
Witness so many Maids with Child are got
By zealous people of your ranting crew,
Which being done, this Virgin up you mew,[10]
Because the wicked thereof should not know,
You nurst her up, and so away did go.
And thus doth propagate your pure elect,
The which is too much used by your sect:

6. The parody of Quaker phraseology is similar to that in *The Secret Sinners*,
Section IV. 7. Jewish high-priest, thus hypocrite. Popularised in Johnson's
The Alchemist. 8. Stone; I suspect this is a variant of stand, meaning insist
on high points of doctrine. 9. Sc. but in private. 10. Conceal, coop up.

Our learned[11] Reverend Divines you hate,
And say the Language of the beast they prate,
Because your blockish weak capacities
Cannot conceit[12] the secret misteries,
The which are written in Gods sacred Book,
Which is the cause so many are mistook:
Yet some of you that hardly knows a Letter
Stick not to say you can expound it better;
Your learned teachers that do all disjoint,
That know not how to spell, to read, or point,
Are they not reverend botchers, or som weavers
some zealous coblers, hatmakers, or glovers?
These are the Saints that do the Scriptures wrest
Nay some of them of it do make a jest:
They make a Cloak of true Religion,
And a false Vizard[13] o re their face put on:
Do but unmask them, you shall plainly see
Their cheating tricks and base Hypocrisie:
The wicked for to rob they hold no sin,
And careth not who lose so they do win.
And now I say (yet speak under the Rose)[14]
Those snotty fellows that speak in the Nose[15]
Like to the Papists silly women tice[16]
For to undo their Husband in a trice:
As by experience I have found of late,
You amongst them have impoverisht my estate;
And therefore now I mean to mold you new,
Huswife i'le make you leave your ranting crew.

11. The fundamentalism, impatient of the niceties of biblical and theological
scholarship, of the sects, was a major target of critics. 12. Comprehend.
13. Mask. 14. Sub rosa, in strict confidence. 15. A general puritan idio-
syncrasy. 16. Entice.

5. Fridays Lecture.

Delivered Dialogue wise between bold Betteris and
Welch Guintlin,[17] two Fish-wives, in Newgate
Market, upon a Market day, where they had
store of audience, and great attention.

Bett. Away, away thou impudent Welch Runt thou, thou comest
from a Forraign Nation, I do not know where, beyond Pennin-
mar,[18] a tother side the Mountains, thou mealfac'd Bawd thou,
dost thou think to forestall[19] me in the Market place, that was
bred and born in the Parish, and you come to eat the bread out
of my mouth with a pox to you.

Guin. Marry hang you with a Tevils name, the bold Betteris,
was stand here in spight of her pelly and prafe face, was give her
fine Languages, was her not? was call her Welch Runt, and
Apple-fac'd pawd, and the tevil and his tam, like a shade[20] as
her are.

Bet. Dost thou call me shade thou whore thou? I would thou
shouldst well know, that I was never such a jade as to tire[21] as
thou didst, thou common Hackney thou: for when thou and a
fellow was a doing I know what, thou didst cry dig on, dig on,
which is enough, enough, in your pocky welch language, and
then the fellow told thee, he had almost dig'd his heart out,
that was the trick of a jade to tire.

Guin. Now her was take her self by the noses[22] faith law,[23] was
call her self to remembrance, how her was lye with a fellow in a
tark night, upon a Coblers Stall, and when the fellows Breeches
were down and he got up, thou wast ask whether he was ride a
gallops or a trots?[24] and then the Cobler as he was at work by
candles light was hear her, and he was thrust up his Aul into her
blind cheeks,[25] (with a pox to her) and when her was prickt, her
was give such a kick upward, that her was threw the fellow out of

17. Gwendolyn in pseudo-Welsh. 18. Penmaenmawr. 19. Here, quite literally,
to take her pitch by arriving first. 20. Jade, contemptuous of a woman.
21. Here, tire probably means to grow exhausted and give up during
intercourse. 22. Reproach herself. 23. Exclamations. 24. Pun on old hag.
25. Buttocks.

the saddles all along in the dirt, and was not that the trick of a base shade, think her law?[23]

Bet. Away, away thou toad, head and garlick thou;[26] didst thou call thy self to remembrance since thou lay in the Cage by Smithfield pond,[27] with two bastards, thou cage-bird thou, did you not sing sweetly there? and do you remember how thou layst with a Fisherman for a Quardern of Mackarel,[28] and when yon came back agen how you paid the waterman with a pox that carried you, thou bob-tail'd[29] whore thou.

Guin. Thou was a base whores-bird to call her cage-bird; was pray tell her how long it is ago since her did sing *pity the poor women in Newgate,* when her should have been hanged for picking a pocket; besides her do not remember when her was in a black and blew white rose wastcoat[30] and red Spanish peticoat, with half a tozen of lashes at her tail, and her new stockings, and her new shooes, which her was never pay the shoomaker for unless it were with a pox, and as prave as her was, her had never a penny in her purse, when her was fine, her was go sell Oranges and Lemons, and did her not lye with the Spavel Portugal[31] for half a hundred of Oranges and Lemons at Pillingsgate, and so was put her in the stocks when her was poor.

Bet. Thou scum of a Kitchin-stuff pot thou, that when thou camest out of Wales hadst not a tatter to thy tail,[32] and didst pennance all the way to London bare-foot, thou jade thou, and then didst set up in gathering Rags & Marrow-bones, thou base dunghill whore thou, and as thou didst rake thou didst find a silver spoon, and that did put thee in a stock[33] to trade at Billingsgate, for I am sure thou wert a beggarly whore and full of Lice till then, but now you can keep company and spend pot for pot, and be jovial with your companions, as the best of us, thou leather-fac'd whore thou.

---

26. Form of dismissal. 27. On humiliating display for having borne two bastards, a financial charge on the parish relief system. 28. Quartern, quarter measure; mackerel was also slang for a whore or pimp. 29. Cliché for poxed. 30. This elaborate description means that she was naked to the waist and barefoot, being flogged as a whore. 31. Maimed? Portuguese; orange-selling, as Nell Gwynne demonstrated, was only one step up the ladder from cinder-raking. 32. In modern parlance, 'ragged-arsed'. 33. Gained you capital.

Guin. Pox on you old tallow-fac'd wish,[34] the her has cullar[35] now for her knavery, and was paint her ill-favour face, I think with white shake and red prick,[36] to make her look beautiful and was make her rogues and her rascals to follow after her like a bold whore as she is.

Bet. I faith, now your welsh plood is up you will say any thing, but hark Guintlin, let me speak a word in your ear, I will not hurt you.

Guin. I but will her not bite her nor scratch her with her tooths?

Bet. No ifaith: but are we not a couple of fools to fall out and spoil our Reputation, losing our Market, and our fish is ready to stink, and the people laugh at us: hark the Market-bell rings, and we must away, meet me at the Fox, and there we'l drink our selves friends.

Guin. Here was both her hands, her was meet her at the Fox, get a good fire, and call for half a tozen, come Customers and buy all before her go: new fresh Herin, quick a lie, quick a lie,[37] fifteen a groat, was come, was come Betteris.

6. Saturdays Lecture.

Exercised[38] by a Millers wife in her Husbands Water-
mill, instead of a Barn, where her tongue went
faster and louder than the Mill-clapper.[39]

Marry a Miller, marry a Theif, but it is too late to repent now, the more is my grief: what all alone! that's a wonder that you have none of your trollops with you. You forsooth could not stay at home last night, but you must go to the Mill to work in great hast; you had your stones to pick[40] with a vengeance, but I do wonder who helpt you to pick them, not they that should I

34. Witch. 35. Colour, pun on excuse. 36. White excrement (jake)? and red brick; the latter pun is hardly unconscious. 37. Quickly. 38. Used, here ironically, of puritan lectures or meditative exercises. 39. Ratchet in mill machinery, noisy. 40. Stones, slang for testicles.

am sure, and besides you could not stay lest you should want water to grind[41] with, but you did not grind in your own water-mill: I find the old Proverb true, *That much Water runs by the Mill that the Millers Wife never knows on.*[42] O sirrah, who but you[43] amongst the Maids when my back is turn'd, I know your tricks of old since I was a Maid, I can see what pickle they are in after they have been with you, how all their petticoats are whited with meal: I those are the Lasses that shall have their Corn ground toll-free;[44] I know you are as free to them of your flesh, as you are of your fish, for you can give this wench a dish of trotters for restority, and that wench a dish of girts[45] to scoure her maw, whilst I poor soul sit at home with a dish of pouts, and they to requite your kindness, one brings a plumb Cake, another brings a Goose,[46] and thus when you feast together, you are as safe as so many thieves in a Mill, butifaith I will watch your water, and I shall take you napping, which if I do, I will ring you such a peal, that all the Bells in the steeple shall not outjangle me.[47]

The Mans Answer.

Why how now Dame, what is the cause
That you so wide do ope your jawes?
What did some fury you affright?
Or did you not sleep well last night?
if it be so, then prethee tell,
i'le take some course to make thee well;
Doth Jealousie your pate possess
'Gainst him that never did transgress?
And honest Maidens doth miscall,
Who never did you hurt at all:
What if a dish of fish I give
Unto a friend, why should you grieve?

41. Common innuendo. 42. Usually, that the miller; common proverb. 43. Sc. is. 44. In some places there was a tax on milling as well as the miller's charge. 45. Fillets. 46. Both doubles entendres for the female pudendum. 47. Millers were proverbially lecherous. Cf. Sec. III, 'Simon and Cisley'.

Thou know'st I must work night and day,
The water will not for me stay.
I'm sure there's none can say by me,
That e're I ground their Corn toll-free.
But those that have gone once astray
Think others will go the same way.
The Baker he his Daughter sought
i'th'Oven, where himself was caught:
Thou know'st I had thy Maiden-head,
Before that ever we were wed.
But for the same I made amends,
Be quiet Wife and we'l be friends. . . .

[Vol. I, no. 48]

Short-Title Contents of Penny Merriments
as collected by Samuel Pepys.

*Denotes that a selection of it is given in this book.

*19. *Delectable History of Poor Robin, The Merry Sadler of Walden.* Publisher, J. Conyers.

*20. *The Figure of Nine.* Publishers J. Deacon & C. Dennisson.

*21. *Cupid's Posies.* Publishers J. Wright, J. Clarke, W. Thackeray, T. Passinger. 1683.

*22. *Make Room for Christmas.* By Lawrence Price. Publishers W. Thackeray & T. Passinger.

*23. *True Tryal of Understanding or Wit newly Reviv'd.* By S.M. Printed by I.M. (Ioannis Millet?) for I. Deacon. 1687.

*24. *Book of Merry Riddles.* Printed for W. T(hackeray) & sold by J. Back. 1685.

25. *Variety of New Merry Riddles.* By Lawrence Price. Printed for W. Thackeray. 1684. 1st Ed. 1655.

*26. *The Female Ramblers; Or, A Fairing for Cuckolds.* Publishers J. Wright, J. Clarke, W. Thackeray & T. Passinger. 1683.

*27. *The Unfortunate Son; or, A Kind Wife is worth Gold.* Printed by I.M. (Millet?) for J. Deacon & T. Passinger.

*28. *Second Part of Unfortunate Jack.* Printed by M.W. (Wotton or Margaret White?). Sold by J. Clark. 1681.

29. *Pleasant Discourse between Conscience and Plain-Dealing.* By C. H. Publishers J. Wright, J. Clarke, W. Thackeray & T. Passinger.

30. *Distressed Welshman Born in Trinity Lane.* By Hugh Crumpton. Printed for W. T(hackeray). Sold by J. Conyers.

31. *New Academy of Complements . . . Newest Way of Wooing.* Publisher J. Conyers.

*32. *New Garland of Fifteen Songs.* Publisher J. Conyers.

*33. *Cupid's Master-piece; or, The Free School of witty and delightful Complements.* Printed by H.B. for J. Clark, W. Thackeray & T. Passinger. 1685.

*34. *The Figure of Seaven.* By Poor Robin, Knight of the Burnt Island. Publisher J. Conyers.

*35. *John and His Mistris . . . the Wanton Wife and Her Handsom Prentice.* Publisher J. Deacon.

*36. *The Honour of the Gentle-Craft in Three Stories.* Printed by H.B. for John Clark, W. Thackeray and T. Passinger. 1685.

*37. *Pleasant History of King Henry VIII and the Abbot of Reading.* Printed by I.M. (Millet) for C. Dennisson.

*38. *The King and the Cobler.* Printed for C. Dennisson.

*39. *The Compleat Cook, OR The Accomplished Servant Maid's Necessary Companion.* Printed for J. Deacon.

*40. *The Welch Traveller; OR The Unfortunate Welch-Man.* By Humphry Crouch. (Publication details missing.)

*41. *Tom Tram of the West . . . Son-in-Law to Mother Winter.* Printed for W. T(hackeray) & Sold by J. Deacon.

42. *Second Part of Tom Tram.* By Humphery (sic) Crouch. Printed for J. Dacon (sic).

*43. *Cupid's Sports and Pastimes.* By Henry Sparrow. Printed for W. Thackeray. 1684.

*44. *Famous History of Guy Earl of Warwick.* By Samuel Smithson. Printed for J. Clark, W. Thackeray & T. Passinger. 1686.

*45. *Life and Death of Sheffery ap Morgan, Son of Shon ap Morgan.* Printed for J. Deacon. 1683.

46. *Cupid's Solicitor of Love, with Sundry Complements.* By Richard Crimsal. Printed by I.M. (Millet?) for W. Thackeray. Sold by J. Back.

*47. *Cupids Love Lessons.* By H.C. Printed for J. Clarke sr. 1683.

*48. *Vinegar and Mustard; OR, Wormwood Lectures for every day of the week.* By J.W. Printed by J.B. for J. Clark, W. Thackeray & T. Passinger. 1686.

49. *Groatsworth of Wit for a Penny. Or, the Interpretation of Dreams.* By Mr. (William) Lilly. Printed for W. Thackeray and Sold by Ionah Deacon.

*50. *Two Groatsworth of Wit for a Penny, OR The English Fortune-Teller.* Published by those famous Astrologers Mr. Richard Saunders, and Dr. (Nathaniel) Coelson. Printed for J. Conyers.

*51. *The Secret Sinners . . . A Quaker, his Maid and his Wife Sarah.* In their own sanctified Language. Printed for P. Brooksby.

*52. *A Hundred Notabe Things for a Penny.* (sic) By Josh. Croynes, Gent. Publisher J. Conyers, 1680.

*53. *Crossing of Proverbs . . . Newly Corrected with Additions.* By B.R. Gent. Printed for Margaret White.

*54. *First Part of Dr. Faustus, Abreviated* (sic) *and brought into verse.* Printed by I.M. (Millet?) for I. Deacon & C. Dennisson.

*55. *Diogenes. His Search through Athens. . . . (for) Honest Men.* Printed for J. Wright, J. Clark, W. Thackeray & T. Passinger.

*56. *Exact and Wonderful History of Mother Shipton.* Publisher J. Conyers.

*57. *Merry Conceits and Passages of Simon and Cisley Two Lancashire Lovers.* By J.P. Printed by H.B. for J. Clarke, W. Thackeray & T. Passinger.

*58. *Pleasant History of Tom Ladle.* Printed for J. Blare.

VOLUME II

*1. *The Woman's Brawl.* (Title-page missing.)

*2. *The Five. Strange Wonders of the World OR A new merry book of all Fives.* By L.P. (Lawrence Price). Printed for Margaret White. 1683.

*3. *No Jest Like a true Jest ... Merry Life, and Mad Exploits of Captain James Hind (The Greatest Robber in England) Hang'd ... Sept. 24, 1652.* Publisher J. Deacon.

*4. *Merry Dialogue between Tom the Taylor and his Maid Jone.* Printed for I. Clarke. 1684.

*5. *The Gentlewoman's Cabinet Unlocked.* Printed for W. Thackeray & T. Passinger.

6. *Life and Death of the Famous Champion of England, St. George.* Pinted (sic) by J.M. (Millet) for J. Clark, W. Thackeray & T. Passinger.

*7. *Pleasant History of the Miller of Mansfield ... and King Henry II.* Printed for J. Clark, W. Thackeray & T. Passinger.

*8. *Most Pleasant and Delightful Art of Palmistry ... With Mr. Saunder's Art of Dyalling ...* Faithfully collected by J.M. to prevent superstitious ones. Printed by A.M. (Anne Marriott?) for J. Deacon & C. Dennisson.

9. *Whole Art of Palmestry.* By W. R. Practitioner above Thirty Years in the most hidden Sciences. Publisher P. Brooksby. Printed for W. Thackeray and Sold by J. Deacon.

10. *Mirror of Natural Astrology: or, A New Book of Fortune.* By Mr. (William) Lilly. Printed for W.T. and sold by J. Deacon.

11. *Compleat Cookmaid.* Printed for P. Brooksby. 1684.

*12. *Canterbury Tales.* By Chaucer Jr. Printed for J. Back. 1687.

*13. *Mother Bunch's Closet ... Rare Secrets of Art and Nature.* By T.R. (?Robins). Printed by A.M. (Marriott?) for P. Brooksby. 1685.

*14. *Wonderful Adventures and Happy Success of Young Shon ap Morgan, only son of Sheffery ap Morgan, the Welsh Doctor.* Publisher J. Deacon.

*15. *Loves School.* Printed for W. Thackeray, T. Passinger, P. Brooksby & J. Clarke. 1682.

*16. *Art of Courtship.* Publisher I. Back. 1687.

*17. *The Unlucky Citizen; OR The Pleasant History of the Life of Black Tom.* Printed by J.M. (Millet) for J. Blare 1686.

18. *Love's Masterpeice (sic) OR, The Grove of Pleasure and Delight.* By Philo Amoris. Printed by H.B. for P. Brooksby. 1683.

*19. *Lilly's New Erra Pater, or a Prognostication for Ever.* Publisher J. Conyers.

*20. *Birth, Life and Death of John Frank.* Printed by J.M. (Millet) for J. Deacon & C. Dennisson.

*21. *Merry Tales of the Mad-Men of Gotham.* By A.B. Doctor of Physick. Printed for J. Clark, W. Thackeray & L. (sic) Passinger.

*22. *Tom Thumb, His Life and Death.* Printed by J.M. (Millet) for J. Clark, W. Thackeray & T. Passinger.

*23. *Second Part of the Fryer and the Boy.* Printed by A.M. (Marriott) & R.R. for Edward Brewster and sold by Jas. Gilbert. 1680.

*24. *Death and Buriall of Mistress Money . . . What happened to the Usurer that buried her.* Printed for A. Clarke, and to be sold by T. Vere & J. Clark. 1678.

*25. *The Merry Oxford Knight, or The Pleasant Intrigues of Sir Humphry Frollicksome.* Printed by A.M. (Marriott) for James Bissel.

*26. *The Life of Long Meg of Westminster.* Printed by J.M. (Millet) for G. Conyers.

*27. *A Strange and Wonderful Relation of an Old Woman Drowned at Ratcliff High-Way.* Printed for W. T(hackeray), and Sold by J. Blare.

28. *True Lover's New Accademy.* Publisher J. Conyers.

29. *Famous History of Don Quixote de la Mancha.* Printed for G. Conyers. 1686.

30. *Court of Curiosities.* Publisher P. Brooksby (1685/9).

*31. *Excellent and Renowned History of the Famous Sir Richard Whittington.* Publisher J. Conyers? (Title-page shaved.)

32. *Gentlewoman's Delight in Cookery.* Printed for J. Back.

*33. *Country-Mans Counsellor, Every Man made his own Lawyer.* By H.R. Printed for J. Clark.

*34. *Parliament of Women.* Printed for T. Passinger, J. Deacon and G. Conyers.

35. *Lovers Academy.* Printed for T. Passinger.

*36. *True Tale of Robin Hood.* By Martin Parker. Publishers J. Clark, W. Thackeray & T. Passinger. 1686.

37. *Cupid's Court of Salutations.* By W.B. Printed for J. Deacon. Sold by R. Kell. 1687.

38. *Cupids Garland.* Publishers J. Clark, W. Thackeray & T. Passinger.

39. *Royal Garland.* By T. D(eloney). Printed by T.H. (Haley) for W. Thackeray, T. Passinger, J. Clark & P. Brooksby. 1681.

40. *Shepherds Garland.* Publishers J. Wright, J. Clark, W. Thackeray & T. Passinger. 1682.

*41. *Country Garland.* Printed for P. Brooksby. 1687.

*42. *New London Drollery.* Printed by A.M. (Marriott) for P. Brooksby. 1687.

*43. *The Golden Garland.* Printed for J. Blare.

44. *Loyal Garland of Mirth and Pastime.* By S.M. Printed by J.M. (Millet) for I. Deacon. 1685.

45. *Garland of Love and Mirth OR a Pacquet of New Songs.* By Thomas Lanfier. Printed for I. Deacon. Sold by R. Kell.

46. *True-Lovers Garland.* Printed for J. Back. 1687.

47. *Maidens Garland.* Printed for J. Back.

48. *England's Fair Garland.* Printed for R. Kell. 1687.

49. *Neptune's Fair Garland.* Printed by I.M. (Millet?) for I. Deacon. 1676.
*50. *Most Delightful History of the Famous Clothier of England called Jack of Newberry.* By W.S. F.C. Printed by H.B. for W. Thackeray. 1684.
51. *Cuckolds All A-Row.* Printed for R. Kell.

VOLUME III

1. *Garden of Delight.* By Thomas Deloney. 30th Edition. Printed by T.H. (Haley) for W. Thackeray & T. Passinger. 1681.
2. *Garland of Good-Will.* By T. D(eloney). Printed by Francis Clarke for Geo. Conyers. 1688.
3. *The Crown Garland.* By R. Johnson. Printed for M.W. (Wotton). Sold by Dorman Newman & Ben. Alsop. 1683.
4. *Robin Hood's Garland.* Printed by J.M. (Millet) for J. Clark, W. Thackeray and T. Passinger.
5. *History of the Seven Wise Masters of Rome.* Publishers M. Wotton & G. Conyers. 1687.
6. *History of the Seven Wise Mistresses of Rome.* (By Thomas Howard, fl 1663). Printed by M. Wotton & G. Conyers. 1686.

C3